EXPLAINING THE NOR

For Chairman Meow,
and in memory of Socrates, Claiborne, and Bailey,
who taught me about empathy.

EXPLAINING THE NORMATIVE

STEPHEN P. TURNER

polity

First published in 2010 by Polity Press

Polity Press
65 Bridge Street
Cambridge CB2 1UR, UK

Polity Press
350 Main Street
Malden, MA 02148, USA

ISBN-13: 978-0-7456-4255-0 (hardback)
ISBN-13: 978-0-7456-4256-7 (paperback)

A catalogue record for this book is available from the British Library.

Typeset in 10.5 on 12 Sabon
by Servis Filmsetting Ltd, Stockport, Cheshire
Printed and bound in Great Britain by the MPG Books Group

The publisher has used its best endeavours to ensure that the URLs for external websites referred to in this book are correct and active at the time of going to press. However, the publisher has no responsibility for the websites and can make no guarantee that a site will remain live or that the content is or will remain appropriate.

Every effort has been made to trace all copyright holders, but if any have been inadvertently overlooked the publisher will be pleased to include any necessary credits in any subsequent reprint or edition.

For further information on Polity, visit our website: www.politybooks.com

CONTENTS

INTRODUCTION

My book *The Social Theory of Practices* was published in 1994, as was Robert Brandom's *Making It Explicit*: the first was a small book with intent to demolish, the second a large and in every sense constructive book. *The Social Theory of Practices* was an argument against the appeal to what it called collective objects, with a modest constructive message about emulation as an alternative explanation. *Making It Explicit* was an account of linguistic normativity, in which the "it" being made explicit was a paradigm case of a collective object, but it bypassed tough problems about how the account fit into the world. I thought the arguments of *The Social Theory of Practices* applied to Brandom and, *mutatis mutandis*, to much of the flood of "normativity" thinking of the time. Joe Rouse wrote me a letter that claimed that they did not, because the structures Brandom and he were talking about were "normative." Saying this amounted to giving these arguments a free pass from the questions raised in *The Social Theory of Practices* – questions about how collective objects could possibly work in the way they were supposed to, given the causal features of the world, our cognitive processes, ordinary features of social interaction, and the kind of feedback we get in the course of learning how to get around the world.

I found Rouse's claim deeply puzzling, not least because so much of the argumentation in the texts of the normativists appealed to notions that were taken over directly – or slightly modified – from the social sciences and in particular from classical social theory. Wilfrid Sellars, for example, used Durkheimian notions. And one could not read philosophers like Philip Pettit without hearing Durkheim, for example in Pettit's appeal to common knowledge. Saul Kripke's account of rule-following in Wittgenstein wound up with puzzles about a problematic concept from social theory, namely community. And the borrowing from classical social science was explicit in such works as Margaret Gilbert's *On Social Facts* (1989), with its discussion of Georg Simmel.

The puzzle extended to my own earlier writings. There was a strong relationship between the writings of normativism and the claims that I had made in my (Wittgensteinian) dissertation, published as *Sociological Explanation as Translation* (1980), in my (more Quinean) "Translating Ritual Beliefs" (1979), and in my critique of the Strong Programme (1981). Indeed, there were two columns of text (last column of 190 and the first of 191) in Brandom's "Freedom and Constraint by Norms" (1979) that could have served as a summary of my own arguments in these texts – though in the next pages Brandom took them in the direction of *Making It Explicit*, where I would not have taken them, for reasons having to do with the social theory implicit in Brandom's argument, particularly its own appeal to notions of community. The links between my earlier writings on translation and normativism and on the Strong Programme in the Sociology of Science (e.g., 1981) were close enough for me to be identified as a normativist myself (e.g., by Henderson 2002), though of a more Davidsonian kind.

Clearly there were issues to be worked out, both as a matter of philosophy and as a matter of social theory, and for myself as well as in the larger community of readers of these literatures. During the decade after the publication of *The Social Theory of Practices* I wrote a number of articles and review essays on various aspects of the problem of normativity (mostly collected in *Brains/Practices/Relativism: Social Theory after Cognitive Science*, 2002, 74–107), watched Brandom present his views at various places, and presented my views on these issues in a rough form at an NEH Summer Institute with Brandom present. Among the elements of that discussion was the case of legal normativity. Brandom himself suggested to me at the time that this was a line of argument worth pursuing, and indeed it was. I was also paired with Joe Rouse at a number of philosophical events, reviewed his books (1989, 2005a), and commented on his notion that the concept of practices was a normative one (2007a). This book is the product of these exchanges, though the form of the text itself is an attempt to locate these issues in a much larger and different historical picture: not as a vindication of idealism and Kant, as it is usually presented, but as a story about the attempt to recapture ground that had been lost in the sometimes friendly, but often nasty, divorce between philosophy and social science in the late nineteenth century. Hans Kelsen was the poster child of this divorce, so he plays a central role in this text.

This material has been presented in a variety of places, as part of talks. I am grateful for the opportunities to discuss the arguments that attendees presented, the comments, the objections, and particularly the puzzled looks. I am in particular grateful for the response of students in the University of South Florida Philosophy department, who have put up with this little obsession for more years than I care to remember. I am also especially grateful for such old friends as Paul Roth, who have responded to these concerns in a philosophical language I understand, and George Mazur, who was kind enough to argue with me at length about Hans Kelsen. Eileen Kahl provided her usual competent support in putting the manuscript together. My family, decade upon decade, has put up with stacks of books and slips of paper in the wrong places. For their forbearance I am grateful. Thanks also to Gerhard Preyer for permission to use much of "What Do We Mean by 'We'?" (*Protosociology*, 2003) in Chapter 5.

Pass-a-Grille January 31, 2009

— 1 —

WHAT IS THE PROBLEM OF NORMATIVITY?

Normativity pervades our lives. We do not merely have beliefs: we claim that we and others ought to hold certain beliefs. We do not merely have desires: we claim that we and others not only ought to act on some of them, but not others. We assume that what somebody believes or does may be judged reasonable or unreasonable, right or wrong, good or bad, that it is answerable to standards or norms . . . We find ourselves at sea because there is a huge disagreement about the source and the authority of norms on which we all constantly rely.

Onora O'Neill (1996, xi)

Normative facts (e.g. about who is committed to what) are just one kind of fact among others. Normative facts are facts statable only using normative vocabulary (compare: physical facts).

Robert Brandom (1997, 197n6)

No one bears away from this Sacrament more than is gathered with the vessel of faith.

John Calvin ([1536] 1960, IV.xvii.33)

Normativity is everywhere. The sign of this, as Onora O'Neill's reasoning suggests, is that normative terms are ubiquitous, and we constantly and necessarily rely on them. Correct and incorrect, right and wrong, good and bad, rational and not rational, valid and invalid – the list is long. The normative is a special realm of fact that validates, justifies, makes possible, and regulates normative talk, as well as rules, meanings, the symbolic and reasoning. These facts are special in that they are empirically inaccessible and not part of the ordinary stream of explanation. Yet they are necessary in the sense that if they did not exist, ordinary normative talk, including such things as claims about what a word means or what the law is, would be unjustified,

1

nonsensical, false, or illusory. To say that something has meaning requires that there be such a thing as a meaning. To say something is a real law is to say that there is something that validates the law as real.

But beyond this way of thinking about the normative as a realm of fact lies a vast muddle. What is the character of this normativity that is everywhere and signaled by the presence of these terms? Is it a non-natural, noncausal property of things? A force that attaches to things, such as claims, that gives them some obligatory power? Are norms part of the furniture of the world, a part which is merely odd in some respects, or is it an aspect of things that are otherwise normal? Or is normativity something else entirely? Is it best understood as a kind of shadow system of rules, proprieties, scoring systems, presuppositions, and so forth that stands tacitly behind our normative usages and regulates and justifies them in a way that is a hidden analogue to the way that explicit rules, scoring systems, and the like regulate and justify? And if we are bound by these things, how are we bound? Do we bind ourselves under norms by our own commitments, or in some other way? A danger with these questions, pointed out by John Mackie, is that by answering them in the wrong way we could make normativity into something so queer that it could not be accommodated to the rest of our ideas about the natural, explainable world (Mackie 1977, 38–42, 48–49). But understanding normative language in terms of normativity forces us to ask such questions.

The usual way of getting at metaphysical questions of this kind is to ask about explanation. What does the stuff explain? What explains it? How does it explain? O'Neill alludes to the problem of explanation in her comments about the "huge disagreement" over sources of normativity. Are the sources natural, and if so does that mean that there is no special force answering to the name of "normativity"? Or are the sources normative? Does using normative terms commit us to some sort of complex metaphysics that goes beyond the natural and causal? O'Neill's language points directly to this problem: "Sources" is an explanatory term, tracing something to its source is a way of explaining it. But what sort of explanation is this going to turn out to be? If the explanation is rooted in the causal world, how does it explain something that is part of the noncausal world? Is there is some kind of transformation from causal to normative? If there is some other kind of source of normativity – for example, moral intuitions – we are faced with questions about where the intuitions came from, and, inescapably, with questions about where and how their causes, if they are caused, manage to produce something "normative," and, if they are not caused, how they came about.

These are problems about the explanation of the normative. But there are questions on the other end, about the norms or normative facts that normativity consists in, and what explanatory work these facts do. What do these facts, if they are facts, explain, if anything? And how do the kinds of explanations that involve norms relate to other explanations? Should anyone care about normativity who is not answering normative questions? Are normative considerations merely part of some sort of circular, closed system of thinking? Are they inescapable – part of the business of explanation itself? And does this inescapability imply that everything, or everything expressible, is part of a closed system – what Wilfrid Sellars calls the space of reasons – that is in the end normative? Or is their inescapability a feature of our subjective experience that is not itself factual – a feature of the task of explaining but not of the world that is explained?

Issues related to these questions dominate the present philosophical landscape, where they are often cast in David and Goliath terms. The normative is the small boy with the stone against the massive forces in modern philosophy of naturalism, materialism, physicalism, and causalism; forces that draw their power from the success of science. This imagery gives epochal significance to what might otherwise seem to be a parochial dispute among professional philosophers. Nor is the imagery misplaced. The long history of secularization, bound up with the history of modern philosophy, has largely consisted of desupernaturalizing explanation. Claims about "normativity" seem to imply that this project can never be completed, that the project of desupernaturalization will always be defeated by the small stone of normativity.

Robert Brandom captures this sense of the significance of the issue in a reference to Max Weber's account of the process of rationalization in the West and the consequent disenchantment of the world. Weber located the precipitating cause of modern rationalization in the theological rationalization of the Protestant reformation. It is no accident that at the core of this rationalization was the rejection of the mystery of the real presence of Christ in the Host – the subject of the third epigraph to this chapter. But Weber traces this process back to the origins of the West, and to such rationalizing accidents of history as the alteration in oracular practice in ancient Judaism which forced the Priest to construct yes-no questions, thus sparing the West the less rational superstitious methods of discerning the truth of the sort that prevailed elsewhere. Brandom gives a different reading of the disenchantment of the world. For Brandom, disenchantment went too far, to the point where

3

the meanings and values that had previously been discerned in things are stripped off along with the supernatural and are understood as projections of human interests, concerns, and activities onto an essentially indifferent and insignificant matter. (Brandom 1994, 48)

Brandom proposes to re-enchant the world by reinstating the belief in normative powers, which is to say, powers in some sense outside of and distinct from the forces known to science.

Normativity against social science

The term "normativity" is a relatively novel addition to philosophy. But the question of the relation between the normative and nonnormative, with which this book is concerned, has a distinctive history of its own. Brandom points to this history by mentioning Samuel von Pufendorf, who defended a system of Natural Law against Thomas Hobbes's disenchanting mechanistic account of sovereignty (Brandom 1994, 46–50; Pufendorf [1688] 1964). The philosophical discussion of law over the course of the subsequent centuries produced an extraordinary collection of variations on the conflict over the source and nature of the binding character of law. Much of this discussion involved regress problems. Pufendorf and his school ended this regress in norms. They argued that the normative fact of Natural Law prevailed before the State existed, that it supplies the guiding principles of all legislation, and that it binds the sovereign himself (Gierke [1880] 1939, 319). Hobbes thought the force of law followed from the nonnormative fact of sovereign power, which necessarily preceded law. The discussion was inseparable from the larger project of secularization. The theme of the critics of natural law was to rid discussion of the law of its superstitious, theological, and mystical elements, as physics had been cleansed.

The defenders of the older traditions pointed to the binding character of the law, and argued that for there to be normatively binding law, there had to be an ultimate source that was itself binding. Kant, who is usually given as a source of the idea of normativity, contributed to this discussion by arguing

> that the absolute law of reason is binding on all rational beings by virtue of its rationality, that the state freely legislates the law of reason into positive law, and that it does so because the state's own nature requires it to act rationally. (Gierke [1880] 1939, 321)

This reasoning is characteristic of normativism. Pufendorf, Kant, and the *Naturrecht* tradition that lies behind this play a double game.

They explain the realities (of the state, in this case) in terms of a deeper reality hidden within (for example, in the form of an intrinsic nature). This hidden reality is systematically distinct from and different than the empirical reality – in this case, the reality of actual law and the actions done by actual states. The intrinsic features provide normative standards, which are systematically discrepant from what actually occurs. But this double game is also what gives the disenchanters their opening. They can deny that there is anything intrinsically there, or necessarily there. This is the core of the issue of normativity: normativity is a name for the non-natural, non-empirical stuff that is claimed to be necessarily, intrinsically there, and to in some sense account for the actual.

The social sciences play a special role in the twentieth-century part of this larger story of disenchantment, and place this particular philosophical literature in an unusual relation to "science." The empirical material that is associated with the current problem of normativity, that is, the things that normative notions explain, was already addressed by the social sciences by the time the term "normativity" was introduced. There were social-science explanations of such phenomena as the state and law, and these explanations were designed to replace both folk and *Naturrecht* conceptions of the state. So present normativism, as I will call it, is a more or less self-conscious attempt to take back ground lost to social-science explanation.

One of the central points in the normativity literature is that normativism competes with social science explicitly. The empirical fact of normativity is called "sociological" to distinguish it from real normativity (Brown 2001, 160–61), and it is expressly argued that sociological normativity, which is often dismissed as "mere" sociological normativity, is not the subject of the normativists' discussions, which in turn means that facts of sociology cannot refute claims about normativity. This is a way of conceding the explanatory point to the social scientists and taking it back at the same time. It sets up the problem of normativity in a certain way: the empirical sociological phenomenon of normativity is not denied, but it is not enough to explain what needs to be explained. The thing which must be explained varies, but the usual formulations involve obligation. The mere sociological fact that people believe a given practice to be obligatory does not make it so. It is the extra thing that does make it so that needs to be explained.

This line of reasoning preserves the double game. And it opens the door to a particular claim of dependence: that the normative concept of, for example, the law, is indispensable to *empirical* explanation of legal phenomena, that to speak nonnormatively about such a thing as the law is to "change the subject," that "sociological" accounts of these things improperly presuppose, or, in present terms, "help themselves to," normative language, and thus wrongly come to their naturalistic conclusions, and so forth. The same kinds of dependence or regress arguments appear, and are stronger, when it is a matter of the normative character of reason itself. How can one reason, even "sociologically," about anything at all without reasoning according to reason in the normative sense of correct reason?

These are compelling arguments. But O'Neill's mention of "huge disagreement about the source and authority of norms" should serve as a warning that all is not right with this reasoning.

These claims have regularly come to grief when the time comes to explain what normativity means, where it comes from, and why it is that what is normative in one social setting or intellectual context is not normative in another. The last issue, the problem of local norma-tivity, is especially important. Different groups of people, different professions, users of different languages have different norms. The fact that what counts as correct, true, or valid differs from setting to setting compels us to recognize that this variation is, in some sense of this problematic term, "social."

Unsurprisingly, answers to questions about the source and authority of norms traffic in sociological concepts. Community plays a central role in Saul Kripke's discussion of rule-following in Wittgenstein (1982, 56, 79–81, 89–109 passim) and in subsequent discussions of the problem. Collective intentionality is central to Sellars, who reinterprets Kant's notion of rational beings in terms of a rational col-lectivity of rational beings whose collective intentions are the source of the binding character of reason (DeVries 2005, 266–67; Sellars 1968, VII § 144: 225, 226; 1967, 411).[1] Do these usages mean that the end of the regress is in sociological facts? Kripke's seems to – it ends, or appears to end, in actual communities. Sellars's community of rational beings, however, is entirely virtual. The normativist can deny that there is an issue here and say that the relevant sociologi-cal concepts, such as community, are themselves dual concepts, with both a normative and a sociological sense. This allows them to say that the sense of community needed to account for the normativity of rule-following is the normative sense rather than the sociological. Or they can argue that such concepts as "practice" are normative rather than causal (Rouse 2002, 19–22).

Each of these arguments has problems. But the dual-character argument opens a door that normativists do not want to open; a door to a dualism in which the normative has no explanatory or meta-physical significance at all. The issue appears in a particularly sharp form in connection with the program known as SSK, the sociology of scientific knowledge. SSK operates with what it takes to be a natural-istic notion of reason, in which reasons figure as causes of the beliefs of scientists. But SSK wishes to remain neutral with respect to questions about validity, and objects, in the words of David Bloor, to "the intrusion of a non-naturalistic notion of reason into the causal story" ([1976] 1991, 177, cited in Friedman 1998, 245). This insistence, Michael Friedman suggests,

> rests on a misunderstanding. All that is necessary to stop such an "intrusion" of reason is mere abstinence from normative or prescriptive considerations. We can simply describe the wealth of beliefs, arguments, deliberations, and negotiations that are usually at work in scientific practice, as Bloor says above, "without regard to whether the beliefs are true or the inferences rational." In this way, we can seek to explain why scientific beliefs are in fact accepted without considering whether they are, at the same time, rationally or justifiably accepted. And in such a descriptive, purely naturalistic enterprise, there is precisely enough room for sociological explanations of why certain scientific beliefs are accepted as the empirical material permits. Whether or not philosophers succeed in fashioning a normative or prescriptive lens through which to view these very same beliefs, arguments, deliberations and so on, is entirely irrelevant to the prospects for empirical sociology. In this sense, there is simply no possibility of conflict or competition between "nonnaturalistic," philosophical investigations of reason, on the one hand, and descriptive, empirical sociology of scientific knowledge on the other. (1998, 245)

This is a very rich statement, and it provides an alternative picture, with a distinctive but nevertheless impeccably Kantian pedigree, for an account of the relation of the causal or sociological and the normative that does not invoke normativity as something in the same explanatory domain as the causal, that is to say as a fact which is relevant to explanation.

Friedman prefaces this statement by asking "why SSK represents itself as in conflict or competition with traditional philosophy. Why do we not simply acknowledge the fundamental divergence in aims and methods and leave it at that?" (1998, 244). The question has the effect of putting the normativist, as distinct from the normative philosopher of science, out of business, for it treats the normativity that is all around us as something we impose on a causal world that is unaffected by our "fashioning a normative prescriptive lens" through which to view it. If Friedman's picture is right, there is no problem of finding the place of normativity in the causal world because the idea that there is such a place is simply false.

The presence of normative language and normative belief, from Friedman's point of view, tells us nothing about the presence of some sort of shadow realm of normativity. We are the sources of normativity. The normativity we find in the world, "the meaning and values that had been previously discerned in things," were put there by us, and we had no effect on the things themselves. Normative reasoning is and should be trapped in this circle of imposing, and then falling for the illusion that we are discerning that which we have imposed. The normativist rejects this picture, and even on the basis of the little that has been said here about the idea of normativity, one can see why. Friedman, in his first sentence, insists that we may abstain from normative or prescriptive considerations. The normativist, in contrast, says that such considerations are ineliminable and are an integral and inextricable part of the phenomena to be explained, and part also of the explanations themselves. The normativist denies that we can simply describe the wealth of beliefs, negotiations, and the like that go into scientific practice without reference to normative considerations, such as whether an inference is rational. Even identifying the beliefs requires us to attribute rationality to the scientists we are studying. Explaining their inferences without reference to their rationality, the normativist would say, is not possible. Applying decision theory to account for their errors, for example, requires an appeal to the normative model of decision theory itself. Science, the normativist would say, is a normative concept, not a sociological one, and distinguishing science from voodoo requires the normative sense of science, something that the causalist as Friedman describes him cannot appeal to. The SSK model of explanation uses the notion of belief as a cause. But belief is itself, normativists routinely claim, a normative concept, as is the concept of concept. And the SSK model relies on the idea that explaining a belief can be done on the basis of beliefs alone. But the explanation of scientific beliefs as science necessarily involves the normative relation of truth between the objective world and the beliefs in question, since science aspires to truth, not merely to the satisfaction of one or another subjective belief about truth. The normativity that is everywhere is a matter of some kind of fact, or a condition of facticity itself: the idea that normative considerations can be understood as a matter of "fashioning a normative lens" is anathema.

The door Friedman's argument opens is to a way of making sense of normative language *as* normative without invoking a shadow world of normativities, or a dualistic metaphysics of the normative standing in some problematic relation to the natural. The normativist wants this door closed, because it looks like an attractive option when we begin to inquire into the difficulties of normativism. It is these difficulties that are the focus of this book.

The standard argument form

My concern in this book will be with the common form of argument underlying various assertions about the necessity or indispensability of the normative, and therefore of "normativity." O'Neill's comment about disagreement, it turns out, is partly true and partly false. What is true is that there are a variety of normativity arguments, each of which accounts for a different kind of normativity, which are not easily reconciled with one another. There are also different ideas about the sources of particular kinds of normativity, such as legal or semantic normativity. But there are, nevertheless, extremely strong family resemblances between these arguments. And the family exhibits a large number of genetic defects. In the rest of this chapter I will briefly describe a standard-type or ideal normativity argument and then describe the defects to which this family of arguments is prone. In the following chapter I will do something similar for the naturalistic, social-science explanations of the normative. In Chapter 3, I will discuss a specific, paradigmatic case – as it happens, the case of one of the progenitors of this family – in detail.

The structure of normativity arguments can be summarized in terms of a series of steps with a major disjuncture in the middle: the point where the normative fact appears. The background to normative facts is ordinary, involving the kinds of facts that are part of the ordinary stream of explanation. There is nothing binding, compelling, or constraining about these facts. So these new normative facts constitute a rupture in the world of ordinary fact. The normative, however, arises out of ordinary facts: meanings, obligations, rationality, and so forth come into existence through actions, learning, and the like but have the special added properties of norms: of binding, constraining, and the rest. Once the norms are established, they have consequences for behavior. They do not directly cause behavior, but they regulate it normatively, by specifying what is the right way to say something, what obligations one has, what one owes to others as a result of one's meaningful actions, and what is justified for others to do in response to your actions.

The beginning point of the structure is that which can be naturally or causally explained. One can, as a kind of shorthand, refer to these as dispositional explanations, because they typically involve dispositions of some kind – expectations, for example, that are produced by some finite process such as learning. It is important to note that normativists ordinarily do not deny the existence of these causes, or say that they explain nothing. Instead they claim that the phenomena to be accounted for, which the normativist takes as distinctively normative, are more than these kinds of considerations can explain. Expectations may have, for example, a role to play in the creation of obligations, but obligation is *more* than expectation. The "more" is taken to be the distinctively normative content, which cannot be accounted for by the causal or dispositional explanations at hand, such as the causal explanations of learning that account for the dispositions that produce people's expectations.[2] For convenience, one can keep a few of these special objects in mind: meanings, binding laws, obligations, rules, and so forth. None of them can be fully accounted for by the available causal accounts, or so it is argued.

Typically there is an issue of description with respect to these facts, an issue over what I have called the double structure of *genuine* and *sociological or empirical*. The issue may take a variety of forms. In the case of law, as we will see, the question is whether what can be explained causally or nonnormatively is "really law." Sometimes the issue is formulated in terms of qualitative differences or differences between the things that need to be explained and the explainers. Semantic normativity, for example, or the rules governing meaning, is infinite in character (in the sense that the meaning of my statement today does not change in the future and I am thus in some sense committed to this meaning in perpetuity), while the explanatory facts that make up such things as the dispositions to use words in given ways, which are the result of learning, are finite, as the learning process itself is. Often this special character is simply assumed or asserted. But the problem of description becomes apparent when a social-science explanation already exists, and is criticized by arguing that the *explananda* does not match the object to be accounted for. In short, the normativist claims in each case that there is a novel thing which social science can't explain, and can't explain because it is of a novel kind.

The novel thing that can't be accounted for in the normal (social science) way must be accounted for in another way. Typically this is done by transcendental arguments, in which conditions of the possibility of this thing are identified. These conditions can then be

10

asserted to have been met by virtue of (the uncontroversial fact of) the existence of the thing itself, such as a "meaning." These conditions for possibility are necessarily different in kind from the conditions that ordinarily operate in causal contexts, or else there would be no need to appeal to the notion of normativity. As noted earlier, the existence of these things is typically supported by *tu quoque* arguments to the effect that anti-normativists "help themselves" to concepts, considerations, and so on that are the property of the normativist, or that they speak about them in a way that "changes the subject." A typical example is the notion of concept. The anti-normativist will refer to concepts or necessarily employ concepts in their own thought, and thus concede the normativists' point: that normativity is real and necessary. Similarly for meaning: the normativist can invoke *tu quoque* arguments: that, for example, to insist that a rejection at the notion of meaning would be incoherent because it would imply that the rejection itself was without meaning. Or the anti-normativist will make the reflexive error of referring to a "good theory" and thus concede the reality of goodness.

Non-philosopher anti-normativists – for example, cognitive scientists who are concerned to account theoretically for the kind of thinking called conceptual – are unimpressed by these arguments for the simple reason that they consider the concept of "concept" to be up for grabs and a matter for future science to determine through the normal process of testing theoretical hypotheses against data. And this was the response of the Strong Programme as well: we are just scientists. In science, nothing hangs on the essential definition of terms; what counts as real depends on the findings and the theories that explain them. And this is also the attitude of philosophical naturalisms, such as Quine's. This is the point at which the conflict occurs. The normativist relies on an argument of conceptual necessity: if one says x, one must accept its conceptual precondition, y. The anti-normativist, typically, argues that there is nothing out of the ordinary stream of explanation, so there are no special facts of the kind normativism insists on. Whatever "meaning" and "concepts" are, accordingly, they are not going to have the properties normativists ascribe to them, such as the power ascribed to semantic rules of binding into the infinite future. The normativist reply to this is that they must have these properties to support inferences, to justify, and so forth: to abandon these special properties is to give up on intelligibility itself.

This is the core issue. Why? Because the claim of the anti-normativist is that the normative moment in the middle of the standard story, the source of all the issues, *is* eliminable. *Can* the social scientist provide explanations that get from the inputs, like learnings, dispositions, beliefs, and so forth, to the outputs, that is to say, the empirical facts of communication and behavior which need explanation, without appealing to the normative concepts of meaning, obligation, reason, and the like? If this is the case, normativity needs to be understood not as fact but as an explanatorily inert aspect of facts. Joseph Raz speaks in a way congenial to this when he says that there is a normative *aspect* to reasons, and that the goodness of a reason or its normative significance is an aspect (Raz 1999, 113). This way of thinking of normative significance leaves a great deal of scope for reflection and for fashioning a normative lens to better understand this aspect. It leaves no scope for grounding anything on normativity understood as fact. As facts, they are facts solely in the sense that they appear as such in a particular lens. They do no explanatory work and are not part of the mechanism.

The disagreement involves both what is to be explained and how it is to be explained. The anti-normativist accepts that there may be a need for theoretical terms, as in science generally, thinks that the thing to be explained is the observables (such as human behavior), and thinks that normal explanations, such as causal explanations, will suffice, and have to suffice. If they do not, we have a genuine mystery, which doesn't help the normativist either. The normativist thinks that this misses the point. There are things that need to be accounted for that are not only not mysterious, but absolutely central to our life and thought, and thus have to be accounted for. Moreover, the account should occupy a central place in our metaphysics. As Sellars puts it, the problem is to fuse the scientific image with the normative one. If the conditions for the possibility of these essential things are *recherché*, and involve exotic objects, that is a price that must be paid: no one said philosophy would be easy or correspond with common sense. Paul Boghossian puts this issue clearly when he lists a series of peculiarities that arise because "meaning properties appear to be neither eliminable nor reducible," and then suggests that "perhaps it is time we learned to live with that fact" (1989, 548). For the anti-normativist, this is mystery-mongering.[3]

The "does it matter" problem

The key to the appeal of the concept of normativity is that normative facts are irreducible, meaning impossible to explain in nonnormative terms, and at the same time ineliminable. But in what ways are they ineliminable? The normativist needs to say that they are ineliminable from explanation: if "a normative *must* is to have a distinctive place in the world" (Railton 2000, 4; emphasis in the original), the "must" needs to have some explanatory role. Does it? Scientists may be unable to talk about their theories without using normative terms like "good" and "elegant" or even "must." But this normative language does not, in any simple or direct way, require us to believe in normativities. It would be a different matter if we could not *explain* their ways of talking about their theories without appealing to the notion of normativity, and this is what the normativist needs to claim: that a special fact of normativity is presupposed or required in some sense by this talk or to make this talk intelligible. But there is a generic problem with such claims. The problem is that ordinarily the explanation of actions involves beliefs. The validity of the beliefs, normative or otherwise, is not explanatory in itself. Beliefs in non-existent things, such as ghosts, also explain people's behavior, their other beliefs, and so forth.

The issue is not a new one. Weber argued that religious rationalizations of the problem of theodicy had profound causal effects on European history, and, indeed, that this problem set in motion a chain of effects that led to the same disenchantment of the world that Robert Brandom mentions. Weber claimed that the reflections of John Calvin on the fundamental questions of life and the universe, framed, as one would expect, in terms of the theology of the time, were driven by a resolute attempt to make Christian theology rational and consistent, especially with regard to the central (and as Weber argued, for salvation religions, universal) problem of theodicy. This argument, however, seems to involve a normative concept of rationality in which a human drive for consistency can have powerful effects. Weber, it could be argued, has fallen inadvertently into normativism, helping himself to the normative notion of consistency. And this normative notion, in this context, seems to do some important explanatory work. Alasdair MacIntyre made precisely this argument, though not in these terms. He argued that the relationship between Calvinist doctrine and the effects Weber described was "logical" (1962, 55), and credited Weber for having discerned it, but argued that Weber made a mistake by thinking it was a causal explanation. If the explanation was not causal, logic would be doing explanatory work.

But did Weber make this mistake? A final answer to this question will need to be delayed until the last chapter. It will suffice here to note that rationality is another example of a concept that has a dual nature. It is a normative concept. There is also a philosophical tradition that treats rationality as a disposition (Hempel 1965, 469–87; cf. Davidson [1976] 1980, 273). Weber's notion of rationality seems to be dispositional as well as normative. But the dispositional aspect is all that is needed to do the explanatory work. The normative consideration of whether the conclusions drawn by Calvin's followers were *genuinely* 'logical' seems to make no difference at all, and to add nothing, to the explanation, as an explanation. As Friedman's argument suggests, explaining can make do by treating beliefs as causes, and can leave judgments about rationality or theological correctness – in this case the same thing – to the theologians.

The explanatory peculiarities of normativity

The argument form I have outlined here is a composite of various normativity arguments. Not all the arguments in the family of normativity arguments concern themselves with the whole set of claims. Many are concerned only with the transcendental arguments that can be employed to account for normative language, and ignore even the distinction between the sociological and the genuine sense of "norm." In some ethical writers, for example, the normative character of this and that is taken as self-evident (Nagel 1986, 159–60; Korsgaard 1996, 41), and the existence of alternative accounts of norms is not even acknowledged. Ignoring them amounts to taking a free pass on the central problem of normativism: the strangeness of the explanations given by the normativist. But some of the literature on normativity frankly addresses, or at least acknowledges, that the notion of normativity is unusual and problematic. The response to this unusualness has been to say that one must learn to live with it (Boghossian 1989, 548), to embrace it (Brandom 1979, 192), to make it a foundation of a radical normativist antidualist ontology so that everything is ultimately normative (Rouse 2002), to minimize the oddity by contrasting it to even more spooky entities, like those of Platonism (McDowell 1996), or to attempt to separate it from the ordinary stream of explanation (Korsgaard 1996). There are multiple aspects to the problem of this strangeness, which I will simply list and briefly elaborate here.

Queerness

The claim that there are such things as normativities and normative powers is characteristically bound up with claims about special and

14

puzzling objects: self-authorizing principles; rules, understood as tacit rules behind the explicit rules we might invent or propose; mathematical objects, which are not realized in the physical world; objective values; dictates without dictators, the dictates of reason itself, performative utterances which have the property of being able to create a norm, through the act of utterance of a special ritual kind; the nonspatial space of reason; the constraining ideal structure of thought experiments; intentions without intenders, except for supposed collectives, which, despite being wholly analogical, have the power to create and warrant norms; commitments that are unlike ordinary commitments in that they are made without anyone knowing that they were made, in which the person undertaking the commitments could not have understood them as commitments when they made them, or perhaps even afterward. David Lewis, in the paper from which Brandom takes the notions of commitments and score-keeping, proposes a kinematics of presupposition, in which if anything needing a presupposition is said in time t, the necessary presupposition, if it did not previously exist, comes into existence at time t (Lewis 1979, 340). Lewis formulates a "rule of accommodation for permissibility" as follows:

> If at time t something is said about permissibility by the master to the slave that requires for its truth the permissibility of certain courses of action, and if just before t the boundary is such as to make the master's statement false, then – *ceteris paribus* and within certain limits – the boundary shifts at t so as to make the master's statement true. (Lewis 1979, 341)

The range is from these objects whose lifetimes extend only through the utterance of a sentence to immutable Fregean concepts and the Platonic forms themselves. These odd objects, it may be noted, have analogues in social theory and social science, often with equally mysterious features, such as the collective consciousness in Durkheim, or the notion of the central value system of a society in Talcott Parsons, or the "essentially unavoidable and irremediable haecceity of immortal ordinary society" of Harold Garfinkel's ethnomethodology (1991, 10, 19n10).

Dependence on transcendental arguments

The claim that these things exist usually rests on a particular type of argument which is transcendental, or presuppositional. The claim is that such and such an object, space, intention, or the like, is a condition for the possibility of something that is itself indispensable, obviously true, constitutive of our humanity, reason, or the like. The problem with these arguments is their use: they seem to be stand-ins for causal explanations, but fail to live up to any of the standards of explanation that causal explanations are normally held to.

Construction by analogy

Many normative objects, especially those that figure at the end of regression arguments, are analogical. The objects include rules that are not explicit rules, but rather tacit rules hidden behind rules; commitments that are not commitments in an explicit intentional sense, but something given preintentionally or tacitly; laws, such as the *Grundnorm*, which is not itself enacted as law and so forth. Analogical usages are common enough in philosophy – "true" and "norm" are terms from carpentry, for example. But these devices used in these arguments have an odd common structure: they are hidden or tacit forms of explicit things, and are needed to do work, such as justi-fication, that the explicit things cannot do, namely stop a regress.

Externality

The thingness of normativity is the source of its normative force – it is in some sense outside us and inside us at the same time. When we rec-ognize it fully we are at the same time recognizing that we must obey. There is a parallel with the ontological argument for the existence of God here. To merely treat the normative as conventional, pragmatic, or sociological is to fail to fully understand it. To fully understand it is to believe, to accept, or to acknowledge our pre-acceptance of it and dependence on it.

Acknowledgment

The common thread in these claims about normativity is in our rela-tion to it. It is something to be acknowledged and accepted as a con-straint or obligation – something that is, in the Heideggerian phrase, always already there, but which we only express or recognize through reflection, or admit the power of when we reach the age of reason. McDowell formulates this clearly:

> The idea is that the dictates of reason are there anyway, whether or not one's eyes are opened to them; that is what happens in a proper

16

upbringing. We need not try to understand the thought that the dictates of reason are objects of an enlightened awareness, except from within the way of thinking such an upbringing initiates one into: a way of thinking that constitutes a standpoint from which those dictates are already in view. (1996, 91–92)

Duality and Circularity

These objects trespass across the line between *is* and *ought*. They are facts that warrant values or oughts or that are values or oughts, or from which normative language can be derived. But are they normative themselves? The question typically produces a dilemma, which can be seen in the case of Kripke's appeal to community standards of correctness with respect to rule-following. Are these "community" facts empirical or normative? The community here can't be the empirical community, for the whole of the actual membership of the actual community might be in error. Nor can it be the empirical community after the error is pointed out, because the members of the community might also be wrong about this. To appeal to the empirical community leads either to a regress or to the abandonment of an idea of normativity beyond the empirical fact of community assent. But the community can't be a normative fact either – such as the community of those who are correctly admitted to membership in the community by virtue of having correctly grasped the rule. This results in circularity – which is also a problem for the hypothetical community of rational beings.

The claim of surplus force

A major underlying issue with these odd objects – such as notions of meaning or conceptual content – is this: there is a gap, surplus meaning, or what I have called a disjuncture, between the naturalistic explanations – dispositions, paradigmatically – and the thing to be explained. The problem is with what dispositions or anything else could possibly explain: if they explain law as systematic rules with sanctions, they don't explain why the rules are obligatory. That seems to require something more: normative force. By making this distinction, it seems we create a novel ontological realm beyond explanation, which has mysterious properties. But what necessitates the existence of this realm? A real force? Or our desire to appeal to obligations and the like as justifications?

17

The question of whether linguistic normativity serves as the fons et origo of all normativity

There is more than a hint of this idea in much of the writing on normativity (Brandom 1979, 190). But it runs into a stubborn issue within linguistic normativity, which undermines any extension to other domains. What is the logical relation between *counts as* normativity and obligations to speak correctly in accordance with these conventions? (Brandom 1997, 193; Kusch 2006, 51–55). What is the normative force of the conventions? Are they merely conventions, coordination devices, in David Lewis's phrase (1969, 42), which we adopt pragmatically, like driving on the left or right, which derive their normative force from other, in this case moral or legal considerations, such as the fact that by driving on the incorrect side one is likely to kill or be killed or incur sanctions? Or do they derive directly – so that by acknowledging that there is a correct and incorrect way we immediately acquire or admit an obligation to act accordingly? This is McDowell's picture:

> To learn the meaning of a word is to acquire an understanding that obliges us subsequently – if we have occasion to deploy the concept in question – to judge and speak in determinate ways, on pain of failure to obey the dictates of the meaning we have grasped. (McDowell [1984] 2002, 45)

The problem of separating normative from pragmatically successful

For some philosophers, the issue of normativity comes down to the issue of semantic normativity, which can be construed as the source of all normativity. But there is a problem here, which is revealing about the larger question of how various notions of normativity (and various types of normative language) relate to one another. The core reasoning is this: semantic normativity is signaled by the distinction between correct and incorrect application of terms, and the problem of correctness is intrinsic to language, which makes language and anything linguistic by definition normative. The core kind of normativity here is constitutive: it is about what *counts as* something – what counts as a horse or a duck. But what is the difference between using an utterance *successfully*, for example when ordering dinner in a foreign language, and using it *correctly* in the normative sense? And why should one think there is a difference between the two?

18

There are no grammatical errors in a preliterate society – there is simply being understood and not being understood. In one respect – the empirical, pragmatic one – semantic normativity is governed by the same principle: the correctness of semantic use is no more or less than being understood. So how does genuine semantic normativity – correctness beyond mere usage – arise? Or is there such a thing? In the case of syntax, we produce the normativity of grammar by writing grammars and then using them as a guide or norm of correct speech, regardless of what people actually understand. It is an add-on, in which some model of speech is taken as normative, or in which someone's theory of what is right is imposed on actual, divergent, but intelligible speech to stigmatize something as bad, erroneous, and the like. Is genuine semantic normativity more than this? Presumably it is. So we have two basic models of meaning: one is of an ideal object, collectively held, that has the power of distinguishing correct and incorrect usage infinitely into the future; the other is a notion of meaning as *works in interaction*, as speech behavior, a functional summary of the actual behavioral usages that produce a specific set of similar results when used with certain people in diverse situations, and which is open-ended and changes through adaptation and extension.

The transition problem

Each account of normativity that makes a distinction between the normative and the nonnormative – that is, accounts other than those that collapse everything into the normative – involves some sort of transition between a nonnormative or pre-normative state and the normative one. This is even a problem for the metaphysical normativist, who believes that everything is normative, and argues that the evidence for this includes the presence of various kinds of normativity. When this normativist tries to account for the production of one kind of normativity out of another, a form of the transition problem arises. There is a standard successful model for creating norms by relying on norms: as in the case of the norm (such as a constitution) that gives authority to a norm-giver to create norms (such as a legislature). But the chain of normative justification needs to end somewhere. Does it end in something nonnormative, such as Wittgenstein's "what we do," or something normative which is basic – Kelsen's *Grundnorm*, for example? If it is the former, how does something nonnormative produce something normative? Does it have to end in a norm-creating act of will, such as the will of the people, or in norm-creating

19

commitments, on the model of obligations freely entered into? How do these transitions work, exactly?

These accounts model normative commitment and the like on law. But even in the case of law there are problems. H. L. A. Hart recognized that Kelsen's answer did not work – that even *Grundnorms* needed to be grounded in something more basic (Hart 1961, 117; cf. Postema 1987, 89)[4]. J. L. Austin's notion of performative utterance[5] might seem to be a solution to the problem, at least the problem of transition from non-law to law. A law was something said to be law by the appropriate person in the appropriate setting. But this is a purely formal solution. The explanation is missing. One needs to know something about *why* the person or setting is appropriate. Since "appropriate" and similar terms seem to be normative concepts, the problem of normativity is not solved by appeal to them. It is just pushed a step back, and the answers there are problematic. The idea that by going through the ritual of voting and signing pieces of paper, legislatures and executives or parliaments transform utterances by magically infusing them with the collective will, thus making them obligatory, was ridiculed in some of the funniest writing in the history of philosophy by the Scandinavian legal realist Axel Hägerström (1953, 74–116), as Hart knew well. Hägerström's point was that the whole appeal to will in these cases was fanciful. The people who were supposedly doing the willing into existence of laws, such as the sovereign, were ordinarily unaware of the content of the law, much less engaged in an act of infusing them with normative force. He concluded that ideas about will make more sense as political fictions than as true accounts of the nature of law.

The problem of transition arises in a variety of forms other than this paradigmatic one. In McDowell, there is the point at which the child comes to recognize the bindingness of norms of rationality. In Kripke, there is the point at which a person is taken into the community as a competent rule-follower. As with Kelsen, the issue haunts those who seek to evade it, such as Brandom, who places himself in the paradoxical position of basing his conception of the normativity of score-keeping (thus of language proper) on the normative fact of commitment, but denies that prelinguistic conduct is properly intentional, which seems to mean that it cannot include commitments.

The problem of belief

The epigraph from Calvin that prefaces this chapter refers to the central episode in the disenchantment of the world, the denial that

"Jesus Christ is corporeally, really, and in fact entirely and personally in the flesh contained and concealed in the species of bread and wine, as grand and as perfect as if he were living in the present" (Holt 1995, 18). Calvin, as the epigraph indicates, believed that what you got out of the Eucharist was what you put into it in the form of faith. The normativist does not merely urge us to believe and make it so, in the fashion of Augustine, but rather insists that the normativity in question is real *apart from our beliefs*, and a matter of discovery or acceptance, or that something different in kind, a normative fact, is created by our actions.

The problem of description

According to an old joke, a Texas Baptist was asked whether he believed in infant baptism. "Believe, hell," he replied, "I seen it done!" The joke works, if I may belabor the obvious, because there is a difference between the normative and theological sense of "I believe in infant baptism" and the factual sense. In the normative sense, the Texan would have been in error: a true Baptist believes that infant "baptism" so-called is not baptism at all, so in fact he could not have seen such a thing. In another and equally familiar sense, of course, he is correct. He had seen what a non-Baptist would call, and he could also, speaking in non-Baptist terms, call, "infant baptism." The normativist is constantly forced to take the theologians' side of this argument. The arguments for the existence of normative things, and for the attribution of powers to them, begin with establishing a privileged description of the things to be explained. This is a traditional problem of the philosophy of social science, perhaps one of its central problems. Peter Winch's *The Idea of a Social Science* (1958) is based on the insistence that to talk about human behavior in terms other than the (normative) conceptual terms of ordinary action is to change the subject.

The short "scientistic" reply to such arguments is that scientists are under no obligation to employ any particular vocabulary, and it should be no surprise that explanations may be available in one vocabulary and not another. Changing vocabularies is part of the explanatory enterprise. Social scientists, however, may be in a different position, as Weber (1949, 111) argued, and need to use value-related concepts to define their explanatory problems. But they can use terms such as "norm" or "law" in a purposely nonnormative way to denote the empirical equivalent of the term, to bracket the normative aspect, and thus free themselves of the normative implications of the concept. This possibility is not limited to scientists. The Texan could have saved himself from the joke by explaining that what he had seen done was what people mistakenly believed was baptism. And this raises an important point: we use false descriptions that we disagree with all the time. We use them along with an error theory or error explanation which accounts for the difference between the descriptions used by others and those we use.

This response bears on the *tu quoque* arguments routinely employed by normativists. If the interlocutor of the normativist uses a term such as "concept" or "inference" there is no need for this term to be used or taken in the normativist's sense. The normativist can argue that there can be no other sense than the normative one, but in virtually all the cases in which these issues arise, there is an ambiguity between normative and nonnormative senses of the term. A simple example is this: "What makes it the case that we mean what we mean what we say? Nothing, says the sceptic, apparently refuting himself in the process. For if the sceptical claim is true, it is meaningless. And if it is meaningless, it cannot be true" (Lillehammer 2008). The problem with these arguments is that they depend on an equivocation. The skeptic says that there is no such thing as a meaning, in the conventional sense that there is something behind the utterance, a meaning which makes us mean something. But denying meanings in this sense is not the same as denying, for example, that I can understand what you are saying and that others can also understand you. So this *tu quoque* argument fails, as perhaps all of their analogues do.

Underdetermination and privileged descriptions

One oddity of transcendental arguments is this: they work only when there is no underdetermination, which is to say where the logical conditions for some possibility are univocal. But in the kinds of cases discussed by normativists, there are ordinarily a variety of theories of the normative conditions for the possibility of a given kind of assertion. They can't all be necessary; if each is sufficient, none is necessary. So these arguments must proceed by establishing claims to identify the sole condition for the possibility of the normative fact in question. This is then done by knocking out competing alternatives. In this respect the arguments have the progressive character of traditional philosophical analysis, in which the protocol is "present a theory, come up with counterexamples, iterate." Some of the discussion of semantic normativity follows this pattern, where alternative accounts are eliminated (cf. Boghossian 1989; Kusch 2006, 50–236; Miller and

Wright 2002; Wright 1986). But a persistent feature of these discussions is a more radical kind of conflict, in which the examples don't eliminate the alternatives, and don't point to any univocal condition.

The solution to this problem is often to fiddle with the descriptions of the possibilities for which conditions are being sought, and to change the descriptions in such a way that the preferred precondition becomes the only viable solution to the transcendental question. Brandom, for example, revises Wittgenstein by deciding that the builders, whose language game only involves the words "blocks," "pillars," "slabs," and "beams," are not really engaged in language (1994, 172).[6] The same kinds of claims are routinely made about animal communication. In the case of law, the normativist will say even if "law" is extensionally equivalent to "rules with sanctions enforced by a specialized role incumbent," even if everything we normally call "law," and nothing else, falls in this category, it is not the same thing. To call "rules" thus described "law," in this account, is to change the subject.

A problem of underdetermination that creates a different kind of issue arises from speech and culture's diversity. Attempts to draw normative transcendental conclusions about the mind from the usages of folk psychology, for example, are compromised by the fact that there is no one folk psychology, but many languages that translate into one another more or less well yet which may have very different usages for psychological phenomena. Rodney Needham did a study of epistemic terms such as "belief," based in large part on the problems revealed in the course of translating the Bible, which showed how diverse the language of knowledge and belief actually was, and that in some languages no terms corresponding to "belief" or to the belief/knowledge distinction existed (Needham 1972, 47; 1972, 33, 35). This poses a problem for attempts to derive metaphysical results from what are essentially local cultural usages: one gets different results from different cultures, a kind of underdetermination that undermines the whole project. The claim of necessity no longer holds, or rather holds only conditionally, for the speakers of a given culture.

One can say that the issue is not with the surface forms of belief talk, but with the conditions of talk as such. But this creates a problem about evidence. Why is *our* talk a means of access to underlying metaphysical realities through the device of identifying the conditions for talk's possibility, and theirs not? In fact, analytic philosophy routinely assumes that *our* talk and *our* common sense can be used as a stand-in for talk and common sense generally. If they could not be used this way, the analysis would apply only to our group. And asking what

23

the underlying reality is for our group begins to look like a scientific or anthropological question rather than a metaphysical one.

The use of transcendental arguments to make causal claims

Suppose we argue, as is commonly argued in the normativity literature, that the normative character of something is the result of "commitment," and suppose also that the argument for this claim is (and one cannot readily imagine an alternative to this) a transcendental, "condition for the possibility" argument. Are the commitments *causes* of the normative properties that the transcendental arguments account for? Isn't there something odd about getting *causal* results out of this kind of argument? Aren't genuine causal arguments usually subject to other kinds of considerations, such as confounding, underdetermination, the need for additional warrants, and the like? And aren't causal considerations disrespectful of claims based on preferred descriptions? One might style these arguments as causal in the sense that they eliminate all but one explanation. But eliminative arguments are notoriously subject to difficulties over description: if the underlying causal realities are incorrectly described, the eliminative argument may produce false positives – causes that are not causes. So arguing that these are eliminative arguments pushes us back to the problem of underlying causes, rather than solving it.

Circularity, thinly concealed

A typical normativity argument asserts something like this:

> The mark of being a language is that claims can be questioned and justified. Genuine justification is something in which there are genuine warrants. Genuine warranting is, by definition, a normative relation. Hence language is normative.

What makes this argument work is, first, the preferred definition of language in terms of justification, and second, the use of a normative notion of justification. Is there a nonnormative notion? One can, of course, describe the same justification behavior nonnormatively, in terms of challenge and response. And one can make the obvious point that whatever content there is to ordinary cases of justification is something learned – learned in a mundane way, beginning with a child asking, repetitively and without understanding, "Why, Mommy?" in order to get a more favorable result, and eventually learning a more complex use of these terms. But one can then insist

24

that these behavioral facts are not real justification, and thus insufficient to establish the conduct as linguistic.

Two kinds of regress

The case for normativity rests very heavily on the idea that only the normative can account for the normative. As Thornton explains McDowell's account of Wittgenstein:

> Wittgenstein does *not* aim to give an account of norms using concepts that are not themselves norm-presupposing. He does *not* attempt to dig beneath a bedrock of already normative behavior. This is why he describes following a rule as *fundamental* to our language. It is also why he adds, to the well-known comment that reasons or justifications come to an end, the further claim that using an expression without a justification does not mean using it without a right. The ground-level moves made are always within the sphere of norms. (Thornton 2004, 43; emphasis in the original)

Causal regresses just lead back to prior causes. Normative regresses are a different matter. They lead back either to causal facts, which then must be mysteriously transformed into normative facts, or to normative facts. But often what one gets are causal facts characterized oddly, as normative. Why are "practices" normative, when they are the products of ordinary training or learning through feedback? And what does it mean to say that they are normative? Does it mean that they are free of causal considerations? Evidently not, if they are practices, which are learned? So how does the normative element get added in? Is this a causal question? Or a normative one?

If only the normative can account for the normative, is it also the case that the normative can only account for the normative? This would mean that much of what the appeal to normativity seems to be based on – the fact that people can communicate, for example – is itself in the category of normative. It would also mean that the normative and the causal are separate worlds closed to one another, operating in parallel to one another. Brandom seems to reason this way when he says

> the difference between these two "realms" is not an ontological one. The real distinction in the vicinity is between two ways of treating someone's behavior. According to this line of thought, we treat someone as free insofar as we consider him subject to the norms inherent in the social practices conformity to which is the criterion of membership in our community. He is free insofar as he is one of us. Insofar as we cope

with him in terms of the causes which objectively constrain him, rather than the norms which constrain him via our practices, we treat him as an object and unfree. There is no objective fact of the matter concerning his freedom to which we can appeal beyond the judgment of our own community. (1979, 192)

This seems also to lead to the picture of the normative that Friedman gives, that is to say a bunch of explanatory facts which we fashion a normative lens for in order to view them normatively. And this picture can dispense with the idea of normativity as something that has a place in the world. The problems that go with this idea vanish also.

The location problem

The problem of normativity parallels many other problems in philosophy involving dualisms and exotic objects. The mind-body dualism, with its focus on the irreducibility of consciousness and *qualia*, for example, is similar in structure. The special feature of normativity that distinguishes it from the mind-body problem and the case of consciousness is this: the diversity of morals or local normativity. Normativity, at least in the senses in which it is primarily used, changes from one social setting to another. What is normative for Manhattan singles is not normative for Andaman Islanders. So we need an account of normativity, and corresponding objects, that vary in the way that norms themselves vary, or an account of the unity of the normative that accommodates the reality of diversity. In short, there must be some sort of matching up of the normative facts and the people who are bound by them. Are people who speak in a given way bound? Or do they have to be *members* of a collectivity? What does *membership* mean? Can one be a member by the ordinary criteria of belonging in the actual community, but not be part of a collective intention? If not, how does one become a part of a collective intention? Part of the relevant community? This question is usually answered in terms of fictions – fictional acts of accrediting someone, such as a rule or language user, as part of the community. But this just avoids the problem of what *community* means. If one rejects, as some normativists do, the reality of normative diversity, and insists that apparent normative diversity is merely error, one must invent some way to avoid the charge that one is promoting one local normativity over others, and also find a way to accommodate the reality of differences in actual practice, as natural law theory did with the device of calling actual legal practices *imperfect*.

Do the peculiarities matter?

This list of problematic aspects of normativity arguments does not, by itself, refute the claims of normativism or the existence of normativities. It is simply meant as a set of reminders about where these arguments characteristically get into difficulty. The difficulties may not be insurmountable. Or they may need to be swallowed as the price which needs to be paid to preserve one or another relic of the philosophical tradition – mostly relics of the cozy world of Aquinas or of the great re-enchanter Kant.

The number and variety of normativity arguments make even cataloguing them impossible in a short, or even very long, book. But the discussion in this chapter already points to the recurrent exemplary role of the normativity of the law in discussions of normativity. In the third chapter, as already noted, the key argument against the disenchantment of the law, and for its normativity, will be examined. In the next chapter, the disenchanters, both philosophers and social (and other) scientists, will be given a chance to speak in a way that goes beyond the stereotypical construction of naturalism and dispositionalism. The actual explanatory problems faced by any approach to the general problem of norms are substantial. And the adequacy of an account of "the normative" lies in how the account squares up against them.

Notes

1. The intense mutual borrowing and use of such concepts is not new. Bergson's *Two Sources of Morality and Religion* (1935) is a reflection on Émile Durkheim's idea of collective consciousness ([1893] 1964). Ernst Cassirer's concept of an autonomous order of ideas, a realm of pure significance that is binding on us, is attributed to the sociologist Hans Freyer and to Georg Simmel (Cassirer 1996, 186–87; 2000, 74–75; Freyer 1998; Simmel [1908] 1964). And this just scratches the surface. As we will see later, there is a direct historical link from Durkheim's notion of the *conscience collectif* to Sellars's ideas on collective intentionality, and there are numerous common usages.
2. Brandom gives a standard formulation of this in terms of the regress problem:
    > We can still give whatever causal account we like of the objective capacities in virtue of which individuals are able to engage in the complicated practices we attribute to them, for no regress is generated *unless* we seek to explain the ability to engage in those linguistic practices in some fashion which appeals to prior linguistic abilities, e.g., the following of a rule. (1979, 188; emphasis added)

    Why? Because rules, for Brandom, are normative facts, which cannot be causally explained.

3. In much of the discussion of the normativity of reason this issue is considered entirely in epistemic terms, in terms of the problem of how the mind makes contact with these objects, as McDowell puts it (1996, 104–7). The risk is of falling into a kind of Platonism in which not only are the Platonic forms a mystery, our access to them is a mystery as well.

4. These sociological usages raise the regress problem all over again. If the sources of normativity are social, are they not also natural and sociological? This was the bullet that H. L. A. Hart chose to bite in constructing his philosophy of law. The normative character of law, for Hart, was the result of an authorizing rule that made the question of whether a law was valid a legal question to be solved by reference to the rule. But the authorizing rule itself, he conceded, was validated only by the sociological fact that was accepted as an authorizer.

5. Austin's idea of performatives seems to have been inspired by Hart's legal examples (Lacey 2004, 136, 144; Austin 1962, 4–11, 139).

6. "The 'slab' *Sprachspiel* Wittgenstein describes in the opening paragraphs of the *Investigations* is not in this sense a *language* game – it is a set of practices that include only vocal, but not yet verbal, signals" (Brandom 1994, 172; emphasis in the original).

2

THE CONFLICT WITH SCIENCE AND SOCIAL SCIENCE

> *Each Prieft or* Feticheer *hath his peculiar Idol, prepared and adjufted in a particular and different manner. . . . The* Negroe *who is to take an Oath before this Idol, is placed directly oppofite to it, and afks the Prieft the Name of his Idol (each having a particular one;) of which being informed, he calls the* Fetiche *by its Name, and recites at large the Contents of what he defigns to bind by an Oath, and makes it his Petitionary Requeft that the Idol may punifh him with Death if he fwears falfy; then he goes round the Pipe and ftands ftill and fwears a fecond time in the fame place and manner as before, and fo a third time likewife. . . . All which done the Oath is firmly Obligatory.*
>
> Bosman ([1704] 1967, 150–51)

What is the alternative that normativism conflicts with? What sorts of social science or scientific accounts of norms are there, and why are they inadequate? As we have seen in the last chapter, the core problem is one of rupture or disjuncture: the problem of the gap between normative facts and the nonnormative explanations that fail to adequately account for them, and the claim that the appeal to normativity does account for them. We ordinarily hear about this gap from the side of the normativists. The argument was outlined in the last chapter. A paradigmatic form of it is found in the discussion of semantic normativism: the meaning of a term or sentence is an infinite commitment into the future to use the term or sentence in the same way; nothing non-infinite can produce something infinite, so no learnings, dispositions, and the like can account for the fact of a *meaning*. The argument justifies the claim that there is a rupture in ordinary explanation that requires the acceptance of extraordinary kinds of normative facts.

This kind of argument gets the point made from the description

29

end rather than the explanation end. It only works if you accept this account of what a "meaning" is. The naturalistic response starts from the explanation end: if there is no explanation of something to be had within the ordinary stream of explanation, maybe that thing doesn't exist. Perhaps we need to ask then whether the explanatory problem is with the description, and whether the underlying subject matter, the facts of meaningful linguistic interaction, might be better described in a way that does fit with the ordinary stream of explanation. It should be noted that even normativists understand the issue here is not between them and some sort of philosophical doctrine called naturalism that groundlessly denies the possibility of nonnaturalistic explanation. It is rather a conflict between normal explanations – of a kind both normativists and skeptics about normativism accept – and abnormal explanations – which, as Boghossian says, "we must learn to live with" (1989, 548) as the price for accepting something else, such as "meaning" understood in a particular way.

So what are these supposedly inadequate explanations, and why do they fail? One might expect that there would be a large literature on this subject, debunking these failed accounts and showing why they fail on their own terms, and addressing these "own terms." But there is very little. There is instead a routine appeal to the notion of dispositional explanations, a notion that ordinarily stands in for actual explanations and is rarely elaborated.[1] There are some exceptions to this, in relation to the literature on science studies mentioned earlier, in a discussion of the role of normative rationality in the explanation of rationality as an empirical phenomenon, and in the discussion of linguistic idealism as formulated by G. E. M. Anscombe ([1976] 1981; cf. Bloor 1996). There is also an extensive philosophical discussion of legal normativity. These are interesting exceptions. The problem of normative rationality in decision science will be dealt with in the final chapter. The discussion of science studies, as we have seen, leads to the question of whether the normative is merely a point of view that causal accounts may ignore, except in the form of such things as the normative beliefs, valid or not, that actually do explanatory work. The large literature on rules and dispositional explanations of rules, in contrast, says virtually nothing about language learning, and writers like Brandom have ignored the problems that the acquisition of language pose for their views (cf. Rouse 2002, 109–11; Turner 2005a). Law will be the subject of the next chapter.

The muddle over the relation between normative and nonnormative explanation, however, is much deeper than this list indicates, in part because there is much more overlap in the approaches than appears at first glance. The difficulties involve both the social-science explanations *and* the appeal to normativity, and indeed there are close parallels between the problems faced by each. In this chapter I will provide a general background survey of these problems from the point of view of the disenchanters – and also say something about what they know that the normativists have trouble even acknowledging: that normative phenomena in the real world have little to do with the specific concerns of the normativity argument, and that the normativity argument itself looks very similar to reasoning that we dismiss as superstitious, or magical thinking, when we encounter it in other cultures. The trope of disenchantment and re-enchantment, in short, is closer to the mark than the normativist realizes.

What social scientists (and some philosophers) know, or think they know

Social scientists know that the intuitions people have about the correctness of various kinds of conduct vary dramatically. One example suffices to make this clear. The basic social relations important to most people are kin relations. Kinship structures, who counts as kin, the content of the expectations people have of their kin, vary from social settings in which there is no such thing as marriage to those in which marriage is prescribed on the basis of kin relations. Our most basic sentiments, accordingly, are socially determined in a banal sense: we have strong feelings of connection or obligation to people whose relation to us is specified by the fact of how kinship is structured in our society. These are facts that are, if not arbitrary, neither universal nor the product of rationality in any ordinary sense of this term, or indeed in any reasonably extended sense of it. Social scientists also know that structures (such as those of kinship), rituals of status change (such as weddings), and political forms tend to be much more stable than the theories, justifications, and understandings that the people who enact them have. Theories come and go; institutions, rituals, and practices recur, reproduce, and get ideologically constructed in ever-changing ways. So while the agent's concepts may be closely related to his or her behavior, they are often a poor guide to what is actually going on – which may become evident only when extended comparisons are made between variant forms of institutions. Social scientists know that core moral concepts have histories, and that these histories are typically short, local, and checkered.

We are especially inclined to use terms central to Kant, such as

31

"obligation," as generic moral concepts, but applying them universally is often misleading. As R. G. Collingwood says, speaking of Oxford philosophers, they

> knew that different peoples, and the same peoples at different times, held different views, and were quite entitled to hold different views, about how a man ought to behave; but they thought the phrase "ought to behave" had a meaning which was one, unchanging, and eternal. They were wrong. The literature of European moral philosophy, from the Greeks onwards, was in their hands and on their shelves to tell them so; but they evaded the lesson by systematically mistranslating the passages from which they might have learnt it. (Collingwood 1939, 65)

This practice of mistranslation is a problem even for the Greeks, as Collingwood pointed out:

> ... in ethics, a Greek word like *γϑ cannot be legitimately translated by using the word "ought," if that word carries with it the notion of what is sometimes called "moral obligation," Was there any Greek word or phrase to express that notion? The "realists" said there was; but they stultified themselves by adding that the "theories of moral obligation" expounded by Greek writers differed from modern theories such as Kant's about the same thing. How did they know that the Greek and the Kantian theories were about the same thing? Oh, because *γϑ (or whatever word it was) is the Greek for "ought." (Collingwood 1939, 63)

"Obligation" is a term with a short and local history. Nothing like the Kantian notion of generalized obligation was found in historical societies. It is a distinctly modern idea, though it is rooted in Roman law.

The legal concept of *obligatio* occurs late in Roman legal history. It denotes responsibility entered into or created freely by one's own actions or a ritual action accompanying an act, such as taking an oath that provided for some sort of magically produced automatic harm if the oath was violated. Prior to this, harmful acts, such as the failure to repay debts, were treated in the same way under the law as injuries. The concept of the person, for example, seems to be a product of Roman law as well, and is not only not universal but actually alien to the way most societies differentiate human beings: namely, in terms of ascribed characteristics, such as statuses or location in a kinship system. These statuses are the source of the identity, and therefore the obligations, of an individual. Much of what is translated as "obligation" in anthropological writings is of the latter kind – non-voluntary, and the result of having a particular social status or kinship position, rather than something freely entered into.

Using obligation and similar notions as a template for the normative breaks down completely in translating such concepts as *tabu*, for instance. As Franz Baermann Steiner showed ([1954] 1999), *tabu* is a notion that localizes and defines danger and merges it with the forbidden because *tabus* are ordinarily pronounced by a person who is also *tabu*. The violation of a *tabu* is dangerous because such violation is supposed to produce harmful consequences mechanically and without the intervention of agents or judges. Consciousness or state of mind is irrelevant: *tabu* is like strict liability. This sort of analysis is trouble for the idea of normativity, because this is a paradigmatically normative concept, indeed *the* paramount normative concept in its home societies, yet it is entirely mechanical and natural in every respect.

Given these well-known facts, the procedure of such forms of normativism as Brandom's – taking a local concept of obligation originating from a specific legal context involving agreements freely entered into, and arguing that a form of (tacit) agreement on (tacit) proprieties with a (tacit) score-keeping system underlies all linguistic practice and all communities – seems very strange. It is problematic enough for us to attribute tacit forms of normativity to the mental life of individuals who use explicit normative concepts of the same type. To attribute tacit forms of other societies, to say, for example, that the persons in a Polynesian *tabu* society tacitly possess concepts that they did not possess explicitly, seems to muddle the notion of possession, which normativism usually treats as unproblematic.

Social scientists don't spend much time on the kinds of reasoning that interest philosophers, but the little that is said conflicts with philosophers' universalizations of usages. Basic epistemic terms, for example, vary enormously. When Bible translators try to find analogues to philosophers' standard notions of "believe" and "know" they are often unable to do so (Needham 1972, 32–35). As Needham points out,

> in Navaho there is no word by which the English word "believe," as employed in the scriptures, can be exactly translated. There is a word, "oodlá," meaning "to-believe-something-(unidentified object)," but in biblical translation it is necessary to complement this with other words meaning "to trust in or depend on." (Needham 1972, 32).

Similarly,

> the Kikchi, of Guatemala, express both "believe" and "obey" by the same word (Nida 1947, 4; cited in Koper 1956, 139n15; cf. Nida 1964, 51), and the same usage is reported of the Cuicatec and the Tzeltal

languages of Mexico (Nida 1964, 51). "In the Cuicatec and Tzeltal languages of Mexico there is no way of distinguishing between 'to believe' and 'to obey' . . .. These Indians reason . . . that these words should be one. 'But if you believe, do you not obey?' they say. 'And if you obey, does not this show that you believe?'" (Nida 1952, 21–22). (Needham 1972, 33)

In many languages there is no distinction between "believe" and "know." And in some languages knowledge is represented physically, for example, so that to believe is "to cause a word to enter the insides" (Needham 1972, 34). In Yoruba, the key distinction is between what one witnesses and what one hears from others and "agrees to accept" (Emmet 1986, 2; Hallen and Sodipo 1986, 60, 83). Such distinctions as the know-believe distinction may be obliterated; for example, by assimilating them both to the language of eating, making "he knows that thing" into "he eats that thought."

In one case where a social scientist has tried to describe reason giving, Charles Tilly's book *Why?: What Happens When People Give Reasons . . . and Why* (2006), the result was a taxonomy of responses to "why questions" which included the following: codes, causes involving specialized knowledge, stories, and conventions, by which he meant not conventions in the sense known to ethics but merely politely conventional replies appropriate to the social statuses of the parties to the conversation. Indeed, in general, Tilly suggests,

> reason giving resembles what happens when people deal with unequal social relations in general. Participants may . . . detect, confirm, reinforce, or challenge them, but as they do so they deploy modes of communication that signal which of these things they are doing. In fact, the ability to give reasons without challenge usually accompanies a position of power. (2006, 24)

Reasons do the work of confirming, reinforcing, signaling, and challenging these relations of inequality, as in the phrase "who do you think you are to do such and such?" in a situation in which the answer is not yet clear. The occasion for justification is thus ordinarily a situation of conflict or lack of definition. Appeals to universal principles of morality, or even local normative principles other than codes or rules of etiquette, are not even part of this account, and are extremely rare.

Human reasoning in general bears little relation to the kind of stylized reasoning in terms of principles found in deductive arguments from general principles. When Alexander Luria performed experiments on illiterate Soviet peasants and asked them to respond to

34

questions requiring simple syllogistic reasoning, they either could not do it or refused to do it.

> Subject: Nazir Said, age twenty-seven, peasant from village of Shakimardan, illiterate.
> The following syllogism is presented: **There are no camels in Germany. The city of B. is in Germany. Are there camels there or not?**
> Subject repeats syllogism exactly.
> **So, are there camels in Germany?**
> "I don't know, I've never seen German villages."
> **Repeat what I said.**
> "There are no camels in Germany, are there camels in B. Or not? So probably there are. If it's a large city, there should be camels there."
> *Syllogism breaks down, inference drawn apart from its conditions.*
> **But what do my words suggest?**
> "Probably there are. Since in such large cities there should be camels."
> *Again a conclusion apart from the syllogism.*
> **But if there aren't any in all of Germany?**
> "If it's a large city, there will be Kazakhs or Kirghiz there."
> **But I'm saying there are no camels in Germany, and this city is in Germany.**
> "If this village is in a large city, there is probably no room for camels."
> *Inference made apart from syllogism.* (Luria [1974] 1976, 112)[2]

Yet, with a small amount of schooling, people from the same communities (speaking the same languages) could answer these questions correctly. So, contrary to a central claim of inferentialism, inferential reasoning and language are apparently not closely linked – in this case inferences were linked instead to concrete experience – and, contrary to the idea that there is a universal rationality that everyone properly brought up accepts as binding, the kinds of inferences that are often taken as a model of human reasoning are not even employed and perhaps not understood by large numbers of people.

This applies beyond the cases of deductive reasoning studied by Luria, as the extensive literature on empirical decision-making abundantly shows. The massive evidence shows that

> Faced with even simple sets of options to pick from, human beings make decisions that are inconsistent, sub-optimal, and sometimes just plain stupid. Rather than thinking things through logically, they rely on misleading rules of thumb and they leap to inappropriate conclusions.

Moreover, they are heavily influenced by how the choices are presented to them and, sometimes, by completely irrelevant information. (Cassidy 2008, 32)

In short, the actual rationality of people is different from normative rationality, which consequently does a poor job of explaining what people actually do or how they actually think.

Semantic normativists rely very heavily on ideas about correctness in relation to meaning. But is there such a thing as correctness in this sense? It is a cliché among students of orality that there is no such thing as a grammatical error in a preliterate society, meaning that before writing there is only the understood and the not-understood, rather than a correct and incorrect way of forming sentences. The same point may be applied to semantic normativity and the problem of rules – there is, for these societies, no difference between the correct way of saying something and the intelligible, except perhaps in the etiquette sense of correct. Misuse of a term, accordingly, is not a matter of comparing a usage to a standard – something that perhaps begins to make sense when we have written models and train people in correct usage – but a failure to be comprehended in the course of an actual linguistic interaction.

The gap problem from the side of science and social science

If the key to the normativity argument is a claim of explanatory failure on the part of naturalistic explanation, and the failure is a result of the gap problem – the gap between genuine norms and naturalistic explanations – it should be clear what the nature of the failure is. A convenient example of the gap problem can be found in an area where commentators often naively use the terminology of norms: the study of animal behavior. There are well-known studies of what might be thought of as the same phenomenon that normativists often place at the center of their claims: mutual accountability. In one of these studies, Robert Seyfarth and Dorothy Cheney looked at grooming and reciprocal altruism in vervet monkeys (1984). The question they wanted to ask was, to use the language of Brandom (1994, 141–43), whether the monkeys kept score with respect to grooming, or simply behaved altruistically without regard to payback. Put differently, the question was whether the monkeys learned who paid back their gestures and if the monkeys showed this by acting accordingly.

Vervet monkeys vocalize and other vervet monkeys respond by paying special attention to the vocalization, and by offering aid in the form of grooming parasites off the body or helping in the face of aggression. In many animals this happens largely between kin, so the issue of learning is submerged by other possible mechanisms. In this study, the research found that for kin, the relationship between helping and past help was nil. For non-kin, however, there was learning and reciprocity: "a vervet monkey increases the likelihood that an unrelated individual will attend to its solicitations for aid if it has behaved affinitively toward that individual in the recent past" (Seyfarth and Cheney 1984, 542).

In short, the vervet monkeys kept score for non-kin. Grooming, vocalizing, and support in the face of aggression all seem to be linked by score-keeping. The sanction of not grooming (and also not helping in the face of aggression, which Seyfarth and Cheney also studied) seems to befall the non-reciprocator. Everything seems to be there but the normative language – unless the vervet's vocalizations are given a normative interpretation. As we have seen, normativists are not shy in general about attributing tacit concepts to people who don't possess these concepts in their explicit form, so that cannot be an objection to saying that monkeys keep score. But here the problem of distinguishing normative and pragmatic senses of "correct" intrudes. There doesn't seem to be any explanatory reason to invoke any sort of added-on notion of normativity or normative correctness here. There *is* getting things right, in the causal or pragmatic sense: the monkeys need to understand in the sense of responding correctly to the vocalizations in order to produce the learning. If the responding monkey doesn't groom or help with aggression, they don't do what needs to be done for the first monkey to learn that they will respond, which is to say that they don't act in a way that the first monkey will score as help deserving of reciprocity. But nothing here seems to transcend the causal and pragmatic. Everything that is explained is explained as a matter of learning something new about the world, that is, who will help in response to one's own actions of grooming and helping with aggressors. In this literature, the fact that reciprocal behavior is learned is what makes it a norm, and generally evolutionary psychologists and neuroeconomists (Fehr and Fischbacher 2004) are not shy about using the term "norm" in these and similar situations (Boyd and Richerson 1985; Cummins 2005, 681; Kurzban and Neuberg 2005, 657). "Norm" is used in contrast to "innate" or to other kinds of explanations, such as, in the case of kin reciprocity, closeness during early development.

37

Although the philosophical proponents of normativity don't agree among themselves about what normativity means, they would agree that this kind of empirical normative behavior cannot be real normativity. For Kripke (1982, 146n87) general acceptance of the correctness of applications of a rule is not the same as actual correctness; for Kelsen ([1925] 2006, 177), people behaving as if they are obeying the law, even if they believe they are obeying legitimate authority, is not a sufficient condition for normativity. For Brandom, the issue is accountability, and one assumes that he, like other normativists, thinks that actual behavior is not enough – there needs to be a (normative) relation of genuine calling to account. Just engaging in the causal act of sanctioning people for doing the causally wrong thing, when, for example, they fail to correctly reciprocate or follow a verbal formula to justify, is not good enough, because we are not entitled to terms like "correct" or "justify" on the basis of behavior alone.

The nonnormativist, however, has a reply to this. In each of these cases, an empirical (near) equivalent exists in terms of which an explanation can be given without appeals to problematic normative added elements. There is what actually happens, and there is the added notion of *genuine* correctness that adds nothing to the empirical material or its explanation. The monkeys are a clear case of this. Something causal is going on that we could choose to describe normatively. But it is also true that every time something goes on normatively, something also goes on causally. Something happens in the ordinary world of causal interaction that corresponds more or less with the facts normatively described. And this is also true of human interaction. Winks are distinguished from blinks by some sort of sign that the winker is in control of the eyelid; a causal fact. Promises differ from expectations because the promise-maker actually did something that made the expectation a promise. Courts routinely rule on the facts that justify claims that a promise has been made. Even intentionality has natural signs, and so does the making of mistakes – something Wittgenstein pointed out ([1953] 1958, 26, para. 54). There is a general reason for the presence of external signs of this sort: the fact that everything normative needs to be learned. To learn how to act, even to learn how to act correctly, is necessarily a matter of learning something in the causal world, something like a regularity, perhaps a very complex one, sometimes with a degree of probabilistic causation and always with exceptions that lead to other consequences. These exceptions – that is to say, where things go wrong – correspond to the problem of correctness. Even justification, the paradigm normative concept for Brandom (1994, 11–140), is an activity that needs to be learned, and learned in terms of the more or less predictable outcomes of justificatory acts.

This kind of learning need not be limited to identifying regularities or pattern recognition. Intentions, at least in the sense relevant to distinguishing winks and blinks, are part of the world of even the youngest infant – infants who are certainly prelinguistic and thus, in the picture developed by normativists such as Brandom who link language, normativity, and intentionality, are also preintentional and prenormative. Amanda Woodward performed a series of experiments on seven-month-old babies, which showed that babies reacted differently to a hand reaching for an object than to a robot claw reaching for an object (1998a, 1998b). Woodward, together with Jessica Sommerville and Amy Needham, related this to a kind of mirror system learning (Sommerville, Woodward, and Needham 2005, B2; Hamlin, Hallinan, and Woodward 2008, 493). They found that babies who were themselves capable of reaching for objects were better at distinguishing between a person reaching for an object and a rod or claw touching it. To test this learning hypothesis,

> they gave three-month-old babies "sticky mittens," Velcro-covered gloves that allowed the babies to manipulate Velcro objects. Three-month-olds usually can't reach objects but the sticky mittens magically gave them this ability. Even three-month-old babies who got this experience made the right inferences about the other person in the looking-time experiments. (Gopnik 2008, 8)

Babies learn through, in effect, *assuming* that when they make a motion and other people make the same motion, they are in some sense – a sense that relates to what we call "purposes" or "intentions" – the same as the other person. This "assumption" (about which more will be said in the last chapter) is a causal precondition of a learning process in which the infant improves his or her capacity to manipulate objects, which in turn improves the capacity to recognize other people's actions as like theirs, that is, intentional rather than mechanical. This implies that empathic capacities are based on what one can do, that one learns what one can do through acting and getting feedback from the world, that different people have different experiences and feedback, and thus that empathic capacities are individualized. It also allows for empathic error, and feedback about error: mistaking something as intentional when it is not, or the reverse. I have put the term "assumption" in quotes, as well as the terms "purpose" and "intention," for a reason. Babies are not Euclidean geometers, postulating definitions. It is only by analogy that we can talk about "assumption" here. And it is a bad analogy. The attribution of "intention" by these babies is not a matter of their possessing a theory of mind; it is built into their intrinsically empathic experience of the world, and this way of experiencing the world expands as their abilities to act expand.

If one has a concept of normativity that requires some sort of transition on the part of the acquirer from a prenormative to a normative state – such as prelinguistic to linguistic – and the transition consists of learning in the prenormative state, what is learned must be prenormative facts. This is one reason Wittgenstein invoked the notion of natural signs in connection with intentions and mistakes: the natural signs are prenormative, and allow the "normative" – a term he never used or would have used – to be learned. But the fact that the normative must be learned also implies that it consists in "learnables" that are still part of the ordinary prenormative world. The data from which the prenormative person generates normative understanding or belief is not itself normative. And this implies that for every normative description there is also a nonnormative alternative. So where does normativity come into the picture, and how? For the social scientist, it never does, at least in this sense. When McDowell describes the problem of transition between the normative point of view and the nonnormative one, he does not use causal language, or language about learning. He uses the term "initiation." Learning a rule, as he elsewhere puts it, is initiation into a custom. This produces its own problem: is learning a rule something causal, or something normative? An initiation produces change confirmed by the attestation of the observers. But what kind of change is this?

Social scientists know a lot about the transition problem in general, and initiation in particular. There is a classic anthropological account of transitions, dating from the beginning of the twentieth century, by Arnold van Gennap (1960) and updated by Victor Turner, which is relevant here. As Turner explains,

> Van Gennap himself defined *rites de passage* as "rites which accompany every change of place, state, social position and age." To point up the contrast between "state" and "transition," I employ "state" to include all his other terms. It is a more inclusive concept than "status" or "office" and refers to any type of stable or recurrent condition that is culturally recognized. Van Gennap has shown that all rites of passage or transition are marked by three phases: separation, margin (or *limen*, signifying threshold in Latin), and aggregation. The first phase (of separation) comprises symbolic behavior signifying the detachment of the individual or group either from an earlier fixed point in the social structure, from a set of cultural conditions (a "state"), or from both. During

40

the intervening "liminal" period, the characteristics of the ritual subject (the "passenger") are ambiguous; he passes through a cultural realm that has few or none of the attributes of the past or coming state. In the third phase (reaggregation or reincorporation), the passage is consummated. The ritual subject, individual or corporate, is in a relatively stable state once more and, by virtue of this, has rights and obligations vis-à-vis others of a clearly defined and "structural" type; he is expected to behave in accordance with certain customary norms and ethical standards binding on incumbents of social position in a system of such positions. (Turner [1966] 1977, 94–95)

This model applies, *mutatis mutandis*, to a huge variety of norm-producing and status-changing speech acts such as enacting and pronouncing a law, a marriage, promising, oath-taking. These rituals are underpinned by specific beliefs about the relevant ritual states, the powers of people to change them by way of the rituals, and so forth. These are all cases of norms and related statuses being produced according to norms and statuses: a priest can change a couple from single to married, a legislature can pronounce a law, but they do so in accordance with specific ritual procedures or norms without which the norm or status is not valid. No social scientist imagines, however, that the practitioner of rites of initiation actually transforms the person into something else. Like transubstantiation or initiation, transitions of this sort depend on faith, which is to say on the beliefs of participants in the efficacy and results of the rituals, and no more – as with all proprieties and statuses. The social-science account of initiation is that it is normative, but in the sense of "normative sustained by belief" rather than genuinely normative. McDowell needs it to be something else: a bridge from the natural to the normative.

Diversity: "Good BAD THEORIES" and their functions

With respect to many of the terms used by normativists as evidence of normativity, there is a remarkable and problematic diversity well-known to social science. Consider the notion of truth. According to a classic study of the Chagga, an African group, the core of their notion of truth was the contrast between individual lying and truth in accordance with collective solidarity (Steiner [1954]1999). Their original ethnographer, Bruno Gutmann, "describes the talks preceding law cases, when the clan members assemble and decide to stick to the version of their fellow clansmen. All this is just talk, but the story to which they ultimately bind themselves is *lohi*" (the truth of witnesses under oath) (Steiner [1954] 1999, 248; cf. Gutmann 1926, 706, cited in Steiner [1954] 1999, 248). This exotic concept of truth is intelligible to us. Indeed, it is equivalent to the kind of social constructionism attributed to sociologists of science by their critics.[3] The Western notion of absolute truth can be given an exotic lineage as well, which shows its local and historical character. Steiner derived it from the Old Testament language of witnessing, and paradigmatically from the act of witnessing by God himself, whereby, as he put it, "The manifestation of God of the People [of Israel] is thus explained in terms of jural truth, and thereby jural truth and mythical truth become one" ([1954] 1999, 245). This combined, he suggested, with the Greek notion of truth as nonforgetting, "which refers to the exact rendition of a past event" ([1954] 1999, 244) to form what he characterizes as the western "absolute" notion of truth.[4]

Theories of mind also vary substantially – so much so that the standard Cartesian problem of conscious mind and mechanical body cannot be formulated in some languages, which might have a functional notion of mind, for example, rather than one that produced a problem about thinking substances. Something *like* intention is perhaps universal, but the lowest common denominator of this idea may amount to little more than marking the fact that some objects and beings are not merely pushed around causally, but are directional, at least in the sense that they are responsive to feedback, and in complex ways, so that the processes of feedback cannot be easily reduced to a mechanism, as with a thermostat. But beyond this, there is plenty of variation. It is claimed to be unclear that classical Chinese has a word for intention (Fingarette 1972, 37–56; Hansen 2007). But it is also clear that intentional concepts play little role in some cultural settings, as in the case of the mechanical operations of *tabu*.

What are the implications of all this diversity? In the next section, I will consider the possible responses of normativists to it. But there is a way of distilling it, from an explanatory point of view, which will have some bearing on later chapters. All of the diverse folk notions mentioned here (and this is merely the tip of the iceberg) have two relevant features: they are taken for granted, believed in, accepted, subscribed to, or used, by people in particular, different, social settings. They work in those social settings to enable the participants to interact with each other, understand each other, and co-ordinate their conduct. None of them is "true" in the sense of being scientifically true. It would be odd to claim that out of the diverse array of these vocabularies, theories, ways of reasoning about the world, one is metaphysically correct and the others are not. Nevertheless, there is a great deal of philosophical writing that treats, unreflectively, folk notions of this sort as setting a philosophical standard for judging the correctness of, say, cognitive neuroscience explanations of memory.

We can, for convenience, call these diverse notions "theories", though we should keep in mind that this is only a convenience, and that the whole language of theory, assumption, presupposition, and even belief that we use to describe these diverse things does not necessarily match up with anything like "a theory in someone's head," that is to say, a genuinely explanatory account of what is going on when people use these folk notions. Using "theory" here is merely extending our folk language to talk about our folk language. With that qualification, we may describe these various folk conceptions as "Good Bad Theories", meaning that they are good theories for a particular, unspecified set of purposes in a particular setting, but bad theories if we are thinking of them as adequate explanations of anything, or as proto-explanations that can be turned into genuine explanations with a little empirical vetting and some minor revision. They are, in short, kludges (Wimsatt 2007, 137–38).

The concept of intention is a case in point. As E. R. Dodds pointed out in his discussion of emotion language in the Homeric epics, we find ways of talking about mental causation that are profoundly different from our own. For Homer and his ancient audience, strong emotions were objective, external forces that robbed people of their rationality and were not part of their selves (Dodds 1951, 5–16). Homeric ways of speaking and thinking about the mind can be understood as being like theories: they classify mental events, ascribe causes, and contain many theoretical notions. But they also serve as social coordination devices: we can make juridical decisions within the very specific structure of Greek law using this theory, assign responsibility or blame, excuse actions, justify actions, and obviously also tell stories. One aspect of this making sense, which will prove to be relevant in the final chapter, is this: the vocabulary enables the members of the relevant communities to make sense of each other – for example, through describing actions in a recognizable and empathically accessible way. One can be sure that Homer's listeners could empathize with the wrath of Achilles, and that bringing the listeners into this relation to the actions of Achilles was, in part, the point of the poem.

Discussions of intentionality, for example, normally occur in contexts where, as with justification, something has gone wrong: when empathy fails, or is incomplete or inadequate, for example in the face of a crime, or a misunderstanding, or deception. Gossip about intentions is common, but has a point only because it fills in a gap in our understanding. If we could grasp the point of the actions directly, we would not need to invent intentional explanations. More generally, if empathy did work perfectly, if we were mind-readers who never erred, there would be no need to have the language of intention, assumption, purpose, and the like. In a world where thoughts were empathically transparent there would be no unseen to theorize about. The less empathy we have, the more crutch or surrogate we need. In Oliver Sacks's chapter on the autistic animal science professor Temple Grandin, he quotes her description of herself as an "anthropologist from Mars" (Sacks 1995, 259). When we attribute assumptions, or use our culturally specific language of belief or our technical terms "concept" or "idea," we are doing what she describes herself doing in understanding others – constructing a theory that enables her to predict people's reactions in a situation in which she cannot empathize, or can only empathize in a limited way. The fact that we need these theories, even in connection with our ordinary interactions, is revealing. And we especially need them in connection with the situations in which we are most like anthropologists ourselves, that is, in the face of other and alien cultures. They function and have a function because thought is not transparent, not always empathically accessible to us. And the farther removed from our experience the conduct of others is, the more terminology we need in order to make sense of it, explain it away or repair our understanding of others. We need descriptive language then to serve as a crutch, or a partial surrogate for the empathy that allows us to make sense of others ordinarily.

The take-away messages from this, for the purposes of this book, are two: one is the complex interdependence between empathy and intentional language, an issue that will be considered in the final chapter. The other involves causal-normative dualisms. One of the motives for normativism is the irreducibility of the language of action and intention, and mental language generally, to causal language, with the relevant causal language usually taken to be the causal language of cognitive neuroscience. Irreducibility is then taken to be grounds for a dualism of the normative and the causal, or evidence of the explanatory inadequacy of causalism and naturalism in the face of ordinary human facts, which are then taken to be normative. The discussion here suggests that the dualism in question is a dualism of function, rather than evidence of the existence of some sort of radical difference in types of concepts or explanatory domains.

The functions of mental language obviously vary according to the social contexts in which they are used, and the uses to which they are put. Given this diversity of auxiliary uses, for example in relation to the highly diverse systems of guilt and retribution found in the history of law, it would be strange to expect that the diverse vocabularies of the mental would all correspond to one another, and strange to think that one of them is "correct". It would be odd for us to draw metaphysical conclusions on the basis of the irreducibility of Homeric language about the mind to cognitive neuroscience. It should be equally odd to draw the same conclusions on the basis of the conflict between English usage and cognitive science. Nevertheless this kind of discussion is a staple of the philosophical literature (e.g., Bennett and Hacker, 2008).

Explaining diversity

Most of these social science "facts" are uncontested banalities, at least within social science. But the normativist can ask the following questions: What do they have to do with normativity? And why should they matter? These banalities of social science do nothing to solve the gap problem – the discrepancy between dispositional or causal explanations and the facts of meaning, rules, correctness, rationality, legality, and so forth that need explanation. So what difference do they make? The social scientist can ask some questions of his own: How does the whole range of social science materials fit with any of these notions of normativity? How might they relate to notions like the sacred, and to the facts these notions pick out? How can the notion of normativity as uncaused or beyond cause be made to square with the variations of actual normative behavior and the recognition that what counts as normative comes and goes historically in close relation to social change and varies by community? What does normativism say, or allow saying, or need to say, about *tabu*, Chagga truth, the hierarchical world view, and so forth? Or does it even matter to normativism that there are such things as *tabu* and the like?

The normativist can say, as Christine Korsgaard does, that we base our moral certainties on our confidence in our own beliefs, and the rest of what people in other cultures do is irrelevant (1996, 97). But the existence of alternative cultural attitudes, values, and norms has in fact had a profound influence on Western morality. And one would naively think that the facts revealed by science and social science ought to undermine our confidence in what we take to be obvious – that nothing, but especially not the distillations of our self-knowledge, known as it is to be error-prone – ought to be immunized from refutation, direct or indirect. Moreover, it is a fact that diversity *has* made a difference to ways in which philosophers, including normativists, have constructed their claims, for the simple reason that these claims are themselves counter-arguments or responses to both the facts of diversity and the social scientists' accounts of diversity. Wilfrid Sellars, who will be discussed in Chapter 5, solved the problem of diversity by arguing that we are all members of a hierarchy of collectivities, and that the collectivity of rational beings is the source of the normativity of reason itself. Indeed this is Sellars's reinterpretation of Kant (1968, sec. 7, para. 145: 126, para. 144: 225). A similar argument was made by Hans Kelsen in the face of the actual historical (and present) diversity of legal systems. He argued that the normativity of legality is a feature that is more basic than any system, but that is shared by all systems, despite the apparent conflicts between them.

In short, the problem of beliefs or normative content different from our own has motivated a variety of complex philosophical responses. Why? The basic argument for normativism rests on the rupture argument. Diversity has nothing directly to do with that argument. But the indirect implications of the problem of diversity are not trivial. The motivations for the responses, and the reasons that diversity is a problem for normativism, can best be understood through a survey of the kinds of responses that are available. A simple list of options (which I will simplify to the problem of divergent beliefs, leaving aside such topics as semantic diversity) would include these: in the face of a divergent belief

1. We may decide that we were in error about there being a divergent belief, and that the apparently divergent belief was not really intelligible as a belief, such as when we determine that the utterances made by the parrot do not exhibit the kinds of connections between these utterances that we can construe as intelligible;
2. We may decide that the beliefs are intelligible, but erroneous;
3. We can decide that the beliefs are intelligible, different from ours, but underdetermined by the present facts, so that they cannot be treated as error, but can be regarded as departing from different premises or presuppositions;
4. We can decide that the beliefs are intelligible, but differ solely as the result of the adoption of nonnormative conventions, fictions, or beliefs about the world that are different from ours but not erroneous in any simple sense;
5. We can decide that we had misunderstood the character of our own views, and conclude that they are in fact conventions rather than truths or based on fictions that we had not previously recognized to be fictions.

46

The most extreme versions of normativism assert 1 and some forms of 2. The difference between 1 and the more extreme forms of 2, which I will refer to as fundamentalism, hinges on a narrow question: whether there are beliefs that are not in accord with reason or the moral law that are genuinely intelligible, or whether they merely appear to be intelligible but are in the end not intelligible. If one has an aggressive notion of reason, claiming that much falls under the scope of reason, one will find that many of the things people actually say and believe are contrary to reason. The difference between 1 and 2 is whether the things that fall under the heading of unreason can be understood at all. The adherents of 1 say they cannot. The adherents of 2 say that they can be understood, but as errors. No one actually advocates the solipsism of the 1 kind explicitly, but it is easy to fall into.[5] We can distinguish stronger and weaker forms of fundamentalism. The stronger form (more or less represented by Thomas Nagel [1997] and Korsgaard [1996]) involves the claim that all views other than our own are wrong, and justifies this claim on the basis of our own preferred grounds, such as reflective, self-validating analysis of our own views. The fundamentalist can then claim that his own standards of rationality and reflection are the universal standards of rationality, that no one can escape them, and that there are no alternatives to them, so that by definition any apparent alternative or any belief that conflicts with those that we have generated in accordance with his normative standards of reasoning is in error. The difference between this form of normativism and 1, which is a kind of moral solipsism or failure of moral empathy, is that the adherent of 2 in its strong form thinks there is at least a point to self-justification, as distinct from the outright denial that there are any intelligible alternatives to our worldviews.

For the fundamentalist, the fact that there are masses of people, indeed virtually everyone else in the world, who fail to subscribe to these views and labor under the illusion they are correct in their own views is just a sign that they have not properly applied the binding demands of rationality in a sufficiently reflective manner. For this account, diversity doesn't matter: to disagree is to be wrong. The fact that other people disagree has no relevance to the truth of our own position.[6] It is consistent with this view that we would account for the fact of these failures of rationality by appealing to various error theories, which would account for the specific content of the errors. But the content of these theories or even their success in accounting for the fact of diversity has no implications for the validity of our views. These views we have validated independently by our process of reflective self-validation.

47

One important side comment needs to be made here. The fundamentalist argument sometimes appears to be a normal factual argument about human nature or the commonality among all humans of certain moral standards, ideals, and the like. The earlier natural law tradition made such arguments, though they proved, in the face of actual moral diversity, to be salvageable only by making the common core of moral impulses much more limited than originally envisioned, or by making the claim formal, such as the argument that all people naturally seek the good – which does not specify what the good in question is (Finnis, 1980). The fundamentalist claim is quite different. Arguing that all people have some common moral dispositions is still a dispositional argument. It leaves open the question of whether they should have these dispositions, or should suppress them. The possession of a disposition is not the same as the possession of an obligation: this is a classic example of the problem of the rupture. Natural law arguments are not good enough for the fundamentalist. Something stronger is needed. Older attempts to deal with these issues, such as intuitionism, depended on a psychology that included a moral faculty that enabled them, if they were normal, to discern moral truths from which obligations derived more or less directly, such as the goodness of chastity. The discredit of faculty psychology meant it was a solution that was unavailable to later philosophers, so they supplied their own alternatives which produced more or less the same results. One alternative was the idea that there was such a thing as recognition of the binding character of normative rationality, or the idea that reflection led directly to the recognition of obligations that were already out there. There is no empirical phenomenon of recognition of this sort, but the claim that there is or must be seems like an empirical claim. Similarly, the suggestion that reflection invariably leads to the conclusions favored by the normativist is historically false. So in each case we have something other than an ordinary factual claim, which would be false if it were taken as a factual claim.

It is possible to make fundamentalism more plausible by moderating it in such a way that diversity can be accounted for without supposing that most actual people are bereft of reason. This can be done by combining it with 3 and 4, for example, by saying that actual diversity of belief is sometimes the result of a combination of error and divergences in conventions (which are not subject to rational correction and are not themselves moral) together with the common core of the genuinely normative, which is accessible to all and lies beyond socialization. This revision works by granting the genuinely

48

normative a more limited scope, and reasoning that although errors may occur, the actual diversity of belief is not in general the result of deviations from the genuinely normative. It is rather the result of local differences in empirical beliefs that are underdetermined by the facts or different local conventions, or the two in combination. This is a backhanded concession to the sociological, which raises an empirical question of sorts: how much diversity *can* be explained by reference to conventions and differences in empirical beliefs? It is this question that the other options address in a way that undermines fundamentalism.

The case of egalitarianism

Options 3 and 4 can perhaps best be understood with an illustration from Bernard Williams's writing on the universal moral truth of egalitarianism (1973, 230–49). Williams defends both the moral universality and rationality of equality, and, without using the term, treats it as normative in the sense of binding. He nevertheless acknowledges that lots of people reject egalitarianism, and lots of cultures are deeply inegalitarian both in ideology and practice. Williams doesn't actually consider distant cultures, but deals with this problem by considering Nazi anti-egalitarianism. He admits that the Nazis rejected egalitarianism. But he argues that the very fact that they needed an argument in the form of a doctrine or ideology to reject egalitarianism is a sign of, so to speak, the respect vice pays to virtue – an acknowledgment that anti-egalitarianism is itself an affront to a moral truth. The anti-egalitarian thus needs a (false) theory. The egalitarian does not. Equality, in short, is a kind of default position that allows us to assume that any deviation from it is a matter of error.

Social-science explanations are (usually) more evenhanded.[7] Egalitarianism, no less than its rival doctrines, is open to historical and other forms of explanation. It may be that egalitarianism is a product of evolution, or of a particular religious tradition secularized in a particular historical and political setting, but in either case it is one alternative out of many possible outcomes. The caste system, as studied by Celestin Bouglé (1926) (whom we will encounter later in connection with Sellars) and later by Louis Dumont, produced what Dumont called *homo hierarchicus*, people inured to a way of thinking in which hierarchy pervades all social interaction ([1966] 1970). Dumont explains the system taking Bouglé's definition of the caste system as the starting point:

49

the society is divided into a large number of permanent groups which are at once specialized, hierarchized and separated (in matter of marriage, food, physical contact) in relation to each other. It is sufficient to add that the common basis of these three features is the opposition of pure and impure, an opposition of a hierarchical nature which implies separation and, on the professional level, specialization of the occupations relevant to the opposition; that this basic opposition can segment itself without limit. (Dumont [1966] 1970, 260)

Pure and impure, rather than our ethical concepts, are the foundational organizing ideas of the caste system: its presuppositions, if you wish. They are already anti-egalitarian: they imply hierarchy.

The fundamentalist response is simply that none of this matters – equality, and a specific account of exactly what counts as inequality and what inequalities count, follows directly from reason, objectively, as established by the objective procedures of rational reflection that the given author has adopted, and this fact alone provides all the evidence we need to establish that the opposed views are erroneous. Error theories are a pastime with no epistemic significance for the question of the normative force of the particular account of equality in question. In this case the error is simple: there is no such thing as pure and impure according to the standards of rationality and science, so the system is based on a falsehood. The social scientist who treats the system as resting on a non-factual presupposition and explains the difference between us and them in these terms has succumbed to the error of relativism.

One problem with this response, which motivates the social scientists' evenhandedness, is that it is available equally to opposed philosophical accounts of the normativity of equality (of which there are many), to the opponents of egalitarianism who have other grounds, such as religion, who take the facts of impurities and purity as obvious, and are physically overcome when they are touched by an impure person, and so forth, so that a situation is created in which each argument for or against equality validates itself differently, and claims that only its form of validation is genuine, producing a standoff. The actual history of major philosophers' transcendental arguments for the principle of equality bears out social scientists' skepticism: the arguments vary enormously. Thus in a practical sense, the methods of the fundamentalists do not achieve objective agreement, but actually lead to a proliferation of theories. To list a few: Alan Gewirth derives egalitarianism from the concept of action (1978); Jürgen Habermas, more circuitously, derives egalitarianism from the implied will to tell the truth that is implicit in discursive speech acts, the commitment to the ideal-speech situation implied in speech, and the equality necessary for the realization of the ideal speech situation ([1981] 1984–1987), and Philip Pettit from considerations about the evil of arbitrary power (1997, 55–58). And the list can be extended indefinitely.

This might seem to be a kind of vindication of fundamentalism, since there is at least agreement on the value of equality. But one can find fundamentalist philosophers in the same generally Kantian tradition who reach exactly the opposite, anti-egalitarian, conclusions. Alfred Vierkandt, for example, wanted to base an account of human society on "phenomenological insight, i.e., what we directly experience personally in ourselves and can convey to consciousness with apodictic [i.e., incorrigible] evidence" (Vierkandt quoted in Mises 1960: 56). As Mises characterizes it, Vierkandt's position is that "human society is, so to speak, already foreshadowed in the relationship of the master to the dog he trains. The relationship of leader and led corresponds to the relationship of master and dog: it is healthy and normal, and it is conducive to the happiness of both, the master and the dog" (1960: 56). Similarly, one can get anti-egalitarian results from a consideration of the nature of human action just as readily as one can get egalitarian ones. Action itself, for example, involves choices; choices produce hierarchy – a point made by Dumont ([1966] 1970, 231–38). In short, while objective, univocal results are promised by the fundamentalist, they are difficult to come by. What fundamentalism produces in fact is not a triumph of reason but a Babel in which the opponents each feel themselves to be vindicated by reason itself.[8]

The diversity of theories raises another problem that bears directly on the competition with social science. Much of the persuasive force of the model of objectivity in question depends on the idea that it is close to and in some sense validated by science: that reason in the relevant sense is a condition for the possibility of science and thus validated by the success of science. But this line of argument opens a door to two additional problems. One is the point made famously by David Bloor: that if one makes the case for the special epistemic qualities of science or uses science as a model, one cannot then argue against the application of scientific analysis to scientific belief itself and thus exclude psychological and sociological approaches to science (Bloor 1981). In short, validating anti naturalism by appealing indirectly to the objectivity of science produces a muddle: if science is so great, and reflection is essential, why is the reflexive application of science to science and reason *tabu*? The second problem involves what W. V. O. Quine talks about as one's theory of the world. Is it really consistent with reason and science to say: yes, there is a large set of facts out there about the erroneous beliefs of the vast number of people in the world who don't agree with us, but we are not concerned with these facts, nor do we have any obligation to account for them? Doesn't our quest for a larger understanding of the world require us to understand this large set of facts, and specifically to understand how so many people went wrong? The fundamentalist says we need not. Fundamentalism wants the authority of science without playing the game of explaining facts.

The more moderate version of fundamentalism (more or less represented by McDowell) accepts that diversity needs to be accounted for. And it contains devices for accounting for diversity that protect the central thesis, namely the removal of many of the problematic cases by putting them into the category of convention or false (nonmoral) belief (which might include such things as false beliefs in racial superiority, for example). These devices drastically reduce the explanatory burden: conventions, erroneous empirical beliefs, and the like can then be explained by other means that do not conflict with the central thesis of universal normativity. But if this strategy is used to place every problem case into a separate category, it begins to look like the theory is being immunized from empirical evidence.

To put it another way, there is a question about the theoretical status of such things as the moral/conventional distinction. It is relevant that the distinction is not one that can be constructed on the basis of the phenomenology of moral experience, or the sociological, or descriptive facts about human universals. Whatever is universal – always a hotly contested topic in any case – is not going to match up to the moral or the normative or with normative rationality as it appears in the philosophical literature. It is likely to contain such things as a universal tropism to the acceptance of pecking orders and to the punishment of free-riders. And there is no ground for thinking that individuals distinguish conventional from moral, or that there is a psychological difference between feelings and responses termed moral and responses to the violation of so-called conventions, such as the wearing of head scarves among women in certain Muslim communities. This means that there is no naturally given kind corresponding to "moral" as distinct from "conventional," or at least none that fits the standard usages (Kelly and Stich 2007).

The problem of recognition: Is normativity circular?

The explanatory burdens for the moderate fundamentalist depend on the claim about universal normativity's topical reach: How extensive is this claim? The amount of error that needs explaining is much greater if it is supposed, for example, that the claim of universality reaches in an informative way into such domains as gender relations, political principles, and the like. But from the point of view of the value of the thesis for ethics, of course, its value depends precisely on this claim. Equality is a case in point. To say that equality is universally rational, but also to say that the subject matter of equality – that is, whether it is political, economic, a matter of the distribution of honor, and so forth – is conventional, would be to concede that the informative reach of the normativity in question is not very extensive, because it is largely formal rather than substantive. If we claim that it is extensive and substantive, we quickly pile up examples of error that need to be explained. Indeed, the whole of historical thought on the subject, with the exception of the views of the philosopher in question, will have to be put down as error.

We also run into a serious definitional muddle that threatens to produce a kind of circularity. In the ethical literature, the cases of disagreement we are accustomed to consider are family disagreements, such as those between the Nazis and ourselves, in which there are common points of appeal and enough commonality of language and worldview that arguing, as Williams did, that the difference was a matter of ideology rather than actual fundamental moral disagreement is an option (1973). In the cases of societies in which fundamental moral ideas are contained in notions of purity or *tabu*, however, matters are quite different. Are these moral conceptions or normative at all? For the sociologist, they are; they relate causally to human action and collective life in generally the same ways as our conceptions of obligation, equality, and so forth.

The normativist, however, is in the advantageous – or circular – position of having no independent criteria or definitions of the normative: to be genuinely normative is to possess the properties that the normativist, in his particular account of normativity, ascribes to the normative, for example that it is binding. But the bindingness needs to be genuine, not merely a matter of "believed to be binding," in order to be genuinely normative, and non-genuine norms are not genuinely binding. But what are non-genuine norms? Either they are not recognizable as norms at all, or they are erroneously believed to be norms, to be binding, and so on. But distinguishing between genuine norms and "erroneously believed to be norms" does not seem like a distinction that can be made without reference to the theory of normativity in question. Exactly this problem arises in connection with legal normativity. Situations in the law arise in which courts

53

recognize and acknowledge, or refuse to recognize and acknowledge, the existence of other legal systems. It seems plausible to say that generic considerations shared by all legal systems about the nature of law could, or should, decide such questions. But this, in effect, makes legal *philosophy* into the arbiter. And the "theory" becomes a *definition* of the law. One could imagine a different case: where the definitions of law in one system excluded recognition of other systems, or some other systems, as genuine law.[9]

This kind of possible outcome, as well as the chronic failure of strong fundamentalism to produce anything but a Babel, provides the motivation for the most widely used alternative, the basic presuppositions model, the third item in the list above. The point of this model is to acknowledge genuine normativity other than one's own, something excluded by fundamentalism and solipsism. The roots of the model are in philosophical neo-Kantianism, which had the same motivation: to accept the reality of diversity, which means to recognize a class of facts that are genuinely normative but whose normative character is different with respect to normativity itself, not merely with respect to conventions and different nonnormative beliefs, and to account for it in terms of the different basis of these facts. This model was absorbed into social science, in thinkers as diverse as Émile Durkheim, Georg Simmel, and Karl Mannheim, and turned into commonplaces about worldviews, *Denkgemeinschaften* or thought collectives in Ludwik Fleck, and evolved into Thomas Kuhn's notion of paradigm and its later cognates. But, as noted earlier, it was reimported into philosophy to become a philosophical commonplace as well, in the form of the idea that shared presuppositions were a condition for the possibility of such things as communication and justification.

One motivation behind this model for sociologists and historians was the sheer difficulty of making sense of actual historical, disciplinary, professional, and cultural diversity. The kinds of error explanations envisaged under moderate fundamentalism seemed inadequate to the phenomenon of culture shock, and the radical character of the differences between actual cultures and historical world views. To account for complex ancient civilizations, such as those of India and China, in terms of erroneous beliefs and different conventions, and to insist that they shared rational principles, principles with the kind of the extensive topical reach claimed by Kant and Kantian ethics, led to absurdities: these civilizations didn't possess the same concepts or find normativity in the same places. Even such basic concepts as personhood were different, or absent, in these other cultures.

The problem of recognition was particularly troubling for social scientists: even identifying anything like a morality in the customs, interdictions, rituals, and so forth, of these civilizations required a change in the way we ordinarily think about morality, and the metaphysical views of the mysterious East seemed to be not only radically at variance with Western rationality, but to be unintelligible in its terms. Preliterate societies presented even more difficulties: the concept of a person as distinct from the occupant of a set of statuses, and the consequent notion of personal responsibility, seems to be largely absent, meaning that a supposedly universal ethics based on the notion of the person appears to derive from an ethnocentric perspective.[10] Neo-Kantianism, which was originally motivated by the impossibility of settling such questions as whether the naturalistic or the soul-based model of the human person was correct, provided a powerful solution to this problem. The familiar method of reconstructing the assumptions behind a viewpoint, philosophy, practice, or activity could be applied to a case of activity and thinking one did not understand in order to make it understandable, and to make intelligible the binding force of the normative aspects of these activities for those who shared the presuppositions.

The model had many problems as philosophy – the problems of Kantianism together with the problems produced by making Kantianism local and historical. The key to these kinds of accounts is the special status of the premise-like assumptions or presuppositions behind a practice or activity. These are explicitly not beliefs, conventions, and the like. They are not epistemically normal in the sense that they could be tested, suspended, or replaced, and they are not revisable through ordinary processes of the revision of belief. They are beyond any individual's belief revision because they are beyond individuals: things like shared presuppositions, collective intentions, rules, meanings, and the like are intrinsically collective or community-relative. They define error but cannot be in error. They are truth-making or norm-making but there can be no such thing as a false or incorrect basic norm, since basic norms define normative correctness. For the fundamentalist, this was a fatal flaw, for it accepted the situation of Babel, or relativism, that fundamentalism promised to escape.

But there is a fatal flaw of transcendental arguments generally: underdetermination, the inability to construct a result in the form of an exclusive set of presuppositional conditions for the possibility of the outcome in question. This was, historically, the downfall of neo-Kantian philosophy of physics: it became apparent that it was possible to derive the relevant predictions using different mathematical presuppositions.[11] This weakness can be turned into a virtue, in one sense: problems of fundamental presuppositional conflict, which lead to relativism, can be replaced and downgraded to problems of underdetermination. The possibility of treating fundamental cases of conflict as cases of mere underdetermination, together with the rejection of the idea of unrevisable *a priori* assumptions, is the basis of the fourth approach on the list above, which we may call the Quinean approach. The contrast with other normativity claims may be seen in the arguments used by Quine in his exchange with Sellars over the normativity of mathematics (Quine 1980; Sellars 1980). Quine treats mathematical structures as something akin to conventions, and "validates" them, indirectly, to the extent that they need validity, through their utility in enabling the theory to be formulated and to derive predictions. They are not, in his account, real normative objects.

How would this relate to the problem of explaining error? One possible outcome of an attempt to construct an error account would be this: it would be recognized that the error was not an error, but merely a different outcome consistent with the same facts of the matter, and arising in a way which was epistemically no worse than the way in which the original doctrine arose. This would be a case, or a second-order hypothesis, of underdetermination. In most respects, this is consistent with the neo-Kantian option (number 3 on the list), which would say that the putatively erroneous account was coherent, but based on different fundamental premises, and that these fundamental premises were impossible to decide between on the second-order level at which they could intelligibly be said to conflict. But the neo-Kantian account, in effect (though this is not the language they used) takes the fundamental premises to be normativizing, to make their implications normative, not merely conventional.

The Quinean account eliminates the normative element by treating the fundamental presuppositions like conventions, so that the difference between the two doctrines is conventional, not normative. This in turn has an effect on what kind of error accounts might be offered. Option 3 thus leads to the relativistic end of irreducible conflict between fundamental premises which are normative and, because they are fundamental, not open to further justification. Conventions, as they figure in moderate fundamentalism, although they are closed to "justification," are open to revision and alteration. This might seem to be a merely verbal difference, but it allows for some different possibilities in the face of explanations of difference.

Consider the following case: we encounter a theory that conflicts with our own. For example, it contains statements that are true in our theory and false in the other theory. We attempt to account for the conflict as a matter of the errors of the other theory. So we construct an error theory. This proves to be difficult. So we turn the problem around, and construct an error theory in which our own theory is the erroneous one, and use the conventions and theoretical claims of the other theory to account for our errors. This might involve claiming that our theory is wrong, our conventions are not working, or our observations are incorrect, or a combination of these. Moreover, this actually happens. Something like a demonstration effect operates in such cases: we see people behaving differently, whether it is Lavoisier performing phlogiston experiments and proposing to change the conventions of chemical classification to better suit the results, or Margaret Mead reporting on the lack of adolescent sexual repression in Samoa. We try to explain this as error, by showing that what appears to be the case is not, and why it appears as it does. Or we explain how the other theories or conventions were misconstructed. But when these efforts fail, we start looking at our own views as potentially wrong, and construct an error theory about *them*: that, in our chemistry we ignored the importance of anomalies in the explanation of the disappearance of weight during burning, or we overgeneralized from our own Western experience of adolescence – universalized it.

So what are the explanatory burdens created by this approach? They are somewhat odd ones, or at least different in kind than the burdens created by the other approaches. One is that it seems to leave out obligation, except in the sense that one is obliged to follow the relevant conventions. But if the rules in question are in fact conventions, one is obliged to follow them only in this sense. The normativist has an apparent trump card to use against this general approach, in the form of the following kind of argument.

The attempt to avoid the claims of normativity by treating the normative as a matter of convention is a sham, even in connection with science. The language of this proposal, with words like intelligibility, cognitive values like prediction, and the many uses of "better" as well as notions like coherence, and even consistency, is normative through and through. Moreover, the argument uses, explicitly or implicitly, intrinsically normative concepts such as "concept" itself. The notion of error, obviously, is intrinsically normative. At the end of every argument we wind up with justifications, which are the essence of the normative. None of this can plausibly be naturalized, as Quine thought epistemology might be naturalized into neurophysiology. There is thus no escaping normativity by this route – even the minimal level of self-reflection forces us to acknowledge the indispensability of normativity for talking and reasoning about the world.

The ubiquity of normative language, in short, implies the ubiquity of genuine normativity. Dispensing with normative language is not an option, and thus dispensing with genuine normativity, that is to say normativity that is more than a matter of convention-following, as part of our explanation of the world is not an option. The Quinean option (deciding that beliefs differ solely as the result of the adoption of nonnormative conventions, fictions, or beliefs about the world that are different from ours), in short, is not viable. If it acknowledged the indispensability of normativity, as it should, it would collapse into one of the other options.

Normativists can also point to the apparent defection of Donald Davidson from Quine in the context of the discussion of conceptual schemes, which acknowledges the normativity of reason and shows that any wholesale rejection of a large set of our commonplace true statements – which would necessarily include normative common-places and the commonplace use of normative language – is doomed to incoherence. This means that the rejection of normative language and its replacement by something else, such as the language of convention, or some sort anti-normativist naturalistic reinterpretation of normative language, is also doomed to incoherence.

The development of Davidson's views is, for the normativist, a good indicator of the necessary corrections to the Quinean "conventions" account (number 4 in the list above). Admitting that the gap between reasons and scientific laws, the rational and the nomic, is unbridgeable and that no program of reduction or naturalization of the world of reasons, beliefs, and actions is possible is the first step (Davidson [1970] 1980). Granting that reasons and the like are normative concepts is the next step: something that Davidson apparently does ([1972] 2005; 1985; [1986] 2005; [1994] 2005; 1999; 2004). As we will see in Chapter 6, though, the normativity he accepts is not quite normativity in the same sense of normativists like Brandom, McDowell, or Nagel. The next correction comes from Davidson's "On the Very Idea of a Conceptual Scheme" ([1973–74] 1984). There can be no such things as the incommensurable fundamental premises envisioned by the neo-Kantian option (number 3): the limit of the rational or intelligible is the limit of *our* ideas of the rational and intelligible. The next is to grant the unity or closure of the rational – that there is a space of reasons and that nothing outside it can correct or conflict without beliefs, that only statements imply statements, and statements can only be held up against one another, not against the world. Understanding science itself in terms of the space of reasons becomes the next task of metaphysics: fusing the scientific image with the rational, as Sellars puts it, or overcoming the dualism implicit in the gap. And doing this, for some normativists (e.g., Rouse 2002, 12), requires a monism of the normative, in which we no longer worry about finding a place for values in a world of facts, but a place for facts in a wholly normative world.

If we are to score these arguments as attempts to deal with diversity, we might conclude the following. Normativity is tough to get rid of. But many forms of normativism, notably fundamentalism, pile up enormous burdens of proof by dismissing other opinions as erroneous when the "errors" cannot be accounted for as errors. Moreover, fundamentalism relies on a set of devices, such as the idea of eyes opening to the dictates of reason, that are basically fictional. It fails to produce the results it promises, namely, objective normative conclusions. Treating the normative as conventional and as a matter of beliefs that are different but not irrational and taking account of underdetermination resolves many of these issues. But for the normativist, this is not good enough: the binding character of mathematics, for example, needs to be treated as something more than merely a matter of the kind of binding involved in following a convention. But this insistence on the gap between convention and genuine norms rings a bit hollow when we realize that it is based on a preferred description of the subject, in this case of mathematical objects, and that nothing substantive about mathematics itself is gained by understanding them as genuinely normative. If we look at the problem of diversity from the perspective of social science itself, however, an element of the discussion, and an explanatory burden that has figured in only a small way in this discussion, takes on a central role and poses serious problems for the normativist: a problem of distinguishing the supposedly nonmystical claims of the normativist from the obviously mystical claims made by other cultures when faced with the same problem: justifying claims about obligation.

Is *hau* a case of normativity? Or is normativity a case of *hau*?

In this section, I consider a typical, in this case classic, social-science explanation of a normative structure, and try to reconstruct what it is that the normativist would say about this explanation. The example is Marcel Mauss's account of gift exchange among the Maori. Mauss reports the following Maori beliefs. A mysterious force, *hau*, attaches to the gift, which obliges the recipient to provide something in return.

Hau enforces the obligation it embodies by causing pain or death: it is literally a normative force. The believers in *hau*, which Mauss represents by an imaginary Maori lawyer, explain it thus:

> *Hau* is not the wind. Not at all. Suppose you have some particular object, *taonga*, and you give it to me; you give it to me without a price. We do not bargain over it. Now I give this thing to a third person who after a time decides to give me something in repayment for it (*utu*), and he makes me a present of something (*taonga*). Now this *taonga* I received from him is the spirit (*hau*) of the *taonga* I received from you and passed on to him. The *taonga* which I receive on account of the *taonga* that came from you, I must return to you. It would not be right on my part to keep these *taonga* whether they were desirable or not. I must give them to you since they are the *hau* of the *taonga* which you gave me. If I were to keep this second *taonga* for myself I might become ill or even die. Such is *hau*, the *hau* of personal property, the *hau* of the *taonga*, the *hau* of the forest. (Mauss [1925] 1967, 8–9)

Mauss explains the doctrine in more general terms, and does so in terms of an error theory, in which he characterizes *hau* as a spiritual power rather than as an actual spirit.

> to be able to understand this Maori lawyer we need only say: "The *taonga* and all personal possessions have a *hau*, a spiritual power. You give me *taonga*, I give it to another, the latter gives me *taonga* back, since he is forced to do so by the *hau* of the gift: and I am obliged to give this one to you since I must return to you what is in fact the product of the *hau* of your *taonga* . . .. For the *taonga* is animated with the *hau* of its forest, its soil, its homeland, and the *hau* pursues him who holds it. (Mauss [1925] 1967, 9)

What would the normativist say about this version of the gift relation? The Maori lawyer would reject it, on the grounds that *hau* is real (though, significantly, even the Maori treat it as a kind of mystery rather than part of ordinary factual reality – they also believe there is a gap and that *hau* accounts for and involves a rupture in ordinary reality), and that to describe the gift relation as merely a relation of reciprocity justified by a theory of spiritual powers would be to misdescribe it, because the reality of *hau* is part of an adequate description of the phenomenon.

There are plenty of analogues to this response in other contexts. It is common for theologians to argue that sociological accounts of this ritual are wrong or insufficient *because* they omit reference to the actual presence of God, which is an essential feature of what is happening. The sociologist, in short, changes the subject. The sociologist is not talking about genuine communion. And to describe a social activity in religious terms amounts to helping themselves to a normative concept that they don't acknowledge the validity of. There is no understanding without belief, according to this familiar doctrine. In one respect, the theologians are quite right: describing the gift relation as Mauss does ([1925] 1967) is to redescribe it in a disenchanted way. Mauss's problem is to explain it within the stream of ordinary explanation, and in this context this means that the explanatory problem is to show how the relationship actually operates in light of the Maori beliefs in *hau*.

Mauss does not need to accept these beliefs to perform the kind of explanation he is attempting. When we explain *tabu*, *hau*, and the like anthropologically we don't endorse or reject the claim that there is such a supernatural force. Explaining the effect of such ideas and the reasons there might appear to be real forces of this kind doesn't require us to believe in them. We can explain how the belief is made plausible by the fact that accidental injuries and death do befall the person believed to be under the force of *hau*, and are interpreted as evidence of this force. We can show how difficult it is for someone to reject such a belief and function in the society. We can show the many inconveniences, sanctions, doubts, and so forth that would arise for the unbeliever. We can explain how this belief arises in and is sustained in the epistemic situation of the ordinary Maori, especially by enabling the Maori to interpret their other beliefs and practices. These explanations would not depart from the ordinary stream of explanatory fact, and of course would at no point appeal to the normative fact of *hau* itself.

The sociological explanation, in short, is a rival explanation to the one given by the Maori lawyer. If he had access to the doctrines of normativism, he would complain that it doesn't account for the normativity of the practice: why, he might ask, *should* anyone return a gift if there is no *hau*? He would also insist that the sociological explanation was insufficient, that there were facts that it could not account for. One of the insufficiencies would be the failure to account for the normative facts described in terms of *hau*, "facts" which do involve a rupture in the ordinary stream of explanation. But he would say that this rupture is warranted: if the events that befall the person who fails to satisfy *hau* are described as mysterious, they demand a suitable explanation, in terms of a mysterious force, which *hau* supplies. He would complain that the normative language of the practice, which is a pervasive part of the life of the community, would be bogus if the sociological explanation were true. He might go on to complain that the sociologist has redescribed the practice in such a way that the subject had been changed, and cite the fact that the normative element, the genuinely binding character of the fact of *hau*, had been left out. And he would of course reject the idea that *hau* was a fiction. In these respects, the Maori lawyer would be a classic normativist.

As suggested earlier, one of the most powerful arguments that arises out of the construction of error explanations is this: in constructing an error explanation of a belief that one can explain as false, or as conventional, one discovers that the best explanation is one that turns the tables and requires us to admit that our views are the false ones. Though the example is controversial, this was certainly the effect of such works as Margaret Mead's *Coming of Age in Samoa* (1928), which depicted Samoan adolescence, however accurately or inaccurately, as an untroubled sexual paradise. It was, more generally, the effect of the European discovery of the "primitive" world. In these cases it was clear that the usual error accounts would not work, and that it was our customs and moral convictions that were conventional, and probably conducive to unhappiness, in contrast to what we mistakenly believed about them.

The case of *hau* has similar implications for the normativist. *Hau* has many of the features of normativity. It is apart from the ordinary stream of explanation. It accounts for facts that are visible only within the perspective of the Maori believer in *hau*. The redescription that Mauss provides would be resisted by the Maori as a case of changing the subject. But it is difficult to see how the normativist would account for *hau* in a way that did not at least open the door to an admission that the same explanation applies to his own favored forms of normativity. If he says that *hau* does not exist in fact, and that it is based on an erroneous extrapolation of material which supplies no real evidence of such a thing as *hau*, and that the facts as described by the believer in *hau* have no special claim on us, he concedes the point that such considerations can undermine and overcome similar claims about normativity. When the sociologist applies such considerations to our own normativities, however, the normativist must insist that it is improper, that it cannot be done without reflexive inconsistency, and so forth. The normativist might also say that the existence of normative language points to real normativity, a normativity of real obligation, a normativity that is merely incorrectly described in terms of *hau*. The irreducibility of normativity to something else, such as the false beliefs that sustain *hau*, applies in this case as well: the obligations are real. The sociologist has a simple reply to this: there are many examples of norms being sustained merely by belief. The key to the functioning of fetishes as a means of compelling traders to keep their agreements, the subject of the epigraph to this chapter, was the ritual in which the fetish, a physical object, was created through the taking of oaths, usually with "an Imprecation, that the Fetiche may kill them if the do not perform the contents of their obligation" (Bosman [1704] 1967, 149).

This is an example of a norm created in accordance with a norm: a fetish created by oath-taking. But normativity here bottoms out in the invocation of causes – the kind of causes that can kill the oath-taker. To be sure, these are causes that exist in an enchanted causal world. The disenchantment that Weber referred to was directed at this kind of causal world as it was experienced in the European past – a world in which, for example, the conquests of William the Conqueror were considered to be justified as the fulfillment of an oath taken under duress by Harald of Norway over hidden holy relics, assumed to have causal powers. The burden of proof is on the normativist to show that his normativities do not also require an enchanted causal world, and that normative force is something other than a piece of mysticism.

Notes

1. Among the exceptions, see Philip Pettit (1990a, 1990b, 1996) and some others in Kusch (2006, 228–34).
2. Three factors substantially limit their capabilities for theoretical, verbal-logical thinking. The first is a mistrust of an initial premise that does not reproduce personal experience. There is also a refusal to accept and use the premise as a point of departure for subsequent reasoning. Frequently the subjects ignored the premise altogether. In continuing to reason only from immediate experience, they did not wish to make judgments outside of this experience, referring to the fact that they "hadn't been there," or that they could only say "if they had seen" or "if they knew." They supplanted verbal, logical reasoning with a process of recollection about graphically obtained impressions.

    The second factor was the unacceptability of the premises as universal. Rather they were treated as particular messages reproducing some particular phenomenon. Premises deprived of universality yield, naturally enough, only particular information creating no firm logical system or basis for logical inference. Even when the subjects could remember the premise, therefore, they continued to make independent guesses or resort to personal experience.

    The third factor, a consequence of the second, involves ready disintegration of the syllogisms into three independent and isolated particular propositions with no unified logic and thus no access for thought to be channeled within this system. The subjects had nothing to do but to try answering the question by sheer guesswork or by recourse to immediate concrete experience. While refusing to use the syllogism for logical inference, our subjects could still use the logical relations fairly objectively if they could rely on their own experience. They refused, however, to use the logical relations when the discursive operations were divorced from immediate experience.

Our remarks, however, refer only to those subjects whose cognitive activity was formed by experience and not by systematic instruction or more complex forms of communication. Other subjects yielded a different picture. They could accept the syllogism's initial premise as the basis for further reasoning, and could grasp its universality. Judgments first given in an immediately familiar context were gradually transferred to independent areas, thus assuming the familiar features of abstract verbal and logical deduction. (Luria [1974] 1976, 114–15)

3. The same attitude to legal proceedings caught the eye of W. I. Thomas and Florian Znaneicki, authors of the classic study *The Polish Peasant in Europe and America*, who ascribed it to their immigrant subjects ([1918–1920] 1958, vol. 1, Part 1, 58n.1, 59–62; Turner 2005b).
4. A related lineage is given for belief in Needham (1972, 40–50).
5. Kant himself had problems with these issues (Sagi, 2009).
6. The fundamentalist is fundamentally concerned with warding off "relativism." This book is not concerned with moral relativism. To the extent that the discussion involves relativism it does so only by undermining attempts to build antirelativist arguments on bogus "factual" considerations. As to my own views on relativism, they are largely contained in my chapter "Relativism as Explanation" (2002, 74–107), which argues that the problem of relativism as usually understood – to the limited extent that there is a usual understanding – is the result of an assumed explanatory theory that is defective. The explanatory theory is more or less the one discussed in this book in connection with neo-Kantianism, but which is pervasive in current discussion as well. This explanatory theory holds that different moral viewpoints as a matter of fact rest on different assumptions or fundamental premises that can neither be justified nor reconciled. If one gets rid of this factual theory one can account for differences in belief in ways that are not relativistic in any problematic sense, but at the same time do not warrant the kinds of claims made by fundamentalists.

Fundamentalism ignores actual diversity because it thinks it has no responsibility to account for it. But it is certainly possible to construct a normative lens on human morality as a whole, or at least as it has actually been practiced, that respects actual diversity and allows for it to be accounted for without reaching the conclusion – the conclusion warranted by the "different premises" model – that no moral judgments may be made of different practices or that there are no universally valid moral considerations. Steven Lukes does precisely this in *Moral Relativism* (2008). His account does not rely on the characteristic doctrines of normativism, of which the present work is a critique. I have suggested elsewhere the way in which even Weber, the arch-value relativist in the history of social science, can be understood as having a view of values that is different only in minor ways from that of Davidson (Turner 2007c, 37–62). If I were to confess my own ethical views, they would be close to these.

7. There is a social psychological literature which focuses on distributional issues which also treats equality as a kind of natural end.

8. One is reminded of the famous study by Milton Rokeach in a mental hospital which placed three patients, each of whom believed themselves to be Christ, in therapy with one another. After "the shock and novelty of confrontation had worn off . . .. Each one . . . formulated and stabilized a set of rationalized beliefs to account for the claims of the others" (Rokeach 1964, 190).

9. The problem of recognition does not, in this case, have a theory-independent or standpoint-independent solution. "Law" is either law as defined by a theory or law as defined in a given legal system. The fundamentalist and more moderate fundamentalist options exclude the idea that there are standpoints that would be analogous to alternative "legal systems." So they are limited to identifying normative facts according to their own theories. If there were no question about the theory, there would be no problem: the criteria of normative judgment and recognition would be the same. The implication is that there simply would be no cases of false normativity or "erroneous but still normative." With respect to normativity itself, genuine normativity, there would be no such thing as error. In this respect at least, both the fundamentalist 2 option and the moderate 2 option would be equivalent to the no-recognition option 1. The moderate option allows for us to find, in a putatively normative claim, such as those made by the Nazis, the genuine normativity, in this case the acknowledgment of the demands of equality, concealed under the false beliefs and variant conventions. But with respect to normativity as such, there is no recognition of different normativities as genuine.

10. It is instructive to compare Parfit (1984) with Mauss ([1938] 1985) on the question of the concept of the person (Carrithers, Collins, and Lukes 1985; Dumont 1994, 3–16).

11. Friedman (2000); Howard (1990, 2003).

A PARADIGM CASE: THE
NORMATIVITY OF THE LAW

. . . let us consider . . . the supernatural reality which is supposed to manifest itself in our awareness of an "ought." It can be said, in a Kantian mode: when an ought appears as an absolute demand upon us it reveals the existence of an absolute, or supernatural, will within ourselves, a will which makes demands on us. Being absolute, this will, in each person, is universal and must therefore be determined by the supernatural wills in all other persons. That is to say, they must all constitute a community. From this the principle can be derived that all moral beings should be determined by each other . . .

But if the supposed supernatural will within us is to be thought of as our own will (as it must be if it is to affect us), the question arises how it can be claimed to be supernatural. For it would have to be related to the natural world to which we belong. But, insofar as it has natural predicates it can no longer be said to be above or beyond nature. It may be suggested that it combines two aspects, one towards the realm of natural existence, the other unrelated to it. But this gives rise to the question as to how these two aspects can be combined in one unified will. Such a will is one entity, so the supposed supernatural aspect will after all also be determined by natural predicates.

Axel Hägerström ([1911] 1971)

In the first two chapters, I have dealt with the problem of normativity in two ways. I first presented the general case for normativity together with the many peculiarities of this case, especially the problem of rupture produced by the claim that there is an explanatory gap that requires extraordinary normative objects to fill it. I then presented the other side: first by giving some of the kinds of facts that social scientists (and philosophers, psychologists, and so forth) have taken to be actually relevant to understanding reasoning, folk psychologies, intention, and the historical and cultural diversity of the normative language on which the case for normativity rests; then by considering the responses of normativism to this diversity; and finally by posing the problem produced by error explanations, namely, that the explanations that even normativists accept as applied to other people's normativities can be turned on normativism itself, providing an alternative explanation that undermines any claim that "normativity" can explain the normative.

The sheer variety of normativist claims mocks any attempt to defeat them, or even make them consistent with one another. At best, there are recurrent patterns of argument. But it is possible to see how these arguments fit together, and why the variants vary as they do, if we consider a well-developed paradigm case. In this chapter I will examine what is perhaps the oldest, most elaborate, most discussed, and most fully developed normativist argument against social-science explanation, Hans Kelsen's case, or cases, for the normativity of the law. To understand it, and to understand why it is a paradigmatic example, requires a little historical background.

The neo-Kantian problem of normativity

The origins of the problem of normativity, indeed the term itself, are shrouded in some mystery: one source is Kant, and Kant's critique of Hume in support of the necessity of *a priori* truth. But this is only one part of the contemporary philosophical problem of normativity. The second part is a product of what we may call the neo-Kantian problem of normativity. Neo-Kantianism salvaged Kant in the face of the obvious fact of conceptual diversity by developing a Kantian notion of local normativity. In contrast to Kant himself, who had envisioned only universal mental ordering principles, the neo-Kantians accounted for diversity by treating conceptually ordered domains – of which the law was a typical, indeed central, example – as grounded by distinctive presuppositions. The neo-Kantians accepted underdetermination: the existence of incompatible presuppositions that could not be grounded any more deeply. Subsequently neo-Kantians applied the idea that there could be many such distinctive, object-constituting, presuppositional starting points to disciplines, to historical epochs, and eventually to political ideologies and the like. These discussions did not usually concern themselves with the notion of normativity itself, although many of the presuppositions, for example in the case of law, were explicitly normative. They instead were concerned with the problem of the *a priori*.

67

The distinction between "sociological" and genuine normativity takes its first explicit form in the writings of Kelsen. Kelsen specifically used the term "normative" in this context, and employed this distinction between the normative and the causal. He was commenting on Weber, who made the same distinction, but made it between dogmatic and reality science. There is a reason for this late appearance of the concept. The distinction between sociological normativity and genuine normativity could not arise, at least in its current form, without an appropriate account of sociology as nonnormative. Kelsen was responding to just such an account, elaborated in the methodological writings of Max Weber, including especially his essay "Objectivity in Social Science and Social Policy" ([1904] 1949) and his "Critique of Stammler" ([1907] 1977), which is concerned with the problem of an empirical or reality-oriented rather than normative account of law. Kelsen took account as well of Weber's comment on Kantorowicz at the first meeting of the German Sociological Society in 1910, and Weber's *Economy and Society* ([1968] 1978), first published in 1924, which provided the conceptual materials for a nonnormative account of the historical development of legal orders.[1] The challenge of a sociological account of the law is what pushed Kelsen to formulate a conception of the pure normativity of the law, by which he meant a science of law purified of causal considerations. But he dealt with Weber's challenge in different ways throughout his career.

The problem of the normativity of the law is a rich example. Virtually all of the problematic terms and distinctions discussed in the last two chapters figure into it: ambiguous notions such as "the sources of the law"; the idea of a collective will underwriting the normative character of the law; the idea that the concept of law is intrinsically normative and that any sociological description either changes the subject or is derived from the normative concept; the problem of rituals of transformation in which the utterances of an individual in a specific setting create new laws; the problem of the origin of the law out of nonlegal facts; problems having to do with the relation of normativity to such questions as motivation – in this case, motivations to obey the law; problems of diversity and commensurability that manifest themselves as legal issues in recognizing the existence of law in other legal systems; the problem of the relation between normative facts such as the eternal character of law and the nonnormative facts of revolution and power to compel obedience, enshrined in this case in a parallel set of terms for these two kinds of facts: legality and legitimacy. If anything, the example is too rich to serve as a simple paradigm case, and this chapter is not intended as a substitute for a comprehensive treatment: Kelsen and Weber, the main players, each were prolific writers and difficult thinkers. But the key issues can be separated out.

By the end of the nineteenth century, when neo-Kantianism was at the peak of its influence, the entire neo-Kantian project of understanding domains as conceptually preconstituted and organizable into a scheme of intelligible categories (which could be discovered by conceptual analysis) was beginning to break up, largely over the problem of objectivity. For the neo-Kantians a fact derived its objectivity from its place in an ordered conceptual domain – a concept that applied equally to the scientific, the normative, and the theological. Understanding a domain involved understanding the logical and interpretive dependencies among its concepts. Normally this amounted to showing how a domain was organized around, and dependent on, a single central concept. The fact that there was just one correct construction of the conceptual domain made it objective and thus scientific or *Wissenschaftsliche*, and possessing this structure made a domain a factual, scientific one. This was also the undoing of neo-Kantianism. Einstein created an insoluble problem for neo-Kantian philosophy of science by showing that multiple mathematical structures could be used to construct theories accounting for the same results, making the "single hierarchy" objectivity sought by neo-Kantianism apparently unachievable (Howard 1990, 369–70). But a parallel process unfolded in the social sciences that led directly to the issues addressed by Kelsen and Weber, and this one occurred precisely on the fault line between fact and value, nonnormative and normative.

The issue between Kelsen and Weber arose from applying the neo-Kantian model of science to the science of society. If we look for the single organizing concept for a neo-Kantian sociology, it is easily identified: the concept of the social. And this was indeed the starting point for Georg Simmel, who derived logical forms of the notion – for example, the concept of the social dyad – as a basis for the new science. There were two problems with this approach. The first related to objectivity. It soon became apparent, even to Simmel, that there were multiple ways of construing this conceptual domain, many of which were ideological or visibly connected to political preferences (Simmel [1908] 1964, 25). The choices of descriptions and choices of organizing concepts were interdependent. So the possibility of multiple organizing concepts implied the possibility of multiple descriptions. This proves to be relevant to Kelsen's discussion of sociology. For Simmel, sociology had to say something about law, authority, and so forth. To construe law as a sociological subject "scientifically" in the neo-Kantian sense required that it be thought about under the concept of society, and this is precisely what Simmel produced: a sociological conception of state authority which proceeded by subdividing the concept into logically ordered social categories that differ from the categories of legal sciences, or the domain of law as it would be constructed under a legal concept, such as justice or legality (Simmel [1908] 1964, 190, 254–61). The problem of multiple descriptions of the same thing followed directly from this: sociological descriptions competed with legal descriptions.

Weber's anti-normativism

The unraveling of the standard neo-Kantian model of the domain of the law was the contemporary background to the problems that Weber addressed in "Objectivity in Social Science and Social Policy" in 1904, and also in his extended critique of the then-leading figure in the neo-Kantian philosophy of law, Rudolph Stammler ([1907] 1977). The conflict between the approaches of the social sciences, and for that matter the history of law, which Weber thought of as historical sciences, and the normative, or as he called them, dogmatic sciences, was an important theme of these texts.[2] The difference between historical reality sciences and dogmatic sciences, which for him would include legal science and theology, was not that values had no role in reality sciences. Far from it: for Weber, it was inevitable that historical disciplines, like all disciplines including the natural sciences, began from concerns that could be articulated in the idiom of common sense or the worldview of everyday life. In the case of the cultural sciences this idiom and the central concerns of those seeking historical understanding were especially likely to be specific to the historical situation of the audiences and the social scientists and historians, and the subject matter of these sciences was identified in the language of life of these audiences. The terms, such as "war" and "capitalism," were valuative in the sense that they had valuative significance *in addition to* identifying subject matter, events, and the like. But this kind of value-relatedness did not need to imply, for the social scientist interested in either causal relations or the understanding of action, any kind of evaluation of those actions or events. Causal relations for Weber, it is worth noting, were not law-like, but rather were probabilistic relations that held between facts described in terms of the language of life itself.

70

Weber "solved" the neo-Kantian problem of grounding the constitution of a particular science in a uniquely valid conceptual scheme by rejecting it. He defined sociology in his own way, as the science of meaningful social action, but treated this definition as merely one possible definition among others. His own extensive scheme of terms and categories was presented as only one of the possible schemes, not presented in the neo-Kantian way as the sole and thus objective scheme. It was justified instead entirely by its usefulness to the reader or user. Weber thus accepted underdetermination with respect to conceptual schemes as a starting point, and took an instrumental view of the schemes themselves. This was not an entirely innocent choice, however. The rival schemes with which he was concerned aspired to conceptual closure and uniqueness, in the traditional neo-Kantian fashion. A definition like that of Simmel, which was organized around the concept of society and the question "how is society possible?" is not merely different, but also more encompassing: a full articulation of the notion of society would include the notion of meaningful action, because explaining what "society" meant would involve explaining that it was made of agents, agents who attached meanings to their acts. The situation was similar for the legal-philosophy notions of the state and law: These are concepts which, in their usual articulation, involve citizens or subjects who can obey and disobey the law, which is to say, intentional actors. So the relation between Weber's starting point, meaningful action, and these, is asymmetric, and poses a problem similar to the problem of reduction.

If Weber can account for the state, or the law, or "society," or the actual subject matter comprising these things, without reference to these concepts, they become dispensable. The situation becomes this: the people in history whose meaningful actions he is explaining presuppose his starting point, by treating their own actions as meaningful. But they also value and thus, in neo-Kantian terms, presuppose valuations and a value scheme. Weber, as an analyst, abstains methodologically from these valuations. He does not presuppose their valuation schemes, but treats these schemes as a topic for analysis. By making people's values and presuppositions into factual subject matter, he is enabled to account for the facts they account for. Their beliefs, in short, constitute the subject matter of meaningful action. He incorporates these beliefs into his sociological analysis. This kind of argument is designed to annul a certain class of transcendental arguments. Any transcendental claim of the objective conceptual necessity of valuative presuppositions, such as the concept

71

of legality or justice in the study of the law, disappears, because there is an alternative, the alternative of a sociological system of categories which is a classification of valuative presuppositions rather than another scheme of valuative presuppositions. This is the general form of the social science case against normativism: it treats such things as meanings and values or beliefs about, in this case, the law and the state, as the things to be explained, and thus avoids the claim that the legal descriptions are privileged or uniquely valid.

These problems are especially acute in relation to the law, because legal practice and legal reasoning turn on issues of the description of actions and on the definition of legal terms. Using these terms in a nonnormative way invites confusion, but is not fully avoidable. Weber addressed these difficulties in part by providing alternative nonlegal vocabularies for describing legal facts. This solution to the problem leads to such devices as the following: Instead of using the term "legality," which is fundamentally a dogmatic or valuative term, he uses "legitimacy," which he then defines in a purely nonnormative way. The question of whether a regime is legitimate is a factual question to be answered in terms of the probability that a command believed by at least some people to be legitimate will be obeyed. The difference is this: courts settle what for them are factual legal questions about legality, but do so in terms of dogmatic doctrines that are themselves valuative rather than factual, or involve valuative facts. These valuative facts or doctrines are in turn to some extent legitimated by public acceptance. But nothing about public acceptance in and of itself solves or replaces such questions as whether the purported law, the law that is actually written and obeyed, is genuinely legal. That remains a legal question. The concept of legitimacy does not answer this question. Public acceptance is a nonnormative fact, and nothing about the rituals of legislation believed by people to produce law transforms these acts into phenomena of a new kind – namely, genuine norms.

Where does this leave us with the notion of legality (or legal validity)? Weber never describes legal phenomena in terms of genuine norms, because he does not need to do so to explain meaningful action. He needs only to be able to account for the beliefs of others that there is such a thing as genuineness or legality. This means that there was a large indirect role for the concept, by virtue of the fact that *belief in* legal validity was a way in which historical persons attached meaning to their actions and the actions of others. The way legal history is actually done reflects this distinction, and involves understanding past legal doctrines.

. . . if I have before me a "legal source," by which I mean a source of knowledge of the law, be it a legal code, ancient legal sayings, a judgment, a private document, or whatever – I must necessarily first get a picture of it in legal *doctrine*, the *validity* of which legal precept it *logically* presupposes. (Weber 2000, 53)

Weber outlines a two-step process of reconstructing past legal doctrine for explanatory purposes. The first step involves a kind of empathy. "I find this out," Weber says,

by transporting myself as far as possible into the soul of the judge of the time; and by asking how a judge of the time would have to decide in a concrete case presented to him, if this legal precept which I am construing doctrinally were the basis of his decision. (2000, 53)

The second step is to construct an idealization of the meanings. Judges often actually behaved in varying, even contradictory, ways in different courts, so the functional legal doctrine of a past era, as it was understood by actual historical agents, cannot be simply read off of court decisions. It is itself a double abstraction: from the beliefs of individual historical agents to characterize a group and time period, and from the messier realities of individual causes and actions. The important point is that this kind of idealization of past meanings of legal doctrines is interpretive and sociological rather than normative. We are concerned with understanding what past judges *took to be* valid and the doctrines and law as they understood them, and not with the actual legal correctness of their juridical decisions.

Questions of validity of this kind, Weber thought, though unavoidable for judges and lawyers operating within a legal system dispensing judgments, were inappropriate to a reality-science inquiry. For him they were necessarily based on dogmatic considerations. But actual historical questions about the emergence, character, and success of legal orders were for Weber questions that could be entirely separated from considerations of legal validity themselves. What makes this confusing in the case of the law is that usually the sociological sense of legal validity and the dogmatic one are very close to one another: to understand the doctrines judges reason from is pretty much the same thing for the neophyte lawyer learning the meaning of the law as it is for the sociological interpreter concerned with the actual meanings in use. This is why it became possible later to construct a sociological jurisprudence which held that, in the end, the law is what judges do (Pound 1911–12). Both the neophyte lawyer and the historian of law must construct for themselves an idealization of a complex and heterogeneous mass of conflicting data about actual legal judgment. But there are occasions where the two ways of thinking about validity peel apart. One such case is the making of judgments, the topic of jurisprudence, where our interest in the idealization is to correctly extend it to novel law situations. The traditional objection to sociological jurisprudence is that it cannot explain how judges do this (though one response might be that they themselves necessarily master judicial practice just as the neophyte lawyer does, by idealizing applications of doctrines). Another case is the question of the legality of revolutionary law. This is a typical example of a question that could be addressed dogmatically: Was the revolutionary regime entitled to take power? But the normative legality of a regime in itself is of no significance historically and the entrance into historical discussion of dogmatic considerations, as explanations of actions by agents in history, is a category mistake. Of course Weber did not reject explanations in terms of *beliefs* about legality. This was, after all, the topic of his famous categorization of forms of legitimate rule. Nor did he deny that historical agents acted in terms of such beliefs. But for him these beliefs were something to be explained rather than accepted as givens.

Kelsen's regress argument

Kelsen, as Norberto Bobbio showed in a classic essay (1981), accepted the basic terms of the relationship between social science and legal science as Weber constructed the problem, with one exception: like normativists generally, he tried to establish a privileged description that establishes an explanatory necessity that can only be met by a normative explanation, and to argue that because this description was indispensable and indispensably normative, he was sensitive to the need to do this without overtly falling into circularity. As has been suggested, the template for the problem of description is the claim that a sociological description of a church service is incomplete because it fails to include the fact of the presence of the living God. This is clearly circular. It is a fact only for a believer. Kelsen needs to do better than merely describe the facts about the law in a normative way consistent with his own legal theory and then insist that only the normative description is acceptable. He must show that this description is in some sense necessary. In the course of a long career he returned to this problem repeatedly, and in a variety of ways, some of them conflicting. So in considering Kelsen we get to consider a wide range of arguments about this problem, each with its own difficulties.

The core of Kelsen is the model of regressive reasoning about legality. The law itself produces a problem of regression. The paradigm case of legal justification, around which Kelsen's model of legal systems is built, is this:

> When the validity of one norm founds the validity of another norm in one way or another, this creates the relation between a higher and a lower norm. A norm stands to another norm as higher to lower, if the validity of the latter is founded on the validity of the former. If the validity of the lower norm is grounded on the validity of the higher norm in that the lower norm is *created* in the way prescribed in the higher norm, then the higher norm has the character of a constitution with respect to the lower norm, since the essence of a constitution is that it regulates the creation of norms. (Kelsen [1979] 1991, 257; emphasis in the original)

In short, there is a hierarchical chain of validation in the law. Ordinary laws are governed by laws of enactment, which validate them. The problem for this two-tier account of the law is getting it going in the first place. What justifies rules of enactment? If there is no justification, it seems as though a band of robbers could assert authority, announce itself as a state, announce rules of enactment, enforce the rules it enacts, and be legal. Legality, a normative fact, would be no more than the sociological fact of the successful assertion of authority. The regress of legal reasoning would end, not in a normative fact, but in a sociological one.

These kinds of considerations were the basis for Kelsen's distinctive argument about the law contained in his famous thesis of the *Grundnorm*. The reasoning is this: only a norm can validate a norm. No empirical fact can validate a norm. The norms of ordinary law are valid. Hence it is a condition of the possibility of their being valid that there is in fact a norm that validates them. Some norms are validated by other norms, norms of enactment. Norms of enactment may be validated by other norms of enactment that are more basic, such as the norms of a constitution. But the ultimate norms of the constitution must themselves be normatively validated – assured to be genuinely legal. This requires a further norm, a basic norm or *Grundnorm* that is a regress stopper. Hence there is a *Grundnorm* that in fact validates every genuine legal order. Without assuming this, the whole notion of legality collapses, along with the distinction between legality and the sociological fact of legitimacy.

This is a transcendental argument, and has the characteristic problems of transcendental arguments, namely underdetermination with respect to the conclusion – the thing that is established as necessary

75

– and with respect to descriptions. Begin with the problem of description: we must accept that there is a genuine distinction between legal states and organized systems of coercion passing as states, a distinction that cannot be captured by attending to causal facts about them or their history, which is to say that this is a normative distinction. We thus accept that there is something that needs a normative explanation. Kelsen's Kantian reasoning has been characterized by Stanley Paulson ([1934] 2002, xvii-xlii; Paulson 1997, 209–12) in terms of a distinction made in the Kant literature between two kinds of transcendental arguments: the first is the regressive form, which is concerned to show that something is logically required for a claim or argument to be made. In this case, the various facts of the law, and the fact of legal validity, require something more than facts from the world of causal explanation. The second kind, the progressive form, is the one that Kelsen wishes to establish. This form of the argument not only establishes that something is logically required that can't be produced out of a certain class of claims, such as, in this case, causal claims, but establishes *what* is required in such a way that this answer excludes all other answers of the same type, and, in addition, allows novel conclusions to be deduced from this newly established claim. Establishing the need for a justification is the easy part; establishing the ultimate justification, the uniquely valid regression-stopper itself, is the hard part.

The problem, generic to transcendental arguments, is that even if one acknowledges the regressive form of the argument, which requires one to have already acknowledged the unique correctness of a particular, loaded, description, one discovers that the answers to the question of what is logically required are underdetermined: a convincing story that *some* presupposition is required does not necessarily lead to a unique solution. And this is a problem for Kelsen as well. It is one thing to establish that a normative account is needed in order to speak of legal validity or *the law* as distinct from *what people believe the law to be*. It is something quite different to establish a single account of this kind of normativity as uniquely valid and therefore objective, and to exclude alternatives by virtue of its intrinsic features. Yet for normative theories, there is no alternative: there is nothing else to recommend a given solution over alternatives, if there are alternatives. There are no extrinsic features, such as predictive power, simplicity, or fidelity to the historical facts that apply to such theories, as is the case with empirical theories.

The concept of the *Grundnorm* becomes less mysterious if we realize that, for Kelsen, it is not a concept with any determinate content. It is instead a name for the thing that stands in the place that is created by his reasoning: the regress argument establishes that something needs to warrant the normative distinctions he takes as fact, and that this something must itself be a norm, or normative fact. Moreover, it must be a single fact, not, for example, a grab bag of possible justifications for legal order or the state. In short, it must be a genuine truth-making norm, not merely a "reason for". But when we begin to think about the content that the *Grundnorm* might have, and the way it might get content, we are back in a muddle. What confers normative validity on the *Grundnorm* itself? If it is normative, this content must be conferred according to a norm. But the *Grundnorm* is not, by definition, based on any further norm. So where does it come from? The sociologist of the law can answer the parallel empirical question, and do so in nonnormative terms. The sociologist can describe, as Weber does, causal conditions under which normativizing beliefs arise, for example, the charisma of lawgivers in a situation of crisis. But this kind of explanation does something else entirely – explains people's normativizing beliefs, that is to say the beliefs that lead them to accept acts as legal. So this kind of explanation does not validate the beliefs.[3] As we will see, Kelsen responded to this problem of origins and the problem of the validation of the *Grundnorm* in various ways, each of which was intended to preserve the normative character of the *Grundnorm* and to avoid a nonnormative explanation, such as Weber's. Each way reappears in the normativity literature.

Legal questions, legal answers

Why did Kelsen think that the distinction between legality and legitimacy was such a strong support for normativism? And how does it work? Consider his response to the problem of revolutionary law. As Kelsen explains it,

> After the victory of the French Revolution in the eighteenth century and after the victory of the Russian Revolution in the twentieth, the other states showed the distinct inclination not to interpret the coercive orders established by the revolution as legal orders and the acts of revolutionary governments as legal acts, because the one government had violated the monarchic principle of legitimacy and the other had abolished private property of the means of production. For the last named reason, even American courts refused to acknowledge acts of the revolutionary Russian government as legal acts; the courts declared that these were not acts of a state, but of a robber gang. (Kelsen [1925] 2006, 49–50)

The example contains a series of key Kelsenian points. Whether a state is a state or a gang of robbers is a normative fact rather than another kind of fact. Why? Because it is decided by courts. It is thus distinct from the recognition of one state by another for diplomatic purposes, something that states rather than courts do, which is not automatic or factual but a political act (though one enjoined by international law). It is not a sociological fact, either, because it is decided by courts through the application of legal norms. As Kelsen puts it, "In the realm of law, there is no fact 'in itself', no immediately evident fact, there are only facts ascertained by the competent authorities in a procedure determined by law" (Kelsen [1925] 2006, 221). It is "fact" precisely because courts can be wrong or right about their application of these norms. Thus when we perform the necessary logical regression, and trace the fact of legality back to its logical determinants, we are asking who gives a final determination to the question of whether a state is a genuine legal order or a gang of robbers, and how they do it. So this fact is ultimately juridical – it becomes an operative legal fact because a court makes a determination that it is a legal fact – and also normative, because courts do not do this arbitrarily but by the application of law.

This is, in one sense, an immaculate "normative all the way down" argument. Legality, in this case the legality of a revolutionary regime, is a legal question, to be decided on legal grounds. The legality of the state itself might seem to be a meta-legal question, to be decided, as the dominant naturalistic legal theorist of Kelsen's youth, Rudolf von Ihering, put it, by the tribunal of history ([1872] 1915, 189). But there is the raw, actual, fact that courts do decide questions like this. They do not defer to the tribunal of history – or if they do (as we will see they in fact do) – they do so only in accordance with a norm. The norm in question in this case is a basic principle of international law: that states must recognize other states. International law is used and thus validated by courts, making it genuine law, and the factual issues it decides are questions of genuine legal fact because they have decided that they are on the basis of legal norms. The distinction between legality and legitimacy is thus real, normative all the way down, and factual.

The appeal to international law, and the fact that international law is recognized by national courts, allows Kelsen to make two additional important claims: first, that law does not need a state to enact it; second, that the recognition of the legal norms of another state as legal means that the principle of legality is acknowledged and that it is thus a *legal* principle that transcends particular legal systems and also comprehends them, assuring that there can be no legal conflict between different legal systems. In this way he overcomes the neo-Kantian problem of local normativity: local legality is properly legal only by reference to the universal legal facts of international law.

This is an account of the present normativity of law – of how law can be construed as a normative unity, which works as a jurisprudential doctrine, that is to say, as an account that justifies courts making the kinds of decisions they make when they acknowledge other legal systems. But as an account of legal normativity as such, it is strange, not least because the determination of legality is entirely retrospective. It is one thing to say that courts recognize other states as legal orders or that courts recognize international law – courts, indeed, follow precedents or established rules. It is another thing to say *how* these rules and precedents are law. A genuinely normativist account of the legality of treaties would say, as Kelsen does, that "law regulates its own creation. So does international law. Its creation is its own function. When two States conclude a treaty they function as organs of international law" (Kelsen [1925] 2006, 354). But treaties themselves – the analogue in international law to enacted law within a domestic legal system – must in order to be "law" be created in accordance with legal norms. International law stands behind, and legalizes, treaties.

> It is international law, as a legal order superior to the States, that makes possible the creation of norms valid for the sphere of two or more states, that is, international norms. It is general international law, especially by its rule *pacta sunt veranda* [pacts must be respected], which establishes the norm which obligates the States to respect treaties, to behave as treaties concluded by them prescribe. (Kelsen [1925] 2006, 354)

This tells us how the courts must interpret facts: namely, in terms of this normative principle. But it does not explain where the normative principles of international law that stand behind and legalize treaties come from. By definition they can't come from treaties, for treaties presuppose them. There is no world state to enact them. But Kelsen says that such things as the principle that treaties must be kept is genuine law, and that, like much of international law, it has the character of customary law.

When we work our way up the chain of regress arguments, this is where we arrive. But Kelsen needs to acknowledge the validity and normative character of customary law to make this "legality without states" argument work. Without it, he has no way to ground international law. Where does customary law come from? Kelsen has a general answer to this:

The norms of customary law, on the other hand, are created by the behavior of the individuals who are subject to the legal order. In the former [statutory], the norm-creating authority and the norm-subjected individuals are not identical; in the latter [customary] they are, at least to some degree. To consider the fact of a law-creating custom as being existent, it is not necessary for all individuals obligated or entitled by the custom-created norm, to participate in the creation of the custom; it is sufficient that the overwhelming majority do; thus it is possible that individuals are bound by a custom-created norm in whose creation they did not take part. This is particularly true in a norm of customary law that had become valid some time ago. For this reason it is incorrect to interpret customary law as "a tacit contract," as is sometimes done, especially with respect to international customary law. (Kelsen [1925] 2006, 229)

The "constitutive, that is, the law-creating, function of custom is as indubitable as that of legislation" (Kelsen [1925] 2006, 227). Customary law is created by behavior. The "norm-creating" authority is not a legislature, for there is none, but resides in the fact that "an overwhelming majority" of participants behave as if this behavior is normative. Kelsen does not say "as if" in these early writings. But it is a natural interpretation of the passage. It is relevant to what follows in the discussion of Wilfrid Sellars (in Chapter 5) that the source of normative authority is not, as Kelsen pointedly remarks, "an imaginary *Volksgeist* or *solidarité social*" (Kelsen [1925] 2006, 227). For Kelsen, as for Weber, these are fictions.[4]

It is at least somewhat mysterious for a normativist to claim that behavior alone could create *any* normative phenomenon, or the specific normative phenomenon of law. But it is not behavior alone: it is the norm-creating authority of an overwhelming majority expressed in this behavior and presumably, though Kelsen is not clear on this, in their normative attitude toward this behavior. We may leave this line of reasoning aside for a moment and return to it later. It produces a specific form of the transition problem, the problem of how something genuinely normative comes out of something apparently non-normative, in this case attitudes and behavior. But there is another problem produced by inverting the historical order of the production of legality.

Why should the retrospective decisions of a court in another country be determinative of whether a given state is a band of robbers or a genuine state operating legally? This is not precisely Kelsen's claim. He would say that the courts recognize the legality that is already there. But this leads to its own problems. If legality is to be understood as a fact "in the realm of law," it must, as he says, be "ascertained by the competent authorities in a procedure determined by law." The mere proclamation of legal authority by the revolutionary leaders is not enough because the proclamation would presuppose what it asserts: that the leaders are the competent authority. So what is it that the foreign courts are recognizing? A normative fact about legality or a nonnormative fact, which becomes a legal fact and thus normative by virtue of recognition by a court? For Kelsen's argument to work, it must be a normative fact – a form of the distinction between states and bands of robbers, which he claims cannot be made by a sociological account. The problem with this example, however, is that in this case the dependence relation of the legal and sociological is reversed. Foreign courts have no power to alter the sociological facts on the ground – to rule and enforce a ruling that a state is illegal and to replace it with another. They only have the power, and the obligation, to recognize the fact of effective control, which, as Kelsen admits, they do. In the case of the French and Russian revolutions,

> . . . as soon as the revolution-born coercive orders turned out to be effective, they were recognized as legal orders, the governments as state governments, and their acts as state acts, that is, legal acts. (Kelsen [1925] 2006, 49–50)

Kelsen's answer to the question of when something becomes law, then, comes back to the same idea: a legal fact is a fact when it is recognized as such by the courts, or is produced in another manner that is itself normatively governed, such as through enactment by a legislature or a King legally entitled to make law. But what is recognized? Do courts concern themselves with the discernment of legality according to some specific normative principle? As Kelsen himself concedes, they do no such thing. All they ascertain is the fact of effective rule – the very same "sociological" fact he dismisses as inadequate to express legal reality. The courts (and international law) do not recognize in these effective regimes a special nonsociological quality of legal normativity, because there is none, at least in the ordinary sense of succession according to law, because succession did not occur according to law, but by force.

So this argument depends on an equivocation. Effective control is a nonlegal, nonnormative fact. Courts acknowledge such facts, and assign them legal meaning. The role of the courts in these cases of recognition is thus not constitutive of legal facts about the revolutionary regime itself, but explicitly derivative from the nonlegal fact of effective control. The court adds no factual content to this fact.

So the sociological fact of legitimacy is all the fact there is here, and the legal sense is dependent on the sociological sense – the opposite of the relation of dependence that Kelsen requires. But Kelsen can insist that this fact is given a legal meaning nonetheless, on the basis of a dogmatic or normative consideration by the courts. So despite having no normative content itself, in a sense it is also a normative fact in waiting and becomes one explicitly by virtue of the law that the courts apply to it.

It is an oddity that it is a fact about legality which is meaningful in the jurisdiction in which the decision is made, but not legally meaningful to validate the revolutionary regime for that regime's subjects. But Kelsen has a response to this. There is no such thing as legality that is only meaningful for the courts of the people of one country. Law is, for Kelsen, a unity, despite the apparently diversity of actual laws. International law is what unifies the laws of all countries into one. Legal conflicts can be resolved legally. The international customary law governing recognition of laws constitutes all of these facts as legal facts. So it is the legal perspective that is in the background doing the constituting work throughout. And the relevant facts are all facts within this perspective.

The problem of perspectives

If we embrace the idea of legality as a matter of perspective, we face some new problems. What is the epistemic relation between different perspectives? How do perspectives of different kinds relate? Does the notion of perspectives produce a relativism of perspectives? These questions were hotly debated at the time. Emil Lask, Weber's philosophical companion and interlocutor, wrote a *habilitationschrift* on *Rechtsphilosophie* (1907) addressing this problem at the time Weber was writing his methodological essays. This essay formulated explicitly an account of the relation between sociology, understood in Simmel's neo-Kantian manner, and the neo-Kantian conception of legal science. Lask puzzled over the recurrent distinction between the substratum of the ordinary, quotidian, vital, living, and social concrete realities that law forms into concepts, and the fixed, rigid, universal, and eternal character of the concepts themselves. He put the problem of perspectivalism in a particular way: legal and sociological perspectives are distinct ways of constituting something, the living substratum, which has its own distinct, and at least partly conceptual, character. Sociology and law, or the legal perspective and the sociological one, begin on an equal footing in relation to this substratum. Lask constructs this problem by asking how the substrate of conceptually unformed reality meets and mixes with our concepts to produce the objects of our concrete experience (cf. Schuhmann and Smith 1993). This move serves to invert the problem of conceptualization: concepts have a role in the constitution of objects, but the (rigid) conceptual order itself no longer fully determines its content. Verbal, definitional stabilizations of terms are placed upon the moving, living stuff of experience, and are necessarily inadequate to it.[5]

Kelsen responded to this problem of the difference between sociological and legal perspectives in a variety of conflicting ways, and the conflicts are closely connected to the stages that commentators have discerned in his work. The formulation quoted earlier, which says that there's no fact for the law other than those recognized in a legal process, comes from his earliest attempts to grapple with the problem, in which he treated the legal perspective *as* a perspective, but a privileged one ([1925] 2006, 221). In this period, he stressed the contrast between the objectivity of the law and the subjective character of Weber's account. This led him to claim that

> Max Weber's definition of the object of sociological jurisprudence: human behavior adapted (*orientiert*) by the acting individual to an order which he considers to be valid, is not quite satisfactory. According to this definition, a delict [legal wrong] which was committed without the delinquent's being in any way conscious of the legal order would fall outside the relevant phenomenon. ([1925] 2006, 178)

This is misdirected. Weber does not say, as Kelsen thinks, that the subjective meaning in question must be the meaning given the act by the agent. For Weber, the fact that a judge would do so also qualifies an act as subjectively meaningful. But Kelsen also has an argument that is a better fit to Weber's texts:

> Human behavior pertains to the domain of the sociology of law not because it is "oriented" to the legal order, but because it is determined by a legal norm as a condition or consequence. Only because it is determined by the legal order which we presuppose to be valid does human behavior constitute a legal phenomenon. Human behavior so qualified is an object of normative jurisprudence; but it is also an object of the sociology of law insofar as it actually occurs or probably will occur. ([1925] 2006, 178)

The reasoning here is that the domain of the sociology of law is defined by the legal order. The legal order is normative. Sociology inquires whether something that qualifies as "an object of normative

83

jurisprudence" actually happens. It is thus dependent on the normative perspective but fails to acknowledge this dependence. As it stands, this is not very different from what Weber himself says. For Weber, notions like "law" are both valuative and indispensable in constituting the subject matter of sociology. But the normative question of what the law truly is has a place for Kelsen and no place in Weber. For Weber there are two relevant valuative concepts of the law: one that gives meaning to the actions of the people being studied by determining what they consider to be valid, and one that is shared between the sociologist or historian and the audience for their writings, so that they can communicate with this audience. Whether either of these concepts is in some normative perspective "correct" is irrelevant.

Why does Kelsen persist with the arguments that "normative jurisprudence" is the ultimate determinant of the subject matter? Why can't Kelsen concede that the difference between sociological and legal constructions of such facts as the state is merely a matter of perspective, of different conceptual developments leading out from the starting point of ordinary language or common usage? This would salvage normative jurisprudence as a separate discipline. And it would fit with the neo-Kantian idea that something becomes a fact, and becomes objective, by virtue of being part of a hierarchically organized conceptual system or science. But it would lose something important. If Kelsen were to concede that the notion of legality is a feature of the world produced by and bounded by legal science – which Weber branded as a dogmatic science – he would be conceding that the normativity of the law is a feature of a specialized discipline's form of reasoning, rather than of the general factual character of the world itself. [6] He would adopt the Friedman solution of treating normative jurisprudence as a normative lens (1998) – the normative lens of the dogmatic discipline of legal science. But this organization of the facts is binding only on legal science. And this is precisely what he wants to avoid. The perspective of legal science is not binding on anyone but the practitioners of legal science. And it is binding only epistemically, in terms of the reasoning one can do with the objects that the perspective constitutes, not normatively.

So Kelsen must deny the possibility of any construction from the substratum of ordinary facts that is not the juristic one – to say the substratum of facts is already normative and that, correctly described, its facts are binding. He bases this argument on an explicit thesis about the nature of description and conceptualization – a thesis that is rarely found in such an explicit form, but is implicit in the argument for normativism generally.

84

> There is no sociological concept of the State besides the juristic concept. Such a double concept of the State is logically impossible, if for no other reason because there cannot be more than one concept of the same object. There is only a juristic concept of the State: the State as-centralized-legal-order, is not a concept of the State, it presupposes the concept of the State, which is a juristic concept. (Kelsen [1925] 2006, 188–89)

Sociological studies of the state, in short, are perfectly acceptable, as long as it is acknowledged that the sociological concept presupposes the juristic concept as the only correct one.

In his later work, *Pure Theory of Law* of 1934,[7] he shifts ground, perhaps in response to Weber's substantive writings on the law published in the 1920s. In these writings it is apparent that Weber can redescribe legal phenomena in exquisite detail, as well as give a sociological account of what is taken to be valid in different legal orders, as well as construct a theory of the state which comprehends and explains the juristic one, that is to say explains it as a "believed-in" phenomenon. Kelsen's new position seems to concede this point by admitting that the substratum, the material that concepts organize, is not normative. He thus comes even closer to Friedman's normative lens:

> The external fact whose objective meaning is a legal or illegal act is always an event that can be perceived by the senses (because it occurs in time and space) and therefore a natural phenomenon determined by causality. However, this event as such, as an element of nature, is not an object of legal cognition. What turns this event into a legal or illegal act is not its physical existence, determined by the laws of causality prevailing in nature, but the objective meaning resulting from its interpretation. The specifically legal meaning of this act is derived from a "norm" whose content refers to the act; this norm confers legal meaning to the act, so that it may be interpreted according to this norm. The norm functions as a scheme of interpretation. To put it differently: The judgment that an act of human behavior, performed in time and space, is "legal" (or "illegal") is the result of a specific, namely normative, interpretation. And even the view that this act has the character of a natural phenomenon is only a specific interpretation, different from the normative, namely a causal interpretation. ([1925] 2006, 45)

The "external fact" seems to be the new substratum, and it is non-normative. These facts become normative facts only by virtue of interpretation, or rather of a normative scheme of interpretation.

This reasoning allows Kelsen to introduce a new way of formulating the relationship with sociology: in terms of parallelism. In the sociology of law, he says

> The object of . . . cognition . . . is not actually the law itself, but certain parallel phenomena in nature. Similarly with the physiologist: he investigates the chemical or physical processes that accompany certain feelings or give rise to conditions under which these feelings occur, but he does not comprehend the feelings themselves, which, as psychological phenomena, cannot be comprehended chemically or physiologically. The Pure Theory of Law, as a specifically legal science, directs its attention not to legal norms as the data of consciousness, and not to the intending or imagining of legal norms either, but rather to legal norms *qua* (intended or imagined) meaning. And the Pure Theory encompasses material facts only where these facts are the content of legal norms, that is, are governed by legal norms. The problem of the Pure Theory of Law is the specific autonomy of a realm of meaning. ([1934] 2002, 14)

This represents a step back from the aggressive claims of the earlier writings. The "actually intended norms" are not determined by anyone's actual intentions or beliefs, but exist autonomously in the realm of meaning. These autonomous normative facts are the subject of the pure theory. What people really think is specifically *not* the subject matter here. That domain is left to sociology.

As we have seen, meaning is not alien to Weber's approach: he defines sociology as the study of meaningful action, and writes on understanding what judges are doing when they reason about ideals of validity, but he does not make the normative sense of "validity" relevant to the explanation and understanding of judges' actions. Kelsen is distinguishing his own project from this with the phrase "not to legal norms as the data of consciousness, and not to the intending or imagining of legal norms either [i.e., Weber's specific definition of meaning], but rather to legal norms *qua* (intended or imagined) meaning." Weber is concerned, to put it differently, with meaning in use, meaning as it actually figures in social action and as it is intended and imagined by the people involved. But what is Kelsen concerned with? And how does it relate to actual law? Kelsen seems to assume that there is in fact a structure that answers to the name "legal norms" that is separable from the "data of consciousness" and that is *common* to the intending of some unspecified group of people. Perhaps this structure is the written law plus the *Grundnorm* that is presupposed. Perhaps it includes the conventions and maxims of the law. Without the assumption of a common structure, however, there is no subject matter here. And Weber has no need of this assumption: for him, speaking about the legal order in an explanatory sense is aided by the construction of ideal-types of orders of *Herrschaft* or domination, but these have no normative significance, except for

86

those who live under them and believe in the validity of the forms of authority that they underwrite. The types are constructed for purposes of explanatory utility.

Kelsen shifts ground in the course of his career, but the core problem remains. To understand law as normative in a special sense – not merely as some set of social facts interpreted normatively or understood normatively, but as a novel kind of fact that is intrinsically normative – one needs an account of the normative which is closed, or self-generating, by the rule of norms generated by norms or of facts recognized under norms, for example. And one also needs to be able to say that this set of facts cannot be reduced to or explained by the nonnormative. But the closure turns out to be something of a sham: there are what we might call nonnormative moments: either the rule of norms generated under norms breaks down, or closure fails. In the case of customary law, the norms are apparently generated by a nonnormative fact: behavior. In the case of the legality-legitimacy distinction, the legal fact that the court recognizes – the fact of effective governance – is indistinguishable from the nonnormative facts that are the subject of sociology. The idea of a closed order of normative fact, on Kelsen's own terms, is an impossibility. Even the norms depend on nonnormative facts. The idea of a specially constructed normative lens on facts that are not themselves normative avoids this problem. And, as we will see, this is the direction that Kelsen ultimately goes: he saves the idea of the structure of norms, but abandons the idea of closure.

The disenchantment of the law

Kelsen's argument exhibits in a particularly vivid way the odd dual structure of normativity arguments. As he explains it in connection with the pure theory, his interest is specifically *not* in intended meaning, which is Weber's terminology for what people actually believe and understand themselves as meaning. It is with the actual meaning, which exists in a system of meanings that stands above the various individual understandings and beliefs that make up intended meanings.

Why appeal to such a sphere of meanings? For Kelsen's contemporaries such as Ernst Cassirer, it was obvious that there was an autonomous symbolic realm with internal relations, structure, and investigatable properties, and that the individual mind interacted with this realm – though precisely how this interaction was supposed to work was a bit of a mystery. In the case of law, however, the motivation for believing in such a realm is more specific. This account is a replacement for various folk theories of legality and the state, such as the idea that kings ruled by divine right as a result of a deposit of authority originally granted by God. Kelsen of course did not believe in such theories. But he would not, at least in this part of his career, accept the sociological approach to such theories – which was, in Weber's case, to classify them as legitimate beliefs. Kelsen accepted Weber's classification: he reproduced it almost exactly in his own classification of law into the categories of customary, revelatory, and statutory. But Weber had a completely disenchanted view of these beliefs. There was never a question for him of their being true or imperfect approximations to a hidden normative truth. For the purposes of explanation, the fact that people *believed* – in the mystical charisma of a king and the transfer of charisma through ceremonies, or in the sanctity of traditions, or in the rationality of the legal system – was enough.

Their contemporary, Hägerström, was relentless on this point. He delighted in collecting examples of survivals from the magical rituals of ancient Roman law, and treated the normativity of the law as just another magical idea that the philosophy of law ought to rid itself of. This is not so different from Weber. For Weber, as for Hägerström, the origin of beliefs in justice and authority, or more precisely justified authority, is mixed up with magic. For Weber, the original basis of legal authority is charismatic, and has subsequently been converted into traditions that are then believed in because they are ancient usages. The attribution of charisma at its primitive origins is conceptually informed by magical ideas. Its authoritative character and the typical belief in the special powers inherent in the person of the charismatic leader are essentially taken from magic. The category of magic or magical thinking and the category of charisma are closely related, with charisma being in some sense a refined and distinctive subcategory of magic. At its origins the case is the same as *tabu*: interdictions are backed by magical powers attributed to persons who offer the interdictions.

What Hägerström does that is different from Weber is to emphasize the central magical character of all legal activity. Hägerström is providing an error theory. For Hägerström the doctrines justifying the law are not merely superfluous to the explanation of a functioning legal order (as they are for Weber), nor are they, as they are for Weber, properly placed in a separate nonfactual category: the category of dogma. Rather, they are false beliefs. However, they are false

88

in the sense that magical beliefs are false, or in the sense that theological beliefs would be said by a nonbeliever to be false. Hägerström has no stake in either legitimating these beliefs, as does Kelsen, or in providing (so to speak) an alternative intellectual venue in terms of which the beliefs might be treated as true, namely, as a dogmatic science.

These are the kinds of conclusions that Kelsen resisted for virtually his entire career. But at the end, he recanted. Kelsen ultimately acknowledged that the regress argument led, not to a genuine norm, but to a "merely thought (i.e., a fictitious) norm" ([1979] 1991, 256). The *Grundnorm*, Kelsen concluded, was a "real fiction" in Vaihinger's sense. Real fictions were, in Vaihinger's words "not only in contradiction with reality but self-contradictory in themselves" ([1979] 1991, 256).[8] As Kelsen puts it:

> According to Vaihinger, a fiction is a cognitive device used when one is unable to attain one's cognitive goal with the material at hand (1935:13). The cognitive goal of the Basic Norm is to ground the validity of the norms forming a positive moral or legal order, that is to interpret the subjective meaning of the norm-positing acts as their objective meaning (i.e., as valid norms) and to interpret the relevant acts as norm-positing acts. This goal can be attained only by means of a fiction. It should be noted that the Basic Norm [*Grundnorm*] is not a hypothesis in the sense of Vaihinger's philosophy of As-If – as I myself have sometimes characterized it – but a fiction. A fiction differs from a hypothesis in that it is accompanied – or ought to be accompanied – by the awareness that reality does not agree with it (pp. 85ff). ([1979] 1991, 256)

Why did it conflict with reality? Because the assumption of a Basic Norm – for instance, the Basic Norm of a religious moral order, "Everyone is to obey God's commands," or the Basic Norm of a legal order, "Everyone is to behave as the historically first constitution specifies" – refers to something that does not exist, namely, an actual act of will that would make this a norm. It is also self-contradictory in that it produces a regress: "it represents the empowering of an ultimate moral or legal authority and so emanates from an authority – admittedly, a fictitious authority – even higher than this one" ([1979] 1991, 256). The regress needs a further authority – God or the original will-generating fathers of the constitution have to get their authority somewhere. But the requirement that they generate the Basic Norm by their own willing contradicts this. In short, Kelsen recognized that without accepting some sort of mystical general will, which was inherently self-authorizing and referred to no higher authority, there was no way of generating legal normativity.

Myths must meet some minimal standards of intelligibility, and the inferences in them must be capable of being followed. The model of *tabu* meets this standard, especially if we place these beliefs in the context of a premodern world that is not yet "disenchanted." Hägerström and Weber thus converged at the point of the origins of law, offering complementarity. Their treatments of magic (and in Weber's case the magical character of charisma) overlap. But neither of these accounts establishes legality as a real thing. To understand the law, for Hägerström, is to separate the mystical elements from the factual ones, and the effect of this separation is to reduce law to fact and to reduce the legal order to the brute facticity of the actual expectations on which people act. All the rest, such as the notion of binding and the notion of the normative quality of the law (and normativity itself), for Hägerström fall squarely into the category of falsehood.

Kelsen as the paradigmatic normativist

The Kelsen saga may seem far removed from contemporary normativism, but in fact it exhibits most of the basic features, and conundrums, of normativism. It should be noted that when these ideas appeared in Anglo-American philosophy of law, they did so in a modified form, in the writings of H. L. A. Hart, who might be considered a normativist of sorts. But in an important sense Hart merely arrived at the conclusion Kelsen arrived at before Kelsen did, without advertising its implications. Hart preserved the basic idea of norms being generated according to norms. But he ended the regress differently. Ordinary rules of enactment, as exhibited in performatives in which a law is stated by parliament in the name of the Queen, for instance, were based on a further norm, in this case the rule of recognition "In England they recognize as law . . . whatever the Queen in parliament enacts" (Hart 1961, 99). He argued that such rules were in the end only grounded in the sociological fact of acceptance. In short, he made the same accommodation Kelsen did at the end of his life: he preserved the internal sense of the normativity of the law – the norm produced in accordance with norms sense – at the price of the normativity of the starting point. In effect, this was another capitulation to Weber, for acceptance is just legitimacy.

The core issues for legal normativity are the same as for normativity generally. The "explanatory necessity" conundrum is generic: the claim is that there is some aspect that requires some sort of special explanation, in this case validity; the solution is that there is such a thing as legal validity that transcends what people believe to be valid.

But there is nothing but belief in these things. Lawyers have to learn what is legally valid through a consideration of what people say, and what they say they believe legal validity consists in; in the end they have beliefs about validity. It is beliefs about validity that are transmitted. The mundane explanatory facts of what is actually said do not justify the transcendental fact of real validity. Only the *description* of legal facts in terms of validity – a description the sociologist makes in terms of beliefs in validity – requires the transcendental fact of validity.

Of course, it also happens to be a property of the law that legal ideas have a strong association with myth, as do normative ideas generally. The reasons people actually think the law is binding, if they in fact do, are exceedingly various and also peculiar, ranging from the idea that God wishes us to obey the authorities because they represent the divine order on earth to such ideas as *hau* or karma or the idea that one will be struck dead if one violates an oath one has taken on one's life. Kelsen faces this problem directly when he argues that the *Grundnorm* is a very specific type of fiction – an outright false and self-contradictory one rather than a kind of half-truth. One might argue that the diversity of beliefs about the binding character and ultimate authoritative grounding of the law reflects the fact that ordinary people can understand these mysteries only though myth, but the normativity at the core of these mysteries is in fact real. The Maori do incur real obligations, as do the fetish users of Africa. They merely apprehend them through the wrong theories. But to make this argument incurs the burden of explaining how and why they are wrong and came to be wrong, and why the theory of normative force is not wrong in the same ways.

The problem of legal validity thus produces the same kinds of arguments that normativism produces elsewhere. The crucial issue for transcendental arguments is the exclusion of alternatives: sociology purports to give an alternative account of the law. Kelsen gave many of the standard normativist responses to such arguments. The core of the argument is that the sociologist has changed the subject. But making this argument in a noncircular way proved difficult for Kelsen, despite his different formulations of it. The claim of surplus force appears in the case of the law as the binding character of the law, which cannot be accounted for by ordinary explanations. This is a clear example of the problem of circularity: the need to account for the surplus force only arises under the description of the law as binding – a description not grounded in any sort of empirical fact. It is a feature of the law, like normativity generally, that is inaccessible to empirical investigation.

91

Yet the problem of legal normativity is a poor paradigm in another sense. It is routinely claimed that certain kinds of topics, notably rationality and concepts, are intrinsically normative, and thus inescapable regardless of the topic one is considering. In these cases, in contrast to the law, there is no alternative to the normative concept – or so the argument goes. There is also another reason that Kelsen's account of legality is not a paradigm relevant to all normativisms. As we have seen, Kelsen is careful to reject as mythical such collective notions as *Volksgeist* or *solidarité social*. Many normativist accounts, however, appeal to similar collective notions, notably community and the idea of collective intentionality, or to a collective idea of "the social" as the location and source of normativity. Kelsen himself turns to the notion of will as a basis of legality. So the problem of collective intentionality needs to be addressed directly. In the next three chapters I will take up each of these problems, beginning with concepts in the following chapter, with collective intentionality in the subsequent chapter, and with rationality in the final chapter.

Notes

1. Labels like "neo-Kantian" prove unhelpful here, for they apply to all of the participants in this dispute. Weber's methodological texts were themselves critiques, in a neo-Kantian idiom, of other kinds of neo-Kantian conceptions of the problem, during a period in which philosophers and also sociologists, many of whom were by profession philosophers either by training (such as Durkheim) or by both training and professorial appointment (such as Simmel), were either transforming or emancipating themselves from neo-Kantianism. The emancipation was sometimes explicit, as in the case of the Swedish legal realist Axel Hägerström ([1929] 1964, 33–76), or sometimes it arose simply through the workings of their own philosophical development in attempting to resolve the many issues within neo-Kantianism, as was the case with Weber's personal philosophical interlocutor, Emil Lask, his posthumous philosophical exponent, Karl Jaspers, and his close contemporaries and allies, including Simmel.

2. As this book is not primarily concerned with the history of philosophy, I will omit any detailed discussion of the role Weber played in defining the subsequent discussion of history and the social sciences in philosophy generally, or his role as the "other" to the Frankfurt School, Heidegger, and Leo Strauss. But it should be noted that Weber was much discussed in Kelsen's Vienna, that Karl Popper had an intimate acquaintance with Weber's collected methodological essays, and adapted his notion of logic of the situation explanations from Weber, and that, in like manner, the philosophy of history in the form of Maurice Mandelbaum's *The Problem of Historical Knowledge* (1938), restated Weber's views in the guise of analytic arguments. Some of this history is given in Turner and Factor (1984).

3. Even the fact that the command giver is God is not enough. We need a specific kind of validating claim to get an ought out of the mere causal fact of a command:

> The reason for the validity of a norm can only be the validity of another norm. A norm which represents the reason for the validity of another norm is figuratively spoken of as a higher norm in relation to lower norm. It looks as if one could give as a reason for the validity of a norm the circumstance that it was established by an authority, human or divine; for example, the statement: "The reason for the validity of the Ten Commandments is that God Jehovah issued them on Mount Sinai"; or: "Men ought to love their enemies, because Jesus, Son of God, issued this command in his Sermon on the Mount." But in both cases the reason for the validity is not that God or his son issued a certain norm at a certain time in a certain place, but the tacitly presupposed norm that <u>one ought to obey</u> the commands of God or his son. To be true: In the syllogism whose major premise is the *ought*-statement asserting the validity of the higher norm: "One ought to obey God's commands," and whose conclusion is the ought-statement asserting the validity of the lower norm. (Kelsen [1925] 2006, 194–95; underline emphasis added)

4. Would they cease to be fictions if they were recognized as facts by a court acting according to a norm? In the case of "will of the people" in the Florida Supreme Court Gore–Bush election controversy, just this happened. The court asserted that the legislature had "expressly recognized the will of the people of Florida as the guiding principle" for electing officials (*Albert Gore, Jr. and Joseph I. Lieberman vs. Katherine Harris, as Secretary, etc., et al*, SC00–2431, 18, 2000). (The cited support for this claim [*Gore and Lieberman vs. Harris*, 17–18] never mentions the phrase "will of the people," however, but instead describes electoral procedures.) The legislature, not the courts, are doing the recognizing here, but the courts are accepting this will. According to Kelsen's own reasoning, they would cease to be fictions. Legal procedures have the power to make non-facts into facts. The problem of circularity produced by this reasoning will be discussed below.
5. Current work in neuroscience has shown that 75% of the neural contribution to perception is from the resources of the brain itself, and 25% from the perceptual nerves: if we take the resources of the brain to be conceptual, this fits with Lask's picture of the co-production of the ordinary world of objects by the interpenetration of concepts and an unformed empirical reality (Gawande 2008).
6. The secondary literature on Kelsen has made precisely this suggestion. Here is Paulson:

> . . . if the Pure Theory takes its place alongside other normativist legal theories, but without the transcendental argument inspired by Kant and the neo-Kantians, it is perhaps best understood as offering a *legal point of view*. This approach, worked out in some detail by Joseph Raz, has affinities to H. L. A. Hart's theory, as well as significant precursors in the two circles most intellectually congenial to Kelsen: the Heidelberg or South-West School of neo-Kantians, and the positivist tradition in German public law. (Paulsen [1934] 2002, xlii)

93

This idea, that legal science was concerned with the "juridical aspect," was part of the literature prior to Kelsen (cf. Patterson 1950). The issue is whether there is any explanatory relevance to this aspect, or whether all the explanatory work can be done without reference to it. Kelsen clearly wants, in his early writings, to assert that genuine normativity in some sense needs to be part of the explanatory stream. Raz is similarly vague about this point, using the term "normative aspect" and making a similar claim: that acting according to reasons reflects our capacity to, for example, recognize that the barometer is falling is "evidence of forthcoming weather" (Raz 2009, 18). But this fails to resolve the question of whether the recognition and evidence need to be correct to be explanatory, or whether correctness is part of the explanation at all.

7. *Reine Rechtslehre* 1st edn. translated as *Introduction to the Problems of Legal Theory* ([1934] 2002); 2nd edn. translated as *Pure Theory of Law* ([1960] 1967).

8. Weber had said that the state was a fiction. Kelsen had a complex disagreement with the theory that the state and the law were separable, so the analogous claim for him would have been that legality was a fiction.

— 4 —

LUSTRAL RITES AND SYSTEMS OF CONCEPTS

... all abstracta *are now to be counted as delusions. They are useful as ways of speaking. Even Copernicus, for all his enlightenment, found it convenient to speak in Ptolemaic terms of the rising and setting of the sun. And in mathematics, it is convenient to be able to speak of infinitesimals, imaginary quantities, negative quantities, irrational numbers, and improper fractions, despite the fact that mathematicians are fully aware of the intrinsic absurdity of these products of the mind.*
Franz Brentano (letter to A. Marty, March 1901 [1930] 1966, 64)

Legal normativity is a model in one important sense: the usual way of thinking about normativity is based on notions that are analogical to law, such as the moral law, or on notions of obligation that are also analogous to legal obligation. Where they differ is that legal normativity is in some sense an option. The legal thinkers of Weber's time, including Weber himself, were fascinated with people who rejected the law – such as anarchists, or contemporary followers of Tolstoy. The fact that there were such people, and that they had made an alternative value choice, indicated to them that following the law was itself a value choice, rather than necessary submission to a normativity external to the person and not subject to choice. This is the thought that Kelsen addresses in a confused way in his suggestion that Weber cannot account for the fact that a criminal who rejects the law is still a criminal; as I have noted, Weber's reply to this would have been that it is the meaning attached by others (such as judges) that makes someone a criminal, in sociological terms.

The normativist can concede these optional kinds of normativity, especially if she considers the real issue to be nonoptional normativity – normativity that attaches to the fundamental categories of understanding ourselves, or to understanding itself, or to reason, or

95

to something equally fundamental. For this reason, the normativist is likely to dismiss Kelsen's troubles with normativity as irrelevant and uninformative. The normativist can say that it is merely an oddity that the model for normativity in general, the law, cannot be given a genuinely normative basis, and that the supposed normativity of the law collapses into a sociological fact about belief. Basing the claims of normativism on belief itself – which is to say on the nature of belief, understanding, thought – enables the normativist to escape the considerations about the source of normative authority and its origins that so befuddle the legal normativist. Indeed, the argument that belief is a normative concept is the perfect *tu quoque* response to Weber: he relies on the notion of belief to account for legal norms, and is therefore convicted of helping himself to a normative concept that he is not entitled to.

More generally (or so it appears), this stronghold of normativism can be defended by considerations that nonnormativists are bound to accept as a condition for their own thought, such as the fact that "concept" is itself a normative concept, as well as some relatively straightforward factual considerations about the nature of thought and language. There is an interesting parallel to these kinds of considerations in the case of law, which I did not discuss in connection with Kelsen but which nevertheless appears in Kelsen and in his neo-Kantian predecessors, such as Rudolf Stammler. It was routinely claimed by these writers that as a matter of fact all organized societies had law. The implication was that the law in question was genuine law, which meant normative law. The implication was that legal normativity was thus a universal fact. This argument was only quasi-factual. Kelsen or Stammler would not have been impressed by the fact that, say, Polynesian societies were organized around "the big man complex" rather than law. They would either have adjusted the definitions so that this would not count as organized society or stretched the definition of law to make the will of the big man into a form of law. But the appearance that this was a fact would be sustained.

Similar reasoning abounds in the literature about nonoptional normativity. John Haugeland, in the introduction to his influential *Having Thought* (1998), gives a long list of matters about which he doesn't think there needs to be any sort of argument. These include the question of whether there is a basic difference between human and animal cognition, what understanding is, and many other matters of the same kind (1998, 1–2). The essays in the book go on to formulate a long series of arguments designed to elucidate the conditions for the possibility of understanding, language, and so forth thus conceived

– conceived in an unargued – for and unarguable – with manner. The style is signaled by the repeated use of the term "genuine," as in "genuine normativity," "proper," and "essential" in claims like this: "to collapse correctness into propriety is to obliterate the essential character of thought" (1998, 316).

It is somewhat breathtaking to think that we understand "understanding" so well that we can say that people do it but birds, bees, educated fleas, dogs, and dolphins don't do it. But what these claims are supposed to support is even more breathtaking. The point of these claims, as with the parallel cases in legal philosophy, is to establish the fact of the normative character of the things described: that there is a real thing called conceptual content that implies normativity, and that thinking, understanding, and so forth are fundamentally and inescapably normative concepts. There is nothing new about the idea that the conceptual forms a domain that is different from the domain of the natural. But these arguments raise the stakes substantially by purporting to give accounts of the normative that have metaphysical implications that tell us something about the necessary existence of "the normative" as a novel category of being.

One form of this argument is this: society is always conceptually constituted; that "concept" is a normative concept; that to be conceptual is to be part of a special nonnatural domain of fact; that society itself can only be understood through the concepts that constitute it, therefore a social science understood in a naturalistic sense is impossible. Peter Winch formulated this argument in the 1950s, under the influence of a certain (linguistic idealist) understanding of Wittgenstein's recently published *Philosophical Investigations* ([1953] 1958). Winch's classic text, *The Idea of a Social Science and Its Relation to Philosophy* (1958) contains the nonoptional normativity argument that most directly parallels Kelsen's argument against the sociological understanding of the law, and specifically addresses such issues as Weber's accounting for such things as the law in terms of "beliefs in" the norms rather than the norms themselves. In this chapter, I will do with Winch what was done with Kelsen in the last chapter: trace out the normativity claims that were made initially and see how they wound up.

The core problem of naturalism and normativity restated

As I have suggested, the initial move in antinaturalist arguments is to assert the primacy of a particular description. If the concept is

97

recognition, for example, and the issue is what it means to say that a person has recognized something, two kinds of parallel and conflicting claims will be made. One is a naturalist claim that recognition is nothing more than x, where x is a nonnormative, naturalistic description of, for example, a causal psychological process, which can be tested, in at least some cases, by external evidence of some kind. Herbert Simon for many years studied the psychology of pattern recognition. The question Simon's work raises is this: Is this really recognition, or is it something else, something less than *real* recognition? Is there, in the phrase of Wilfred Sellars, surplus value that the naturalistic characterization fails to capture ([1956] 1997, Sec. 9, pp. 30–31)? The antinaturalist will claim that whatever it is that the psychological theory describes, it is not recognition in the full sense, that only some other description of recognition is the correct description, and this correct description implies something nonnaturalistic: for example, that recognition of a thing as one kind of thing implies a variety of other things through the conceptual properties of the concept of that thing – a cat cannot also be a dog, for instance – and that these implications present a logical, and therefore normative, relation between concepts. Such relations, then, by their nature cannot be properly understood as causal. Genuine recognition is thus, in the phrase of Sellars, already in the space of reasons ([1956] 1997, Sec. 36, p.76), and the surplus value consists of its inferential relations, relations that are logical or conceptual and cannot be captured by the naturalistic form of the fact.

Other cases work in the same way. They are cases in which there are at least two descriptions – for example, of an action or a mental phenomenon – which are empirically equivalent but, not equivalent with respect to their implications. One description makes no reference to normative, conceptual relations; the other description is, explicitly, in "the space of reasons." "Understanding" also works in this way. A naturalist might claim that understanding amounts to being able to navigate more or less successfully in the social world, to anticipate and respond to the reactions to one's own utterances and actions and to the utterances and actions of others in a way that conforms to the expectations of others and is predictable to them – to pass the Turing test and apply this test to others. An antinaturalist description of the same thing would insist that understanding, properly understood, implies something more: a merging of horizons, a mastery of common normative or conceptual content, a sharing of commitments (conceived as more than and different from mundane causal psychological facts, such as mere attitudes), or something else that goes beyond the empirical and the external. Some notion of system is central to these arguments: logical or conceptual relations that make up the thing go beyond the empirical; the thing thus constituted can only be conceived normatively, because the relations are normative.

Without such arguments, antinaturalism cannot begin. But there is another kind of argument in which the antinaturalist finds a normative component in the description made by the naturalist. A telltale sign of the normative, according to normativism, is the notion of correctness and error. Thus, if correctness of understanding is part of the concept of understanding, the concept is a normative one. Similarly for other conceptual relations: That cats cannot also be dogs is part of the logic of cat and dog talk. To say "my cat is a dog" is to speak unintelligibly, and unintelligibly not because of some sort of fact of science about the species canine, but because of the logic of the terms "dog" and "cat" and the normative relations between the terms that enable claims about them to serve as reasons. To put this in a slightly different way, the claim is that there is a normative moment even in the explanations the naturalist tries to sketch, which the naturalist cannot, try as he might, exclude. These moments reveal the genuine, normative character of the explanations, or at least the ineliminability of the normative from them. And a naturalism that concedes any role to normativity is not naturalism.

It should be noted that the naturalist is not defenseless against this kind of argument. The concept of "concept" is perhaps conceptualizable in other than normative ways (as, indeed, it routinely is in the context of cognitive science, correctly or not), and the various notions of correctness, which the naturalist may correctly observe are the by-products of a "natural" process of training, may perhaps be substituted for by notions like "belief in correctness." But these defenses lead to a second stage. Is "belief" more nonnormative than "concept" or "correctness"? The normativist would deny this, on the grounds that "belief" is already a term with normative implications. To believe is already to acknowledge a set of logical and therefore normative relations, to be "committed" to certain proprieties, and especially to accept the rational implications of one's beliefs. The antinormativist, in the common saying of these thinkers, has illegitimately helped himself to a normative concept in the course of constructing his naturalism.

The background question in what follows will be the question of whether this dispute can ever be convincingly resolved on one side or the other. Winch is especially interesting in this regard, for he begins with precisely the kind of reasoning from descriptions that I have detailed here, based on a similar interpretation of Wittgenstein, and was eventually forced to concede a key naturalist point, a point which his more modern heirs are, I will argue, also forced to concede.

Winch's problem with social science

Peter Winch wrote two classic works in the philosophy of social science. Both resonated far beyond this obscure field. The first was *The Idea of a Social Science and its Relation to Philosophy* (1958). The second was "Understanding a Primitive Society" ([1964] 1974), which grew out of a celebrated exchange with Alasdair MacIntyre at Oxford, in which MacIntyre defended the idea of universal standards of rationality and the necessity for making judgments concerning the rationality of other cultures.[1] It was in this form that the problem of the rationality of other cultures emerged into the general philosophical literature and became a spur for such classics as Donald Davidson's "On the Very Idea of a Conceptual Scheme" ([1973] 1984). The passage in question in what follows comes from "Understanding a Primitive Society." It is analogous to the passage in Kelsen that declares the *Grundnorm* a fiction, though it is far less explicit and open to multiple interpretations. Like Kelsen's passage, it concedes, or appears to concede, a key normativist claim. The passage itself extends and modifies a section in *The Idea of a Social Science* which criticized Vilfredo Pareto for arguing that baptisms were *au fond* lustral rites. Winch does not explain exactly what was wrong with his original passage on Pareto. This presents us with a little historical mystery. He footnotes his earlier discussion without comment. The question of the relation between the two passages is not answered directly and is answered only very indirectly by the discussion in the paper itself, which is an extensive analysis of a passage in E. E. Evan-Pritchard's prewar book on the Azande dealing with the question of the rationality of their witchcraft beliefs (1937).

Pareto had an explanatory account in which actions of various kinds could be understood by separating them into elements involving the beliefs about them, which are often mystical (or, as he calls them, nonlogical), and their basic or persistent character. His point is that theories about these persistent forms frequently change, while the forms stay the same. His argument is that expressed beliefs are a poor guide to action, people are nonlogical in much of their conduct, and the true explanations of much conduct must be sought in the persistent rather than the variable parts of action. Lustral rites are a case in point. As Pareto puts it,

> Christians have the custom of baptism. If one knows the Christian procedure only one would not know whether and how it could be analyzed. Moreover we have an explanation of it; we are told that the rite of baptism is celebrated to remove original sin. That still is not enough. If we had no other facts of the same class to go by, we should find it difficult to isolate the elements in the complex phenomenon of baptism. But we do have facts of that type. The pagans too had lustral water, and they used it for purposes of purification. (Pareto 1935, para. 863; quoted in Winch 1958, 105)

He goes on to argue that there is, so to speak, a rational kernel to this idea. The human being as a rule has a vague feeling that water somehow cleanses moral as well as material pollution. People do not, as a rule, however, justify their conduct in this manner. "The explanation would be far too simple. So instead he goes looking for something more complicated, more pretentious, and readily finds what he is looking for" (Pareto 1935; para. 863; quoted in Winch 1958, 105–6).

We may take this as a model bit of naturalism. People have a vague prenormative factual idea about purification, which they confusedly extend to what they (wrongly) conceive as the spiritual domain. They then make up a complicated but bogus theory – what I have been calling here a Good Bad Theory – to justify it, and they change the theory now and then without changing the basic ritual actions. The doctrine of baptism is thus like a false scientific theory – an error – which overlays mundane acts by adding supernatural and mystical content, much as Axel Hägerström argues that the law – a real coercive system that operated in the world of cause – was overlain with mystical ideas about binding, wills, and so forth. Not surprisingly, this added content is conceived by the participants in the rites as somehow essential to the phenomenon itself, and essential to its correct description.

Winch's argument is that Pareto's characterization is intrinsically flawed. His reasoning is this: actions are logically connected to intentions; to be an act, rather than a bit of behavior, it must be (subject to the usual limitations of weakness of will, human error, and the like) the act intended. The baptizing priest intended to *baptize*, that is, to initiate the baptized into the community that is also literally the body of Christ through an act in which Christ is not merely represented but, on some theologies, is a real presence. He did not intend to perform a lustral rite. Therefore, the act of baptism is not the performance of a lustral rite. To translate Winch's argument into contemporary terms, he was saying that among the constitutive elements of the act of Holy Baptism, without which we are no longer talking about Holy Baptism but rather about something else, is the intention. It therefore implies that beliefs make it one kind of act rather than another. The relations of belief are in the space of reasons: logical, conceptual, and therefore normative. To describe the act differently, for example, as a lustral rite, and to explain it under this description, is simply to change the subject and obliterate the essential character of the act.

We can distinguish various versions of this "misdescription" argument, but we may begin with the naive form (which Winch not only does not defend, but carefully steers clear of). The naive form is what Christian theologians use. For them, the reason "lustral rite" is a bad description of baptism is that the only proper way of describing the Christian activity of Holy Baptism is in Christian terms, that is to say, by taking the uppercase H and B seriously. Only by respecting the inferential connections between the elements of the activity thus described and other beliefs, such as the belief that in sacraments it is an essential feature that God actually be present, is it possible to grasp the nature of the activity. In short, to explain and understand Holy Baptism one must explain it and understand it in its own, Christian, terms; this requires being a Christian and accepting the validity of these terms.

In our time, we are typically uncomfortable with this sort of reasoning, or even with the idea that the Christian version of Holy Baptism actually makes any sense. Phrases like "incorporate in the body of Christ by these Holy mysteries" and the theology of the real presence were, of course, the source of the century of religious warfare that ushered in modernity, and, as noted earlier, the emblem of the process of disenchantment that Weber named. Accepting this language hardly seems to be the sort of thing that anyone should be told is a condition for any project of explanation or understanding.

But for the naturalist, the same skepticism holds for the traditional language of thought itself. Why should "belief," "concept," and the like be any different from baptism, where possibly bogus content is smuggled in as descriptive fact on the back of a theory-laden description of the phenomenon? The question the naturalist poses for the normativist is this: Is there a salient difference between the language of thought and the language of baptism that allows the normativist thus to avoid this challenge and affirm that the traditional (normative) language of thought, unlike that of baptism, is sacrosanct, and that alternatives to the traditional language of thought (such as naturalistic psychological ones) that purport to be nonnormative are a case of changing the subject, misdescribing, and missing constitutive features of the phenomenon? Why is the normativist's claim that we must swallow normativism in order not to change the subject any different from the Christian claim that describing baptism correctly requires acceptance of the whole of Christian belief? Why, to put it simply, is the language of belief, concept, and the like any more than another Good Bad Theory?

Winch does not tell us why he doesn't accept the Christian account of baptism as the only valid description. But if his preference for his alternative to it is merely a matter of intellectual fashion – that is, the decline of the intellectual respectability of religion, and our wish to substitute descriptions that leave out God except as God figures in the beliefs of the participants – are we not also free to substitute descriptions of other things that suffice for the empirical purpose of identification but leave out implications we don't like? And if this is acceptable for Winch, why is it unacceptable for Pareto, who seems to have done this kind of selective redescription, only in a slightly more extensive way? Why is Winch's redescription the correct one and Pareto's not?

Winch has an answer to the question about Pareto. Pareto has crossed the line of acceptability by describing in a way that loses the logical connection between intention and action. The action description and the intention are linked – they have "internal relations" or, as we might now say, normative inferential relations – to one another and with their actions. This is the basis of the preference for these descriptions, and for the exclusion of other, merely causal descriptions. Here, however, we reach our little historical puzzle. The term "internal relations," which was key to the argument in *The Idea of a Social Science,* is dropped in "Understanding a Primitive Society." The term is largely equivalent to what is currently meant when it is said that logical relations or relations between concepts are normative. Internal relations are logical relations between concepts, or concepts and actions, which are intrinsically normative: they specify the standards of correctness and are conceptual rather than merely psychological and causal. Had Winch given all this up, and if so, why? Or had he arrived at a better formulation?

Winch's concession: The end of internal relations

The Azande posed a serious problem for Winch. The reason was simple: the Azande failed to reason in the normative way that their

103

own concepts, according to the internal relations that hold between these concepts, required them to reason. They appeared to be a society that as a whole violated the norms of their own thought. The Azande had an elaborate system of thought organized around the practice of using poison oracles to detect witches. But the system and its inferential connections led directly to obvious contradictions that the Azande themselves ignored. Their beliefs about the detection of witchcraft by the poison oracle should have led very quickly to the conclusion that everyone was a witch, because the evidence of the poison oracle, taken to be infallible, together with the dogmatically accepted theory that witchcraft was inherited, would have quickly led to the conclusion that everyone was a witch because everyone would have had someone in their lineage who had been determined by the poison oracle to be a witch. But they not only did not draw this conclusion, they refused to consider the contradiction when it was pointed out to them.

From Winch's own viewpoint, what were his alternatives in the face of this odd case? One of the key motivations for normativism and against dispositional interpretations of rules in Kripke and the subsequent literature, including the Sellarsian writers mentioned earlier (the idea is also key to one of Sellars's own papers, on collective intentionality, to be discussed in the next chapter), is the question of whether group opinion about what is, for example, a correct application of a rule or meaning, is the final arbiter of what is correct. If it is *merely* group approval, the phenomenon of correctness seems to collapse into a natural fact – the approving behavior of members of the group – a behavioral analysis that Quine himself would be comfortable with, and which, as we saw in the last chapter, Kelsen was driven to in the case of customary law in order to avoid appealing to collective intentionality. The normativist wishes to preserve the theoretical possibility that these opinions might be wrong, and to argue that the members of a group, and even all the members of a group, may in fact be wrong about the application or meaning of their own terms, and come to discover their error. The empirical facts about group approval, in short, are insufficient: the surplus value in this case is the normative fact of the correct application of the group's norms. Correct application and meaning are normative because the final arbiter is the norm that would allow them to discover their error. The norm is not itself potentially erroneous, in contrast to group opinion, which is potentially erroneous. But the Azande confound this argument by not only persisting in their error but by acting in ways that quite consistently were in accordance with another pattern.

The case of the Azande is thus a perfect example of the case that is central to the discussion of Kripke on rule-following: the community itself, according to us, is in error about the application of its own rules. But what Kripke says (that Wittgenstein says) about this is not very helpful to normativism:

> ... if the community all agrees on an answer and persists in its view, no one can correct it. There can be no corrector *in* the community, since by hypothesis, all the community agrees. If the corrector were outside the community, on Wittgenstein's view he has no "right" to make any correction. (Kripke 1982, 146n87; emphasis in the original)

The Azande, in any event, agree: when the error is pointed out to them, they refuse to discuss it. But one might doubt that they would persist in this agreement. Kripke asks whether this would be possible within Wittgenstein's framework.

> Does it make any sense to *doubt* whether a response we all agree on is "correct"? Clearly in some cases an individual may doubt whether the community may correct, later, a response it had agreed upon at a given time. But may the individual doubt whether the community may not in fact *always* be wrong, even though it never corrects its error? (Kripke 1982, 146n87; emphasis in the original)

The latter is the Azande case: the question is whether it makes sense to say that the community could be wrong in perpetuity. And this is what the normativist seems to need to say. Kripke points out that

> It *is* hard to formulate such a doubt within Wittgenstein's framework, since it looks like a question, whether, as a matter of "fact", we might always be wrong; and there is no such fact. (Kripke 1982, 146n87; emphasis in the original)

But he adds that

> On the other hand, within Wittgenstein's framework it is still true that, for me, no assertions about community responses for all time need establish the result of an arithmetical problem; that I can legitimately calculate the result for myself, even given this information, is part of our "language game." (Kripke 1982, 146n87)

The fact that calculating the result for oneself is part of our language game means that calculation itself is subject to the same considerations: if the entire community agrees in perpetuity with my method of calculation, there is no additional test of correctness to be had. This is all there is to the normativity of the norm governing, or embodied in, the method of calculation. The possibility that "they" have norms they never follow, and choose not to follow even when it is pointed out to them that they are not following them, is an enormity not envisioned even in Kripke. But this is what the Azande are accused of.

What are our options here? One would be to decide that the Azande are, as a group, irrational. But this won't do. In the first place, it seems merely to echo Pareto, who said that nonlogical thinking abounded in society. But for the normativist, nonlogical thinking is an oxymoron, and if a society was in fact nonrational it would also be nonnormative, because the thing that makes for normativity is the inferential connection between such things as intentions and actions, and between beliefs. Without these, people would be like animals, ruled only by causality. This is Winch's core argument. More important, it severs the exclusive, special, rational link between intention and action, on which the whole argument to the effect that Pareto's description of Baptism as a lustral rite was illegitimate depended.

But what about this special, exclusive – and irreducibly rational, conceptual, and normative – link? One can imagine the following kinds of cases: those where the concepts do match perfectly with the conduct, in which case there is no error, weakness of will, and the like. In these cases, because the link is perfect, there is also no difference between the rational link and a causal interpretation of the action; or those in which the link is imperfect, in which there is error, weakness of will, failure to live up to intentions and beliefs, which is to say individual irrationality, which is the classic model of rule-following, concept-using action. But the Azande fit neither of these. The idea that a people could be systematically irrational as individuals, which is to say that they routinely and almost always do not mean what they say or do what they mean to do, also seems like an impossibility: they would never be able to understand one another, or themselves. This is important, inasmuch as this consideration constitutes a second line of defense for normativism: that without some common fact of rationality, a normative concept, there is no understanding at all. In any event, this is not the problem with the Azande, for they are rational outside of this context. So the problem is systemic, or collective: the Azande's actual practices themselves in relation to witchcraft do not fit their own avowed concepts of witchcraft.

The problem thus takes a different form: why should one of our interpretations of Zande witchcraft concepts be favored over another? Pareto, after all, is himself giving an interpretation of baptism that is sense-making: it claims that there is a rational kernel to the practice of baptism, which consists in the idea of cleansing, which is being erroneously (but intelligibly) generalized. Why is this different in kind

106

from Winch's attempt to find the rational kernel in Zande witchcraft beliefs? The usual answer, which works in the baptism case, is this: the activity is constituted by a set of concepts that are intelligible; following them and acting in accordance with them amounts to a form of life; and understanding them requires us to master the concepts and their application, so that we can determine errors and failures of rationality in terms of the concepts themselves. This doesn't work for the Azande: we seem to have mastered their concepts and their criteria for applying them, but they don't seem to understand that they are making an error by applying these concepts in a way that precludes the recognition that everyone is a witch.

This means that there is a problem with making empirical claims about the rules or concepts of a given group. Interpretation necessarily involves identifying the rational kernel of a practice, of cutting through the errors and failures to act in accordance with one's beliefs and intentions; why is Pareto's approach to doing this, which is specifically concerned with error, ruled out? Winch's original answer had been that the relation between act and belief was an internal one, and that when Christians performed baptisms they intended to perform something other than lustral rites. But here the internal relation deviates from the conduct not just in identifiable cases of error, such as baptizing the wrong child or sprinkling the wrong water, but whenever a clear logical implication of the concepts is invoked.

Winch saw that this meant big trouble for the doctrine of internal relations. But what were his alternatives? He could have preserved the doctrine of internal relations by making it into a regulative ideal or analytic truth. He could have said, "We have just misunderstood their concepts." His response to Evans-Pritchard would have been, "Whatever they mean, they can't mean what you think they mean.". But this would have landed him in a worse situation: there was no alternative understanding of their concepts, and if the method by which Evans-Pritchard got the translations Winch worked with were wrong it raised questions about all translation done with these methods. In any case, the translations were not incorrect in the usual sense. The Azande didn't correct the ethnographer, or fail to understand the questions they were asked. And there were no alternative translations that would have made any sense to us.

Winch's response, however, takes a different tack – though the difference is unannounced. He abandons, or perhaps supplements, the theory of internal relations by appealing to dispositions or habits. The crucial text is this: "it is the European, obsessed with pressing Zande thought where it *would not naturally go* – to a contradiction

– who is guilty of misunderstanding, not the Zande" ([1964] 1974, 93; emphasis added). In the course of giving background to this claim he appeals to the notion of "our intellectual *habits*" (1964]1974, 93; emphasis added). And he is compelled to make a crucial concession, one that amounts to giving up the idea of internal relations as originally understood:

> the forms in which human rationality expresses itself in the culture of a human society cannot be elucidated *simply* in terms of the logical coherence of the rules according to which activities are carried out. ([1964] 1974, 93; emphasis in the original)

This means, first, that understanding requires *understanding more than concepts and their internal relations* or, in present language, the relevant inferential relations. But correcting for the error of pushing other people's concepts, in this case Zande witchcraft concepts, where the Azande themselves would not "naturally" push them, namely, to the point where their contradictory character was visible, is a matter of attending to something natural: the "intellectual habits" which are the presumable determinants of where their thought would "naturally" go. Understanding requires knowledge of the dispositions, the habits, which govern the use of their concepts. But there is more. There is a difference between the connections that hold between concepts in the abstract and the actualities of the inferences that people actually make and actually accept as correct. If this sounds familiar, it should. It is the same problem we encountered in the last chapter with Kelsen and Weber in connection with the discrepancy between the way to correctly interpret of the law – the one that accorded with normative fact – and the way that judges actually interpreted the law.

Here the situation is similar: the anthropologist, in this case Evans-Pritchard, understood the Azande perfectly well. It is on the basis of this understanding that he was able to translate what they said and report on their witchcraft beliefs. In this respect he was like Weber's legal historian entering into the soul of the judges of the past to understand how in fact they interpreted the laws. The problems occur when we talk about this understanding. Weber did so in terms of ideal-types, in much the manner of Lask as discussed in the last chapter – as an imperfect rigidification and idealization of the living stuff of judicial thinking. Evans-Pritchard, at least as he was discussed by Winch and MacIntyre, operated with a different model, the model of normativism, in which a people possess a set of concepts with internal or logical connections with one another. These connections are such that the concepts can be said to form a system, with properties such as externality. We are familiar with the use of these ideas in the context of transcendental arguments, to the effect that there must be such structures in order to have justification and valid law. In the context of interpreting another culture, however, a claim about the witchcraft concepts of the Azande must be treated as having a different status – perhaps as something like a hypothesis, which may or may not accord with the actions they are supposed to constitute and give meaning to, and to in some sense explain.

Thinking of this as a kind of hypothesis helps clarify some issues. Begin with the idea of who has a right to decide whether a concept is used correctly, or what the concept is. Kelsen had the idea that there was a fact of legal normativity that judges should refer to. But this assumes that anyone has access to these facts – or at least anyone with the proper training. Given the structure of continental law, this was a natural assumption: professors of law provided interpretations judges relied on. Precedent played a less formal role, and interpretation was itself not considered a prominent part of jurisprudence. The judge had the job of applying the law in a particular case, but not to define it by establishing a precedent. It made some sense to think that the person possessing the best understanding of the norms – law professors, for example – could instruct others in their meaning. In the anthropological case, things are different. It is part of the hypothesis that there is a system of concepts. The concepts constructed by the anthropologist and imputed to the Azande give content to this hypothesis. But the right to decide what is correct or intelligible does not belong to the anthropologist. Nor, one might also add, does the anthropologist have a right to say what a term means, except in a derivative sense based on what others say it means or what they enact as its meaning through their speech and actions.

This matter of rights has implications for the idea that there is some sort of fact about normativity to which the Azande could be held by others. Telling the Azande that they were misapplying their own concepts would not be a Socratic exercise – reminding them of their own norms and getting them to act in accordance with them – but instead an effort at retraining them into a new sense of what is natural. It would involve the exercise of a kind of authority over their application of their concepts akin to that of the schoolteacher. But the schoolteacher would only be teaching his own habits, making them feel natural with these new habits. And his habits rest on no different authoritative bases than those they replace. They represent, so to speak, his group's opinions about what is correct. This is why the Wittgensteinian idea that the outsider has no right to do this is apposite. This admittedly strange notion of rights will be given some sense in Chapter 6.

What are the implications of Winch's concession? It is a concession that the conceptual, the normative, do not have the last word, even in the context of understanding. But he does not develop these thoughts. Indeed, his use of the terms "habit" and "naturally" is almost furtive. He could, however, have gone on to ask the question "Is that all there is?" Is the rightness and wrongness of the application of rules, or the use of concepts in reasoning, itself a matter of naturalness in the use of the word "correct" and its kin, which is in the end no more than a matter of habit? This question, the question of who has the last word and how it is assured, will be my concern in the rest of this chapter, and it brings us back to the problem of lustral rites with which we began. The crucial point is this: the normativist account depends on the idea of a set of inferences organized into a system. The relations among the contents of the system (e.g., its conceptual content) must be normative rather than natural, and there must be no alternative to this conception of the relevant facts. Unlike the law, these relations are non-optional. But here we see that there is in fact a parallel order made up of dispositions and habits, and that the actual explanatory work of accounting for such things as Zande witchcraft discourse requires us to acknowledge this parallel order, for it is this order that fits the actions of the Azande. In the final chapter I will suggest that the parallel order, properly understood, in fact does all the explanatory work, and that the hypothesis of a normative system of inferences standing behind language and practice is unnecessary.

Description

The reason the hypothesis of a normative system has seemed to be necessary will by now be familiar. For writers in this tradition, such as Winch, social or natural explanations of essentially conceptual or normative subjects are always inadequate to account for the phenomena properly described in their full conceptual significance. Put differently, sociological or naturalistic explanation always works by substituting or changing the subject and constructing an explanatory object that is less than the thing that needs to be explained. These thinkers are also insistent on arguments that depend on the free use of notions of genuineness and essentialness. What is the connection between these two points of insistence? The connection is very close: these arguments depend on taking a particular description

110

and accepting it in what I called above, in connection with Winch, its naive sense, and rejecting any restatement of the problem as "changing the subject".

Winch at least provided grounds for refusing Pareto's descriptions – the ground of the supposed internal relations between the concepts that were part of intentions and actions. The theory of internal relations turned out to be a bad theory, or at least an inadequate one. And this changes things: without the theory the grounds for the preference for these particular kinds of descriptions vanished. Why? Winch's concession poses the key problem: what is the status of internal relations, normative conceptual relations, and the like, in relation to actual cases, such as that of the Azande? Can we assume that our attributions of internal relations are correct if we have the correct description? The answer in the case of the Azande is no: the supposed internal relations are at most something like a hypothesis which may or may not correspond to the way people actually think; the hypothesis is something external to their thought to which their thought can be compared. In this case the hypothesis failed. It is of course possible that it would succeed; then the comparison would end in agreement, so that the actual inferences they draw will correspond to those in the normative model. In this case, one would say that the norms have been completely habitualized, embodied, and so on. This would permit one to simply ignore as irrelevant the fact of embodiment and the dependence of these inferences on the actual causal processes of inferring that occur in the people performing the actions. The norms, in short, would explain without reference to the natural world.

Arguments from considerations of the adequacy of description are as theory-dependent for Winch as they are for Pareto. And in this case, what we see is that the relations are circular. *Because* Winch assumed the existence of genuine, noncausal, internal relations between conceptualized intentions and action, he could claim that the description of behavior as action, because it included the conceptual relation between the particular beliefs of Christians and the action of Holy Baptism, had logical priority over other, naturalistic descriptions such as Pareto's which were inadequate because the performers of the actions did not intend a lustral rite. But the case of the Azande shows that the assertion that the actual reasoning of the subjects accords with the normative model can only be a hypothesis. But this means we are forced to change our descriptions, and decircularize them. The subject matter about which we are hypothesizing when we give our account does not consist of facts that are already described in normative, internal-relations terms, but is rather the raw behavior of the subjects, the Quinean level that normativism wished to escape. Winch's concession amounted to an acknowledgment that one cannot claim to reveal the internal relations in the thought of one's subjects simply by examining concepts. The claims must be tested against the evidence of what they do, and the test may well reveal that they think differently.

If the normative model is only a hypothesis, the playing field is leveled. There is no privileged description that necessitates the truth of the normative model. Description is separated from hypothesis, the circular reasoning of normativism is broken, and the naturalist is entitled to give other hypotheses. The naturalist is not compelled to take pronouncements about what is genuine and what is ersatz seriously. He can ask whether there is anything there at all, and suggest that meaning, concepts, and the like, be construed differently. He may even, as the epigraph from Brentano suggests, abandon the notion of "concepts," while permitting it as a convenience in the way that terms from past physics continue to be used after the theories have been supplanted. Construing meaning differently and treating the normative language of concepts as passé may indeed prove impossible to do: naturalism offers no advance guarantees of success. But in pursuing this goal, naturalism is no more compelled to accept the terms of discussion offered by the antinaturalist than Winch was to accept the Christian theology of baptism, or Pareto was to accept the participants' terms.

Structures of meaning?

What are we to make of the conceptual order that led to the contradiction that the Azande did not acknowledge? Recall that Winch is trying to account for the concepts that make understanding a primitive society possible. He assumes that these are the concepts that are in some sense resident in that society. He also has in mind, though this is not a primary focus of his thought, that there are logical or conceptual – that is, normative – connections not only between the intentions and actions of members of this society but also between the concepts themselves. Accordingly, the concepts of a society form a kind of inferential network or system that is normative. This is also the way in which normativists who believe in local normativities think.

These common structures are imagined in a variety of ways. The early Wittgenstein, in the *Tractatus*, claimed that "the tacit

112

conventions on which the understanding of everyday language depends are enormously complicated" ([1921] 1961, 37, para. 4.002). Referring to language in this way suggests that his concern is with a local rather than a universal structure. McDowell in *Mind and World* criticizes

> this idea: that when we work at making someone else intelligible, we exploit relations we can already discern between the world and something already in view as a system of concepts within which the other person thinks; so that as we come to fathom the content of the initially opaque conceptual capacities that are operative within the system, we are filling in detail in a sideways on picture – here the conceptual system, there the world – that has been available all along, though at first only in outline. (McDowell 1994, 34–35)

The idea of a conceptual system possessed by the people we are trying to understand is the idea behind local normativity. McDowell has a different point to make: he wants to argue that when we understand other people who are initially opaque to us we are really relying on a deeper set of concepts that we already share with them, so that in coming to understand another we are

> coming to share with her a standpoint *within* a system of concepts, a standpoint from which we can join her in directing a shared attention at the world, without needing to break out through a boundary that encloses the system of concepts. (McDowell 1996, 35–36; emphasis in the original)

This is a way of dismissing the problem of other cultures in its "radical incommensurability" form by saying that we all share some sort of common conceptual framework. As we have seen, McDowell gestures to the idea that evolution has produced this framework, while Sellars appeals to the entirely virtual "community" of rational beings.

Robert Brandom is concerned with local normativities. His focus is on linguistic normativity, and he understands language as a structure of normative inferential moves governed by a scheme of scorekeeping about the commitments generated by the moves. Brandom thinks that the inferential structures are local, community-relative, or as he calls them, "social," and that they take the form of a system of practices. The system is a vast structure that can ultimately be made explicit in the form of propositions. Brandom thinks that every part of the whole structure can be made explicit, in principle, and that in doing so we come to recognize our character as discursive beings bound by norms:

Though all the deontic attitudes and practical inferential know-how involved in scorekeeping cannot be made explicit in the forms of claims and principles at once, there is no part of that content-constitutive practice that is in principle immune from such codification – out of reach of the searchlight of explicitation. Having been all along implicitly normative beings, at this stage of expressive development we can become explicit to ourselves *as* normative beings – aware both of the sense in which we are creatures of the norms and of the sense in which they are creatures of ours. Having been all along implicitly discursive beings, at this stage of expressive development we can become explicit to ourselves *as* discursive beings – aware both of the sense in which we are creatures of our concepts (the reasons we produce and consume) and of the sense in which they are creatures of ours. (Brandom 1994, 641–42; emphasis in the original)

This account is one of the reasons that Brandom endorses expressivism, the idea that in articulating this structure we are not offering an explanation, but instead expressing what we already implicitly are: creatures of our concepts. But what is the nature of our relation, as individuals, with this structure? Do we have it internalized? And is it there at all?

Consider first the fact, to paraphrase an old remark by the anthropologist Edmund Leach, that not one in a thousand of the participants in the ceremony of marriage in the Church of England know more than a tiny fragment of the meaning of the rituals they are performing. This raises a question about ownership. These questions were not a concern for Winch, who seemed to assume that everyone in the relevant group has the same concepts. But it is a concern for Brandom, who realizes that, in the case of language, people do have their own linguistic usages, an idiolect, which is not identical to the idiolects of others. To save the notion of a language as a single normative structure that is in some nonliteral sense shared by all of its speakers, Brandom suggests that there is a single unified language, which includes a full set of normative inferential commitments to mean certain things by the use of words, that is only partially grasped by each individual speaker (and thus by most of them). This allows him to salvage the idea of an external normative structure that is univocal, while conceding that it is not, strictly speaking, "shared." But this produces a variant of the same problem that Winch ran into: the things that exist on the level of concepts and their ideal relations to one another are simply different from the way people actually think, infer, speak, and so forth. Brandom thinks he can resolve this problem by making the differences into a matter of an incomplete grasp, and that a full grasp of the underlying structure would show that the apparent differences are merely differences between parts of a coherent whole. But this doesn't help with the Azande: they don't seem to be failing to grasp anything, and the idea that they as a whole fail to grasp their own concepts is, at least, puzzling. The problem here seems to lie with the analysts, with the concept of a shared structure, and the sense in which it can be said to be shared.

The term "intimate connection" is mine, but the problem it points to is an issue both for the anthropologist employing the notion of shared frameworks and the philosopher appealing to the idea of shared concepts that we misuse. It is important to distinguish the misuses Winch originally had in mind, the cases in which there are shared rules with shared criteria for the correct application of the rule, from the cases of misunderstanding one's own concepts but consistently applying them, as the Azande do, and to distinguish these cases from the case of misusing and misapplying the supposed framework of normative reason shared by all rational beings. In the first case, the intimate connection is there: understanding the rule, both for the interpreter and the rule-follower, is a matter of using the same criteria for correctness, and, both for the analyst and for the member of the community, attributing possession of the rule requires understanding the rule as the user does and being able to understand the actions in accordance with the rule as the user does, that is, in terms of mistakes and the like. For convenience, we may refer to this level as the level of intelligibility. The next level involves a less intimate connection. The Azande case is one in which the supposed structure of concepts is different from what people actually do, and allows us to criticize the bad habits of the users of the concepts, who nevertheless seem to apply their concepts in a way which is intelligible.

It is on this level that conventional analytic moral philosophy operates: it purports to deal with "our" concepts and feeds them back to us in ways that correct our actual usages, which include usages that are intelligible, but not as rational or coherent as the fed-back purified and corrected ones. The third level involves a less intimate connection yet: it involves universal standards of normative reason that constrain us, which we recognize, and which enable us to understand others on the basis of our common possession of these standards. For this account, the separation of what is intelligible and what is rational is radical: languages, cultures, theories, bodies of practice, and the like, which are intelligible, share only a common core of normative rationality.

The Azande are intelligible, despite the oddity of the discrepancy between "their" witchcraft concepts and their use of these concepts, and not merely because we can figure out: how to apply their concepts in terms of their habits. Why? Because we can understand them: the theory of witchcraft is just another Good Bad Theory. It serves the purpose of coordination. It is a way of proscribing certain actions. It justifies and explains. And, like other Good Bad Theories, it is, as Paul Veyne says about the Greeks and the Greek myths, "believed in," in a way that scientific theories are not. It is foundational to, or part and parcel of, a body of social practices of blaming, punishment, and evil-finding. In this respect it is no different from our own culturally specific notions of intentional harm, personhood, bad will, rights, and the like. We do not challenge such notions by pushing them in directions that we could by asking to see laboratory evidence for personhood or intentions.

What the Azande acquire in the course of their own learning of their own culture and language *are* the habits of inference and speaking that *we*, for our own theoretical and interpretive purposes, call concepts and conceptual content. What the Azande have is a mass of individual inferential patterns that we can abstract from and attribute to the group. Linguistic usage itself is not especially consistent or uniform. It is constantly changing. The job of the lexicographer is to keep up with these usages and to explain what they mean. But this amounts simply to saying what some sufficiently large or high-status group of individuals take them to mean. This we can think of as the lexicography model. Dictionary writers are in the business of tracking usage and presenting it back systematically. Necessarily this involves simplification, selection based on frequency of appearance of a usage, some judgment about how widely understood the usage is, and so forth. To be sure, there are "natural" constraints on linguistic variation: people speak to be understood, so they speak in ways that allow them to be understood.

Unless claims about the concepts some group possesses are like a hypothesis that can be proved wrong by the actual structure of habitual inferences, which was Weber's idea, what sort of hypothesis is it? Or more pertinently, because it is a hypothesis, a claim which can go wrong, what is it a hypothesis about? Expressivism has no good answer to this – it assumes that there is something to express, and that this thing is normative, but provides no criteria for determining whether the expression is correct. In some sense, I can say what I mean, and I have some sort of authority for doing so. But unless I assume that my expressions of meaning are expressions of a structure, there is no reason to say that this is evidence for a structure, or for the explanatory necessity of such things as "concepts", and no reason to think that my own meaning is an expression of facts contained in a hidden structure. In Chapter 6, I will discuss an alternative to the idea that our capacity to say what the meaning of a term is depends on such a collective structure.

As with Winch, who was compelled to appeal to habits, there is an empirical, nonnormative, and explicitly causal moment for Brandom, as we will see in the next chapter, and it is the same moment that Kripke and Sellars also arrive at: the problem of the meaning of the notion of community, community responses, and the like. These are the places where the normativity is supposed to reside. The account of the Azande I have presented here, it should be clear, does not depend on any such collective notions. Sellars himself argued that "our common sense world picture [is] a very coarse grained explanatory framework" (1974, 457). What I have called the Good Bad Theory of Zande witchcraft is a theory in the heads of individual Azande. They adhere to it because it makes sense of the world to them. It constrains them in the way our own "coarse grained explanatory frameworks" constrain us – not due to any hidden structure of normative facts residing in the society or the collective mind, but because they are what we believe to be true, in whatever sense of "believe" is relevant. What we use to communicate these beliefs to others constrains us as well, but these constraints need not be understood as a matter of a hidden structure of normativities.

The focus of the next chapter will be the distinction between these two ways of approaching the subject: the *collective*, which is that of Winch, Brandom, Sellars, and many others in the normative tradition, and the *social*, with which it is often confused. But the normativist also has an unrelated line of defense. Even if we construe Zande witchcraft beliefs as a Good Bad Theory, it is still a theory. The connections between the elements are still rational. Even the account given here assumes some kind of rationality. Rationality is a normative concept, indeed the normative concept par excellence. So this line of argument is no escape from normativity. Indeed, it opens the door directly to the kind of rationalization promised by rationalistic accounts of ethics. The Azande could be presented with an argument like this: your accounts of witchcraft are really bad theories of ethics, which can be improved by replacing notions like "possesses witch substance" with "lacks virtue" and by making the notions of harm and social good more explicit and rigorous, arriving at the universal moral truths of the present. In the final chapter, I will deal with the problem of the normativity of rationality directly and extensively, in terms of the arguments of Donald Davidson, which are usually thought to justify the idea that universal rationality is presupposed by any successful interpretation of the thinking of other cultures.

Note

1. A history and discussion of the background to this highly consequential exchange is found in Lukes (2000).

— 5 —

COMMUNITIES, COLLECTIVE
INTENTIONS, AND GROUP REACTIONS

*Such notions as "the will of the people," the true will of the people,
ceased to exist for me years ago; they are* fictions.

Max Weber, letter to Robert Michels (1908, cited in Mommsen
[1959] 1984, 395; emphasis in the original)

*The idea that moral and legal qualities are substances leads to the belief
that evil, like illness, is contagious. Hence, the wrong committed by an
individual assumes a collective character because it necessarily spreads
to those who live with the perpetrator or are in close social relationship
to him. That is the reason for the collective liability which is so highly
significant for a primitive legal order. It is self-evident for primitive man
that retribution is exercised on the whole group, although the delict has
been committed by a single member only; and it is entirely justifiable
that children and children's children expiate the sins of their fathers.
For, like illness, sin is a substance, and therefore contagious and herit-
able. Indeed, even the* collectivum, *the group, is considered a substance.
A man belongs to one and the same group if he shares with others the
same group-substance: the blood is preferably regarded as the seat of
this substance. Blood community, blood brotherhood, the entire blood
myth, still effective today, are ideas based upon this primitive tendency
of substantialization – a tendency which is not entirely overcome in the
scientific thinking of civilized man and plays a fateful part in the social
theory of our time, particularly in the doctrine of the state.*

Hans Kelsen (1946, 14–15)

The social-science account of normativity I have been giving here,
which is to say the account that treats normative beliefs as a Good Bad
Theory, is open to the usual criticisms: that real normativity cannot be
merely believed-in normativity; that merely believing something to be
normative cannot make anything normative; that real binding is not
"believed to be" binding; that it is essential to the notion of genuine

119

normativity, and indeed to correctness, that everyone in a community could be wrong, and be corrected, and so on. The issues may be put starkly by considering the apparent conflict between the giving a "sense to the possibility of everyone being consistently wrong about something" (Haugeland 1998, 315), including the idea that everyone in the community could be wrong about the community's own norms, and the account that Hans Kelsen gives of customary law. Customary law, it will be recalled, was simply a matter of behavior and majority or overwhelming majority opinion about that behavior. Being wrong was rejecting that opinion or failing to behave in accordance with it. There is no room in Kelsen's account of customary law for the community being wrong about their own norms and corrected by an individual who gets it right and appeals to community standards, or standards binding on the community, which are genuine and distinct from those which "everyone" accepts, because the standards simply are what "everyone" accepts.[1]

As Kripke pointed out, everyone may be corrected if that is part of the language game for the thing in question – everyone may be wrong about the big bang, for example, for it is part of the language game of cosmology that new data and new theories may correct what we believe. The language game of constitutional law may even permit such things. But eventually with these games, too, we end up with ungroundable rules of the game for which the game does not allow correction. If we understand the normativity of these rules as similar to Kelsen's customary law, we are still left with a problem: mere agreement in attitudes or beliefs, such as the belief that the rule is valid, does not make the rule valid or produce normativity. Kelsen got into this fix by rejecting collective concepts: he rejected, as we have seen, group wills, except as expressed through actual legal procedures like voting, that is to say the production of norms in accordance with norms. This meant that for him that "group will" in the prelegal sense couldn't ground law. Collective intentionality theorists have generally thought otherwise. Group wills supply both a standard and a regress-stopper – a source of normativity that is primal in the sense that it produces norms without reference to norms. Group will is also distinct from and irreducible to individual wills. In theory at least, every individual will can be wrong about, say, the meaning of the nation, and come to be corrected and brought into accord with the unchanging but obscured genuine group will.

Kelsen's view of collective concepts was, as the second epigraph shows, that they rested on an intellectual error akin to the primitive belief in contagion, in which collective legal facts about retribution, the legal act he saw as basic to primitive law generally (and primitive causal thinking and indeed all causal thinking), arose as a consequence of group moral contagion, leading to the idea of collective guilt and then to collective being. The idea of contagion was itself a staple of primitive thought, a rough picture of disease and evil that was partly false and that served, like other Good Bad Theories, as a basis of social coordination. It was not a specifically normative idea, however, but an account of a mechanism relating facts about evil – witch substances and the like. We retrospectively or anthropologically regard this kind of mechanism, on the basis of our present scientific knowledge, as a way of speaking about normative facts like evil or bad will. This is the kind of example, as Kelsen himself understood, that turns back on its users because the error account we give applies to our own Good Bad Theories, exposing such appealing things as the will of the people and theories of the state and democracy as themselves semi-mythical.

The failure of Kelsen's account to generate real normativity provides grounds for reconsidering collective concepts and collectivities as a source of normativity. If we could strip the mythical content from notions like group will, perhaps there is a remaining core that solves the problem of the sources of normativity. Collective intentionality does appear to provide something objective, at least for a community or collectivity: a standard that is factual in some sense and at the same time normative. But his critique of the mythical elements in these theories is also difficult to refute. Concepts of collective will, group intention, objective mind, and the like have a checkered past. The disputes over these concepts have been bound up with the problem of liberalism and liberal individualism. Collective concepts have routinely been deployed (and adhered to in a genuinely fanatical fashion) by the political left and by various rightist antiliberal ideologies, especially Nazism. They are still deployed for political purposes within philosophy (Turner 2004). It is at least ironic that the "defenders of science and reason" should find themselves with these bedfellows. But the modern intellectual sources for the fascination with collective concepts cannot be reduced to the ideological and political. As we will see, the contemporary philosophical concept of collective intentionality derives not from these sources but, surprisingly, from a source in the history of social science.

Starting from we-statements

The central philosophical intuitions behind the present analytic approach to collective intentionality are grammatical. There are

121

collective intentional facts, such as plans or goals (for example, the goal of victory for a team), which seem to require collective intentional subjects, especially when they are the objects of intentions expressed by "will" and "shall."[2] "I will win the Super Bowl" cannot mean what it says: only teams win football games. Thus to say that there are no genuine collective intenders creates a problem. If all the intenders are individual, and if this means the same thing as all intentions are individual, then apparent collective intention statements need to be analyzed into individual intention statements. Formulating the problem in this way makes it into a problem within analytic philosophy, in which we can consult our grammatical intuitions to provide a test for analyses.

As with many normativist arguments, the case for collective intentionality usually involves stating a forced choice between two doctrines, where the claim that we-statements of intention are genuine expressions of a novel and anomalous collective kind of intention is favored. The alternative to it in this instance is an account of collective statements based on the idea that those collective statements (statements about an orchestra, say), ought to be analyzable into an enumerative list of statements of the individual intentions and actions of the members of the group. Typical examples of this kind of reduction fail when the objects of the intentions are themselves collective. "I will play Beethoven's Fifth beautifully" said truly by all the members of an orchestra, for example, allows for a lot of discord. "The orchestra will play it beautifully" does not follow from these individual intentions to play well, nor is it equivalent to a list of the statements of individuals. The same goes for "We, the Dallas Cowboys, intend to win the Super Bowl." In this case the individual analysis is excluded because only teams win Super Bowls. "I will win the Super Bowl" is of doubtful intelligibility, and it becomes no more intelligible if repeated by each member of the team. Yet it would be very strange to claim that winning the Super Bowl could not be the object of any intention, individual, collective, or otherwise. If it cannot be the intention of an individual, it must be the team that has the intention. So it appears we are forced on grammatical grounds to concede that something needs to correspond to the intention to win that is not reducible to a series of ordinary individual intentions.[3]

The problem then becomes one of characterizing these intentions while mitigating the strangeness of an intention without a normal human intender; that is, having a single intention without having a single corresponding mind. The single intention / single mind model would require an actual group mind. Sellars himself started out fascinated by a particular collective account of morality that appealed to a form of the idea of collective consciousness. His father had written a lengthy and adulatory introduction to his mother's translation of a text by Celestin Bouglé, *The Evolution of Values: Studies in Sociology with Special Applications to Teaching* (1926). The young Sellars not only read but extensively underlined this text, and marked out many of its sources for further reading.[4] The text was an application of the ideas of Durkheim to the problem of morality. In a sense, Bouglé's book was a substitute for the text that Durkheim himself had worked on and intended to write at the end of his life, a fragment of which remains as "Introduction à la morale" (1920). Durkheim had developed an elaborate theory of the collective conscience, meaning both a collective consciousness and a collective conscience, as a normative, causal, mental collective fact, external to the individual but at the same time part of his own consciousness or mind, that was the source of moral constraint, and indeed of the moral intuitions that a person in a given society had. Bouglé, like Durkheim's other followers, accepted this account as expressing a core truth about the social nature of morality, but withdrew, as indeed Durkheim himself had, from the more explicit aspects of his earliest appeal to ideas about collective mentation.[5] Central to this vision was the imagery of constraint that was experienced internally or mentally, but experienced as an external force, and which conflicted with one's individual impulses. For Durkheim the mind was divided against itself, between its collective elements and its individual ones.

Durkheim was regarded, and seems also to have regarded himself, as having sociologized Kant: to have shown how the submission to moral law of the Kantian subject was better understood in terms of what I have called local normativity, and that the conditions of moral experience were in fact social – meaning that the constitution of morality was the product of the collective mental processes of particular collectivities (cf. Schmaus 2007). It should be noted that Durkheim was concerned not only to distinguish his own *collective* approach to social explanation from *social* approaches, but also to *reject* social approaches – such as those which appealed to processes of social interaction and mutual learning.[6] Sellars can be understood as having gone farther down the Durkheimian path, accepting the substantive truth of the collective character of morality, but also rejecting the idea of group mind that the idea of collective intention seemed to require.

Sellars's actual argument, however, is conducted as an exercise in analysis. He classified intentional statements into subsets, and made we-intentional statements into a subset of the class of statements of intentions that might truly be made by individuals. This avoided treating them as the expressions of a mysterious collective being. Yet the analysis led to very similar ideas. Sellars distinguished two possible analyses of we-statements of intentions, the paradigm case of which was "we disapprove of women smoking." In one analysis, the noncollective one, the statement is interpreted as referring to the enumerated individual intentions of the members of the "we." For this analysis, a claim like "we disapprove of women smoking" was simply a descriptive generalization about individual commitments of some set of persons defined by the "we." The "we" need only be a list of people. If the reference to others is simply an enumeration of individual attitudes to women smoking, there would be nothing added by the concept of "collective" because there would be nothing explanatory that was added by the "we" to a list of "Joe disapproves . . ., Bill disapproves . . ., Sally disapproves . . ." sentences. But Sellars thinks he has a decisive counterexample to this analysis: claims like "we disapprove of women smoking, but I don't" ([1956] 1963, 198). This statement would be a contradiction under the first analysis: the speaker "I" is part of the "we," the "we" is a universal state- ment or generalization about individuals which includes the "I," so both cannot be true. An enumeration of individual intentions would contradict a "Bill disapproves" statement because the enumerative statement "people in this group disapprove of women smoking" is a generalization about the attitudes of individuals. Sellars gives an analysis in which the contradiction disappears because the two state- ments of disapproval are different in kind: "we disapprove of women smoking" signifies group disapproval, a collective fact that is univer- sal and binding for the "we" in question; "I do not" expresses an individual attitude, which is not binding on and makes no reference to others. There is no contradiction because the two clauses are about different kinds of facts.

If a statement about collective intentions is not a generalization of the "Sam disapproves . . .," "Sam believes in its legality . . ." kind, how does it relate to empirical reality? The problem exists for any form of the claim that there is collective agency without collective agents. Begin with the obvious: if there is no real collective agent, there is also no real collective speaker who can express these inten- tions in the authoritative way that an individual might be thought to be able to express their own intentions. To use the language of Kripke, no one has the right to speak as a collective agent except the collective agent. If the statements were simply enumerative, matters would be different: it would be an empirical claim: "Joe this" or "Sally that." Sellars solves this problem as part of his general account of collective intention, but it is a problem that recurs when the particular solutions to this problem break down. The usual solution is to insist that there are individual speakers who can express collective intentions, or whose statements can be assessed as expressions of collective intentions. This is Sellars's approach: individuals are entitled to express we-intentions because they are their own individual intentions, but happen to have the *form* of "we" statements. Merely possessing the form, however, cannot be enough. Normally, claims about group intentions, according to Sellars, are related to some ordinary facts about *other* people: "the fewer the people in the group who believe p or intend X do A, the less defensible becomes the statement that the group believes that p or intends that X do A" ([1956] 1963, 203). But "less defensible" is an odd construction: it implies that ordinary facts about people point to collective facts, but not directly – rather, one is tempted to say, in the way that facts indirectly support theoretical constructions.

Reference to other people is important here. Sellars is not a simple expressivist, who thinks that individuals can authoritatively "express" collective normative commitments without consideration of any empirical facts about other people. For him, *neither* introspection with respect to one's own intentions nor sociological inquiry about the (enumerated) intentions of other individuals, nor the two together, suffice to warrant claims about group or shared intentions. So what would? In general the problem is this: an individual intention, even one in a collective or "we" form, needs to have some additional property, call it S, that makes it actually collective or shared. Searle tries to avoid this problem by making S into a "mode" of intention, and denying that it matters whether anyone else actually shares it (1990, 408). But to use a collective intention in an explanatory way – for example, to explain a norm that is binding on members of a community – something needs to be shared in fact. So the problem is how to ground claims that intentions in the we-mode are in fact shared. Even if we take intentional statements to be themselves epistemically unproblematic, we are still left with the problem of the property S, which is a factual claim about others, accessible neither by introspection nor enumeration, which seems to need its own special grounding. What would that grounding be? What sort of facts might there be about S?

One answer to this is that there is no deep problem about S. If we can know something about the intentions of others, we can know

125

about such things as their likenesses to ours, their complementarity, and their mutual consistency. This seems unexceptionable. But empathy cannot tell us about anything other than the individual intentions of others: it yields at most an enumeration. And this is not enough: even an enumeration of intention statements in the "we" form does not seem to be enough for an actual collective intention. Kelsen's discussion of customary law shows where the problem is. If all we had were a list of claims like "Jill prefers that people would not steal" we would be in the situation described by Kelsen. Kelsen was not naive: his thought seems to be that if I believe that people should not steal, I also believe that I should not steal. So this wish is a kind of self-binding. But if it is self-binding it is not collectively binding. And an enumerative list of self-binding acts that express wishes about what others would do is not the same as a binding collective fact. So Kelsen is forced to make the problematic claim that, in the case of customary law, the wishes of individuals about the behavior of others, if they are widely assented to, add up to something binding on all of them. A mysterious transition must occur between individual wishes for others – for example, that they not steal – and something binding on them.

Sellars does not address this transition problem. His key article begins with the sentence "My purpose in this paper is to explore the logic of 'ought' with a view to determining the relation between it and other key terms of practical discourse" ([1956] 1963, 159). In other words, Sellars begins by privileging a description that is itself problematic. And the same considerations that have governed our earlier discussions of this situation apply here. One can ontologize such terms provisionally and attempt to provide a theory that grounds them, as Sellars does. But this does nothing to establish the claim that the concepts do some necessary explanatory work – that there would be some sort of damage to the web of belief if these concepts were omitted from our ontology. Perhaps, as in the case of legality, it is impossible to avoid circularity in explaining them. But this would just mean that in order to explain, one needs to place the facts under a different description. It does not mean that whatever odd explanation the facts under these descriptions require needs to be taken seriously as an explanatory necessity, and taken to warrant claims for a novel domain of facts.

This privileging of descriptions plays a major role in his argument. He assumes that statements like "we disapprove of women smoking" are ought statements that express something that is universally binding when shared by others. So he focuses on questions about how one can be assured of the correctness of these statements. The thinking is very Durkheimian, and not Kelsenian. It assumes that the oughts are experienced by people in the group as oughts, and that the problem is to assure ourselves that we as members of the group correctly grasp this shared experience of oughtness needed for S. Sellars responds to skepticism about our ability to make justified claims about S with arguments like this: if we can know something about the intentions of others, we can also know such things as whether universal intentions, such as those expressed by an ought, are shared (Sellars [1956] 1963, 204).[7] In short, if we can know another's intention, we can also know whether it is a universal intention, and if we know the intentions of many, we can know they are shared, and therefore collective, intentions.

Sellars acknowledges that an individual may be deceived about whether there are shared universal intentions in a given case. Even a member of the group "can be deceived about the group's intention" ([1956] 1963, 205). But to make sense of error in a way consistent with this analysis, Sellars must devise a novel way of talking about the difference between a correct articulation of these intentions and a bad one, and of justifying the claim that an individual member of the collective can speak for the collective in expressing the collective intention. So he characterizes error in articulating a collective intention in terms of a new concept: the "genuineness" of the statement. "Genuineness" takes up much of the epistemic role of "sincerity" in relation to individual intentions. Sellars gives a few hints about genuineness, which he links to awareness of group membership, as when he says, "one who does not intend in the *we* mode, i.e., has no 'sense of belonging to the group' cannot have more than a 'truncated' understanding of ought" ([1956] 1963, 205). So there can be truncated or incomplete understandings of ought that are not genuine, and they are not genuine because the individual intender has no sense of belonging to a group. But this does not get us very far, because the same issues arise with the distinctions on which the reasoning rests: is the sense of belonging to a group an individual feeling, or a feeling about a collective fact about which one could be in error? Isn't the notion of belonging just another metaphorical way of talking about something that we don't fully understand, namely, co-intentionality?

Sellars says that a "person who shares none of the intentions of the group would scarcely be said to be one of us" ([1956] 1963, 203). This seems to imply that sharing intentions is a feature of groups and a logical condition of an "us," which makes these notions circular. He makes the important point that "the actual existence of shared universal intentions is [not] a condition of participating in moral discourse" ([1956] 1963, 205). Getting to the point of agreement is a task; intersubjectivity of intention, S, or real co-intending, is not a given, but an achievement. But agreement doesn't seem to get us any closer to collective facts. Agreement of a rough kind on certain beliefs, which is still individual assent to these beliefs, is not the same as a collective fact. Something more is needed. The historian of philosophy and student of primitive thought Lucien Levy-Bruhl used the Platonic term "participate" in the same context, with the suggestion that this kind of mystical participation was a distinctive feature of primitive mentality. Is that what is needed here? This formulation at least makes it clear what a genuinely collective fact would look like: a univocal ought which different people have truncated understandings of, who interact within a mode like participation, as distinct from people having multiple, distinguishable, but more or less similar beliefs about what they are obliged to do. But this raises a question about the empirical significance of this distinction. Are there facts that distinguish the two cases?

This is a question Sellars does not address, because he thinks the analysis of "we disapprove of women smoking but I do not" rules out the only available alternative. But it should be evident that there is a problem here. The difference between Kelsen's failed analysis of customary law and Sellars's analysis is negligible. Sellars is compelled to concede that not everyone in the "we" will share the universal group ought, so, like Kelsen, he must make do with something like overwhelming majorities sharing the sense of the ought. Kelsen's individual's wishes that people not steal are wishes about others. They just don't bind them. But these individuals can certainly say both that "we disapprove of women smoking" in the sense that the majority does, and say that they do not, without contradiction. So there is an alternative noncollective analysis of this statement. The argument needs something better to rule out alternative explanations. One way out of the question of whether there is an alternative noncollective explanation is this: to say that such explanations are misguided because they reflect an external point of view, when the facts are only visible from within the normative world in question. This argument serves to immunize and circularize the explanation in such a way as to avoid the possibility of an alternative explanation, by making collective intentions into normative facts. The immunized sense of normative facts is this: such facts are normative in the sense of belonging to the category of normative as distinct from the category of explanatory and causal. This describes a closed world in which only norms justify norms. This was what Kelsen had in mind at various times when he wished to construct a pure theory of law, meaning purely normative and noncausal. In the pure theory, normative facts came into view only in relation to other normative facts. Brandom has something similar in mind when he reinterprets "Kant's original suggestion that freedom consists in constraint by norms" so that "the difference between being free and not being free becomes a social rather than an objective difference." His characterizing the difference as "social." means that it is a difference in terms of the normative distinctions of a community that is itself defined by being governed by these norms (1979, 192). Brandom's idea is that the normative is not, so to speak, conditioned on and encased in a set of nonnormative facts, but is normative all the way down. If we treat collective intentions as a transcendental condition that is part of the meaning of "obligation," when we invoke an obligation we are also, necessarily, invoking a claim about collective intention. Collective intentions thus construed would not be an external, objective fact, but a generic feature of all local normative worlds, analogous to a *Grundnorm*, whose specific local contents, the specific norm-generating collective intentions, would be visible only within the framework of norms of the community itself, as a condition of their normative character, just as the *Grundnorm* is only visible by way of the fact of legal validity. In both cases the fact of obligation as a collective reality is assumed: there can be, by definition, no alternative explanation that is not normative.

Sellars seems to want to avoid this kind of logical closure when he calls the capacity for participation a novel form of consciousness – a very Durkheimian way of thinking. This answer also provides a way of solving the transition problem by locating it in a different process, a process of change of consciousness into a different mode. The difference is important: Kelsen's problem was to find a way for wishes to become binding on others and not just self-binding. Getting wishes to bind others will not work. But participating in a binding form of consciousness, if there is such a thing, will. Searle has a similar idea: that we have a special biological capacity for going into the collective intentional mode. Sellars's theory about the capacity for arriving at S, in contrast, is a kind of social theory, not very far removed from what he read in Bouglé. For Sellars, the precondition for the form of consciousness S is the internalization of a concept of a group. A concept of the group is "internalized" as a concept of "us." This internalization produces a change in consciousness which is, or permits, or in Sellars's mysterious term "becomes," a form of intending ([1956] 1963, 203): this change in consciousness is the transition moment for

Sellars. It is deeply mysterious. But Sellars wants to treat these as ordinary factual claims: "internalization" is a term for a causal process, a social science term.

Internalization metaphorically describes a process of responding in a way that shows that the subject has acquired attitudes that are more or less consonant with the group. Nothing about the process of internalization as it is ordinarily studied – for example, by testing people's attitudes in response to a questionnaire – warrants claims about shared intentions or novel forms of consciousness. But the term, problematic as it is, does point to the existence of a general process of regularizing responses through social interaction. The question is whether there is any empirical difference between "collective" and "social" or "interactionist" accounts of these processes: those that involve something like *participation* in a collective fact and those that involve mere intersubjective *agreement* on a Good Bad Theory. Durkheim thought, as Sellars did, that a new psychic unity (though in Sellars's case not a new psychic being) was created through them, and that this was a normal fact, observable (indirectly) by outsiders, not a "social" one in Brandom's sense, visible only through the norms of the community. So Sellars's claim is closer to empirical science, less immunized, and thus open to rival hypotheses.

What sorts of things are collective intentions, and what is the evidence?

If we think of the subject matter of co-intending – the collective normative intentions themselves – as analogous to a theoretical construction for which our only evidence is indirect, we place them squarely in the stream of ordinary explanation. But it seems that there is an obvious alternative explanation for every supposed collective normative intention: an explanation in terms of specific enumerable beliefs about the world of the individual members of the group – the belief, for example, that the government is legal, that it is real, and so on. These beliefs do not produce a new thing called normativity. Genuinely shared normative intentions, however, do: they create a new kind of binding that is not individual but collective. But if the evidence of what people say and do is indifferent between the two explanations, why did Sellars suppose that there are such things as collective intentions in the first place? If there can be no decisive evidence for this hypothesis over its simpler rivals, why accept it?

As we have seen, instead of going down the path of thinking of these shared things on the model of theoretical constructs, and asking what other explanations might be given of the facts that are accessible, Sellars tries to find a collective analogue to sincere expressions of non-collective intentions, and arrives at the notion of genuineness. Here he does begin to sound like an expressivist. He defines genuineness in terms of the logical relations between certain claims, as follows: "the truth of 'Group G intends that people do A in C' is a necessary condition of the 'genuineness' of 'People ought to do A in C' said by a member of the group" ([1956] 1963, 204). He concedes that

> "genuineness" is a more complicated matter than the candor or absence of self-deception of an individual. One can know that *he* intends that people do A in C, and yet be deceived about the group's intention. The group has shared intentions by virtue of the fact that its members intend [in the relevant] mode . . . But the fact that its members intend in this mode does not guarantee that in point of fact there are shared intentions. ([1956] 1963, 205)

Does this advance the discussion from where it was when we were enumerating individual intentions? What is the factual difference between intending in a mode and believing? "In point of fact" implies that there is some sort of fact (what I have labeled S) about group intention to be deceived about, and thus genuineness cannot be guaranteed by anything in the intention itself. It has to involve the intentions of others as well. So how does one "guarantee in point of fact that there are shared intentions"?

Sellars could have said something about empathy, or sympathetic imagination, as Durkheim's sociological rivals did, but he does not. He relies on an indirect way. As we have seen, like those who appeal to the notion of community and genuine community membership as a source of epistemic authority about rules, Sellars appeals to "a sense of belonging to a group" as a condition for having more "more than a 'truncated' understanding of ought" ([1956] 1963, 205). But what is "a sense of belonging to a group" and what is it based on? Is it based on anything but empathy? Can it too be mistaken? What epistemic claims can it be said to warrant? If there is no fact of the matter about group intentions other than what is disclosed by (possibly mistaken) expressions of these norms, which Sellars calls "tellings," we are worse off with the notion of wrongness and genuineness than we are in the case of individual intentions. In the individual case, at least, what people *do* is related, though perhaps in complex ways, to the truth of their expressions of intention. Their actions indicate whether they mean what they say. And we have elaborate conceptual resources, including the folk theory of mind and a complex language for dealing with such things as weakness of will that allows us to deploy this evidence, even if in the end it is insufficient to remove all conflicts among plausible ascriptions of intention. We also have some sort of empathic capacity, and however problematic this capacity may be, it is assumed by Sellars and seems to be assumed by "community membership" thinkers as well.

Matters differ in a significant way with respect to S, and indeed with collective intentionality generally. These are not banal objects of individual empathy, or even of the kind of empathy one might feel for people whom one might identify with and feel solidarity with. The fact that legal theory relies on fictional constructions of collective will is revealing. If the real collective will was so easily accessible, one would need no such fictions, and perhaps no explicit norms. Judges would simply apply the collective will directly. It may be noted that the philosophical tradition itself contains a developed conception of the same material which treats it as something akin to fictions. Philosophers as diverse as G. H. Mead and Slavoj Žižek, who have talked about such things as the "generalized other" or the Lacanian "big other," have treated them as psychological constructions of individuals that are causally produced in interaction, but not the sorts of things that could be taken as mundane veridical facts. The fact that one can describe the actions of others in a way that makes them co-intentional does not exclude the possibility that one can describe them in a way that doesn't make them co-intentional yet allows for the same result. This is precisely the possibility that the sociological (causal) concept of legitimacy exemplifies. Instead of explaining legality, as we have seen, one can explain something under a different description, a "legitimate order," factually indistinguishable from a "legal order." What is missing from the description "legitimate" is the (possibly nonfactual) notion of legality.

The problem restated

Sellars set the problem up by assuming (a) that the enumeration analysis and the collective intentionality analysis were the relevant alternatives for accounting for these statements; (b) that the ontological model of collective intenders, however problematic it was as a scientific theory (or as ontology), might nevertheless provide the right analysis of a large class of collective statements; (c) that the problem was soluble, or properly understood, as a problem of linguistic

132

analysis; and (d) that the problem of collective intentionality had to do with the problem of "ought" and that oughts were the result of collective intentions. I have argued with respect to (a) that the fundamental problem is explanatory necessity, and that the burden of proof for the collective intentionality argument is to show that there is some fact of the matter that cannot be accounted for or understood in terms of an explanation that does not appeal to S. I claimed that the gap between the relevant evidence about what people say and do and the "fact" is large. I suggested that the supposed explanatory problem is an artifact of description, and that we have alternative descriptions that do not require collective intention explanations.

The problem of collective intentionality can be reformulated (and updated and generalized) as resulting from three conflicting groups of considerations, each of which has some strong associated intuitions. One is an intuition of analytic philosophy – that commonplace expressions need to make sense in terms of a relatively simple analysis, and that the ubiquity of an expression is grounds for thinking that it shouldn't be explained in terms of non-ubiquitous facts. We-locutions are, as Margaret Gilbert insists, pervasive (1996, 19). This seems to indicate that they cannot be simply erroneous, and more generally that they cannot be understood to be based on some sort of theory or ideology or cultural tradition that is itself local. It also seems to imply that the usages cannot be merely analogical extensions of normal use. Each of these approaches to we-statements would make analysis too complicated. The second intuition is that the theory of real social wholes, group minds and the like, is false, or worse, metaphysical rubbish, and consequently the explanation of the ubiquitous we-usages cannot be found there. The third intuition is epistemic: that if there is a property S, it has to be accessible in an ordinary way, through human interpretation. We come, through experience of what people say and do, to be comfortable with them, able to explain their actions purposively and predict them reasonably well. But nothing in *this* experience provides grounds for claims about collective intentions in the relevant sense – that we have internalized something that entitles us to "tell" collective intentions, in the sense that it grounds the claims that an S relation obtains between the intentions of others.

The solution proposed by Sellars and the rest of the collective intentionality school is to resolve these conflicting intuitions by making we-statements anomalous, to accept the anomaly, and to demystify it. Is there an alternative that deals with the we-statements themselves? Begin with a famous example. When Joe Namath was asked

133

whether the New York Jets would be victorious over the Baltimore Colts in Super Bowl II, he replied, "I guarantee it." The promise was shocking, but neither unintelligible nor uninterpretable. Like almost all promises, whether they involve individual or collective outcomes, Namath's guarantee was implicitly conditional on various contingencies – that the world would not end, that the game would be played, and, more generally, that the usual sorts of conditions that promise-makers are held to be accountable for would hold. His guarantee can be understood as follows – "if my teammates do what I reasonably believe they will do, I promise that I will do well enough for my team to win". At no point in making this promise would Namath have needed to go beyond the individual, non-S, evidence about his fellow players (that is, to say that this special kind of intention was shared with the individual members of the team, and that he was "telling" this in a genuine way warranted by his sense of belonging to the group), or make any intentional claim about the collective object "the team." Namath was not making a claim about the relations between the intentions of the players, nor claiming to be a spokesperson with special authority to speak for the collective intentions of the team. There need have been nothing collective about the *intentions* at all. He could have been as behaviorist as Quine about his teammates and opponents, and merely made a commitment with respect to his own performance, or even less – his guarantee would have been sufficiently grounded by any evidence that warranted a prediction that the Jets would win. His promise did not need to be an anomalous promise, in an anomalous collective mode. The sports fans of the day took it, in any case, as his promise, a personal promise, as indeed it was.

One may notice some pervasive ambiguities about claims like Namath's. Surface grammar is often misleading. What appears to be a shall statement (Namath could have said "we shall win" and indeed is often quoted as having said just that) may be something less – a prediction, to which the speaker's only commitment is epistemic. The same statement could have been intelligibly made by a bookie, or a commentator. If it had been, it would have been clear that the commitment to it was epistemic, and the response to a question like "How can you guarantee it?" would be to cite the grounds of the belief. The fulfillment of the prediction may as a matter of causal fact require that various people have particular intentions, though it may not. It could be that the statement is an entirely nonintentional prediction about an object individuated as a team. Or it could be a statement about an object individuated as a team and endowed by the prediction-maker with quasi-intentional properties, such as response to feedback that ascribed, analogically, "intentions": such sports phrases as "the Cowboys always find a way to win" come to mind. One may ask whether there would have been any difference if Namath had said "we guarantee it." It *would* be different if the "we" was enumerative – if every member of the team also guaranteed it. The grounds for that claim would be that each member had in fact done so: a banal empirical claim.

These sentences are related causally in such a way that there is a striking phenomenon of interchangeability between them. Such sentences as "the team shall win," "I guarantee it," "we shall win," and "we intend to win," spoken by a team owner or representative, all amount to more or the less the same thing, in the sense that none of them is likely to be true without the others also being true. This puts such statements as "we intend to win" in a somewhat different light: the burden is to show that they are not interchangeable for causal reasons. There needs to be a causally relevant fact that makes them non-interchangeable. If there is no such fact, there is no special mystery about what we mean by "we." If collective intentional statements could be justified by showing that S *is* causally relevant, this burden could be met. But this returns us to the epistemic form of the problem. If we are unable to find a way to warrant factual claims about S in the first place, we are going to be unable to show that it is causally relevant.

Representation: Who has a right to "tell"?

The Namath example involves a collective aim, and not a collective intention. A large class of we-statements, however, *is* intended to express collective intentions. These statements pose their own problems. Sellars constructed, as we have seen, an elaborate way around the problem that only a collective agent should be able to express a collective intention or speak for a collective. The "tellings" model involves access to some primitive set of facts. To make the parallel between collective and individual intention-telling succeed, it is necessary to claim that genuine expressions in the we-mode are direct expressions of commitments. So part of the burden of this analysis is to make S similarly primitive, which is to say, independent of theories of various kinds. In Chapter 6 I will discuss various cases in which it does make sense to talk in something akin to this way: claims about the meaning of what I am saying and the terms I use, for example. In these cases, there does seem to be some sort of authority that is not based on ordinary empirical inquiry that gives us a right to make statements of this sort. The analysis given in that chapter, which will be based on empathy, might also be applied to other claims of representation of a community, such as the representation of the emotions or responses of the community. But a different group of cases involving assertions about representation works in a different way.

In the beginning of this chapter, I mentioned the problem of who speaks for the collective agent as a motivation for Sellars's choice of the notion of "telling." "Telling," in Sellars's hands, involves a complex account of the way in which a sense of group membership is a source of authority to speak genuinely about the norms. The nature of these appeals needs some attention. The argument from the ubiquity of these claims implies that they must be in some sense true, and deserving of a proper analysis – a general account for a general linguistic phenomenon – rather than an explanatory social theoretical account that treats them as local ideological formations, or as part of the content of the beliefs of agents rather than of some sort of general, analyzable logical relationship. But the role of Good Bad Theories in these cases indicates that these issues can never be simply grammatical. Two things need to be said about these nongrammatical issues. One involves what might be called the ideational, the other the subideational. By "ideational" I mean this: collective claims are not based, as Sellars and others (notably Searle) often imply, on a "group sense" in some sort of raw, preconceptual mode, but on a fully developed set of ideas about the group – a theory, if you wish, about the existence of nations, races, and so on. These ideas are Good Bad Theories. The fact that these groups and the sense of group consciousness that is connected with them are ideational, that the group consciousness needs to be taught (and that the teaching precedes the sense or makes an inchoate sense articulate as an ideological construction), that there are endless variations on the theories that justify even such a notion as nationhood, suggests rather strongly that these groups are objects by virtue of the beliefs that surround them. Such beliefs are social constructions, in a banal sense. Analyzing the claims made about them, in the light of theories about them, ought to proceed not in terms of some sort of alternative theory invented by an analyst, but in terms of the beliefs themselves. Beliefs about the special properties of the persons speaking are not merely ornamental – they are the justification for the "we" and the use of the collective voice, without which the usages are unintelligible. Similarly, the idea that someone can speak for "society," indeed the idea of "society," is an idea with a history, and not some sort of natural feature of social life. We are more used to the idea of someone in authority speaking for the thing they have authority over, but these sorts of "speaking for" relations have an ideational – and typically theological – background as well – in such ideas as the "head" of the family speaking for the family, for instance.

If we-language is pervasive, in short, it is because the various ideas that warrant it are commonplaces: that there is a huge variety of Good Bad Theories that serve purposes of social coordination, of making sense of social experience, justifying authority, justifying claims to speak for others, and so forth. But this does not mean that they are anything but extended metaphors, or that they warrant a general analysis. Nor does it make sense to treat them as true. The idea of group is not a natural one, but is rather constructed, ideological, and often mythical; group concepts are perfect instances of Good Bad Theories. The concepts of representation that go along with them are Good Bad Theories as well. This is not to say that these theories are not Good Bad Theories *about something*. But the problem of representation, and the justificatory need for backing by theories of representation, doubles back on and puts a different light on Sellars's analysis of the basis of we-statements in feelings of groupness. Sellars is not so much providing an analysis of the sources of normativity as producing yet another theory of representation, which is to say an account that purports to authorize someone speaking for others, for collective entities, and so forth. It presupposes relevant content: it appeals to ideas about collectivity (hidden in the notion of group sense, in his case) that are historical, questionable, and perhaps mythological, rather than merely to intrinsic nonlocal features of language. The same goes, as we will see, for an important argument of Brandom's.

The intentional bias

The non-ideational or sub-ideational – the level signified in its vestigial form by the term "sense" in Sellars's "group sense" – is nevertheless relevant to an understanding of the ubiquity of collective language. Let us begin with some cognitive science banalities. Human beings have very powerful capacities for emulation, mirroring, and therefore empathy. Our most important interactions involve these capacities. We are probably disposed, at some very basic, prelinguistic, cognitive level, to the following: to think of the world as made up of agents, which is to say anthropomorphically; to seek agents behind results that could have been intended by agents, and to objectify the agents,

137

imagine them, and identify them with something in the world. This is a disposition that experience validates much of the time. Many of the entities with which we deal are causal systems endowed with feedback. By the same token, many of the facts and objects with which we deal could have been produced intentionally (or produced by an entity with feedback). "Could have been produced intentionally" is a category that is very capacious, if one allows for the intentions of God and considers that people do not start out with a strong *a priori* sense of the difference between something caused by intenders and something merely caused. When we tell a child who has hurt herself by running into a chair that the chair is "bad" and punish it on her behalf, we enact a little ritual that depends on these banalities. A hurt is a "could have been intended" fact; a chair could be a causal system endowed with feedback. Only a more advanced knowledge of the world than that of the young child would allow us to comfortably say which is which. If a chair can be so readily personified, or intentionalized, it is hardly surprising that collective objects are, or that we have many elaborate entrenched agent-centered metaphors for talking about the putative causes of "possibly intended" outcomes.

This is one way in which we might arrive at a sense that there is collective agency, and therefore real collective intenders. Kelsen, in the second epigraph for this chapter, proposed a different one. And there are others. I observed my own children learning collective concepts, and it was notable that they first employed terms such as "team" observationally rather than functionally, as in "we are on the same team, we are wearing the same color socks." This is suggestive, as is the fact that collective identities so often rest on external identifiers such as emblems. Personifying the notion of team is a natural next step. Collectivities are often personified or analogized to the body, as the group "Christian" is understood as the body of Christ, or a nation as the "body politic" or as a mother. Perhaps this is simply because we choose to understand and communicate about abstractions in terms of personification or bodies because it is easy – we are all embodied and are persons.

These considerations allow us to deal with a number of standard examples in the literature. David Velleman gives the case of the dean who asks the department what it intends to do about a vacancy (1977, 29). This is a query in the same class as a query about what the church is going to do about something – an entrenched metaphor with a meaning that is sufficiently fixed by virtue of the fact that we have a theory of representation, of what it would be to speak for the department or the church, that we have an idea of who can give an answer to it and therefore what it means. This gives us an alternative answer to the problem of ubiquity. We are cognitively disposed to see the church, or the nation, or society as something that has a purpose, and has a reality because it has a purpose.[8] But we should not succumb to this disposition to the extent of ontologizing collective purposes. Ontologically, we can place these statements on a par with those of an adult who personifies a chair that they stumbled into as a "bad chair."

Nevertheless, people do make serious claims about collective purposes. What is the status of these claims? One approach is to validate them by drawing a parallel between them and mental concepts, and suggest that there is a "folk sociology" that parallels folk psychology. If a case can be made for intentions as part and parcel of an indispensable folk theory, it is reasoned, the same case can be made for collective intentions. This parallel, however, is defective. Although it does appear that something like intentional language is more or less universal (Needham 1972),[9] there is no universal folk sociology. Indeed, social concepts vary so radically – from totemism, to such historically specific ideas as the nation, to a bewildering array of ideas of kinship – that what is more impressively consistent are the sources of social metaphors, such as the body and kinship. There is every reason to say that these claims are false or metaphorical (i.e., literally false but with some true implications), and that they have precisely the same cognitive status as claims about God's will, speaking for God, and so forth. It is only a prejudice of analysis that pervasive usages of this sort cannot be dismissed as false, and that their pervasiveness means that they require a grammatical analysis. In short, there are good cognitive-science reasons to expect "us" to personify society. Knowing them, however, gives us reasons for doubting that the usage points to something explanatory, especially when it appears in such a problematic form as a statement about a collective intention that is pervasively interchangeable with many other claims that lack the problematic implications of the concept.

Explaining obligation: Analytic theory, social theory, or circular definition?

The issue of theory-infection is relevant in other cases involving collective claims. Consider Gilbert's summary of her analytic argument: social groups are plural subjects; plural subjects are constituted by joint commitments, which immediately generate obligations (1996,

139

368). In what sense is this an "analytic" argument? Terms like "constitute" and "generate" are systematically ambiguous between "produce" and "define," so it is an important question. If it is a matter of term definition, the argument is analytic only in the sense that it is circular: obligations are obligations if and only if they result from joint commitments. Presumably this is not what is meant. If we take "constitute" and "generate" as causal terms, or something akin to causal terms, this formulation is a rudimentary social theory: a story about how joint commitments simultaneously produce both obligations and social groups.

Whether it is plausible as a social theory is only intermittently addressed in this body of thought, but it is never far away. "Obligations," after all, *are* the subject of explanatory attempts, even theories, in the social sciences, and these attempts compete with the "joint commitments" explanation, though it is not always clear how, since they are typically directed at other well-known aspects of what is usually understood as morality and normativity that the collective intentionality account ignores. As I discussed in Chapter 2, the classical social theory accounts of the origins of morality were concerned with "primitive" morality. In primitive societies, people believed in the existence of impersonal forces that would punish those who violated norms, such as *tabus*. As we have already noted, even in much more developed societies, such as the communities described in Marcel Mauss's *The Gift* ([1925]1967), the obligation to reciprocate was was based on impersonal forces produced by the act of giving a gift, which obliged the recipient to give something back. An explicit feature of these systems of morality was the insistence on their impersonality, which is to say that they are not understood by their adherents as a matter of "commitment," collective or otherwise. Promising, similarly, is historically and ethnographically connected with oath-taking, for example, in relation to fetishes or in legal practice, itself a paradigm case of invoking impersonal mechanical forces of punishment that will operate as a result of a failure to fulfill the terms of the oath. More generally, folk accounts of morality are bound up closely with distinctive beliefs, often about God or magic. These are the subject of epistemic commitment to beliefs about impersonal forces, rather than the normative commitment to a common intention that is central to this account of morality.

Suppose that we take the "joint commitments" theory as an empirically meaningful account of morality, rather than as a closed and circular scheme of definitions making the account analytically true (as would be the case if we tried to save the argument by claiming that concepts of *tabu* are not really "moral"). It would be possible to claim that the impersonality of moral forces that is such an impressive feature of these moral systems is simply an error on the part of the participants, and that what they are conceiving as impersonal forces are merely the reified, misrecognized products of their own joint commitments. Durkheim famously does something analogous to this when he suggests that the worship of God in primitive society is a misdirected form of the worship of society. But Durkheim had a more general account of the nature of the collective mind that would sustain the idea that individuals with their cognitive limitations would fail to grasp the reality of the collective consciousness and misrepresent it to themselves. In the hands of the thinker who has to say, "well of course moral systems are the result of joint commitments, after all, since even the potlatch system would only work if people were jointly (normatively rather than merely epistemically) committed to it," matters are different. This now seems to be a claim impervious to evidence, true only by virtue of the meaning of the terms, and thus nonexplanatory. At best it is a definition of morality, and a tendentious one at that.

Community reaction

As we have seen, Sellars uses social science language such as internalization, and thus situates collective intentionality within ordinary social processes. His "expressivism," meaning his account of tellings of collective intentions, is a factual kind of telling, empirically correctable, and about something tangible. Some of his uses of the notion of collective commitment, however, involve virtual or hypothetical communities. The normal properties of a community in a natural sense are captured by such definitions as the conventional social science notion that a community is dominated by relations of face-to-face interaction. This distinguishes a community from a society, which is dominated by impersonal relations, for example, the relations of customers in markets or citizens in a state. When Sellars describes Kant, as Willem DeVries puts it, in terms of the belief that "membership in the moral 'we' included all and only rational beings" (2005, 266), this "moral community" is a virtual one. Sellars asks how this community could be taken to be a real one, and points to two conditions: that "to think of oneself as a rational being is (implicitly) to think of oneself as subject to epistemic oughts binding on rational beings generally," and "the intersubjective intention to promote *epistemic* welfare implies

141

the intersubjective intention to promote welfare *sans phrase*" (1967, VII, §144: 225, quoted in De Vries 2005, 266). Sellars himself concludes that although the first of these conditions is not implausible, the second, "despite Pierce's valiant efforts, remains problematic, and without it, the argument for the reality of an *ethical* community consisting of all rational beings, the major premise of which is 'the fact of reason' remains incomplete" (1967, VII, §145: 226; quoted in DeVries 266–67).

I argued earlier that this discussion of community turns the social science notion of community on its head. A community is defined by its adherence to certain norms, rather than the following of the norms being an empirically observed property of the life of a naturally defined group, such as a *Gemeinschaft* defined by the fact of face-to-face interaction. This assures that there are shared norms – they are there by definition. But intersubjective relations, a "naturalistic" fact, remain part of the definition, however, and this is revealing. One reason such riders need to be present is to connect the definition-based notion of community, community as defined by conformity to the norm, to any actual community. This is a variation on the problem faced by Kelsen in dealing with revolutionary legality. It doesn't help much to have a definition of legal authority that designates some set of people as the representatives of the legal state if they have no authority in fact. "Legality" would be an exclusively theoretical notion, and it would be unclear what the point of the theory would be – one would have as many people running around as legal representatives of states operating on different theories of legality as pretenders to the thrones of Europe, with as little chance of having the claims accepted. Kelsen admits that international law completely ignores such claims – that the raw sociological fact of effective governance makes revolutionary regimes "legal" under international law. More generally, there must be a connection of some kind between the normative account and the substantive thing it is an account of.

The connection between the normative community and the actual community is made in different ways in different accounts of normativity, and with the same kinds of ambiguities between the normative and the factual accounts. Saul Kripke refers to community and appeals to the notion that membership is decided by mastery of the rules – a circular, start-with-the-norms notion of community rather than a sociological one. But his intention is not to provide an image of an ideal or virtual normative community. It is rather to follow Wittgenstein in describing actual behavior. The Kantian forms of this connection, however, are different. It was one of the points of the

Kantian account of the limits of reason to exclude as irrational – as not part of the community of beings bound by the norms of reason (or failing to live up to them) – various religious doctrines of which he disapproved. This intention led to the incident in which the Prussian authorities (correctly, according to Ian Hunter's 2005 analysis of this case) disciplined Kant for the practice of theological disputation under the guise of philosophy. John Rawls, similarly, has a doctrine of political discussion in the public sphere as rational, but this is not an account of what actually happens: Rawls excludes anti-abortion political expression, which is a part of real, accepted political discourse in actual liberal democracies, as irrational and thus unfit for discussion in the public sphere. Kantians like Jürgen Habermas regard all actual present public-sphere reasoning as less than fully rational. The ideal speech community provides the normative standard for public-sphere reasoning.

The sociological conception of community and community norms is this: norms are recognized by the sanctions that are provided against norm-violators. This "response" notion corresponds to ideas concerning error recognition. Error is understood, to the extent it is discussed at all, in terms of the reactions to erroneous acts – which might range from incomprehension to various kinds of sanctions, depending on the Good Bad Theory that the members of the community are operating under. It may also be perceived, simply and pragmatically, in the failure to get the expected results from one's utterances. Durkheim went so far as to suggest that deviance was necessary for there to be norms in the first place. The social science tradition makes a full range of distinctions between types of norms, between norms and usage, between tacit and explicit, and so forth. To the extent that there is a fact of the matter about normative error, it is going to be describable in terms of these distinctions. The crucial issue is this: someone needs to learn the norms, and they must do so as the social scientist does, by observing them as they are actually used, seeing what is understood, what the reactions are, and then understanding them.

The more interesting question is whether the normative conception can be characterized apart from these considerations. Robert Brandom, like Wittgenstein and Kripke, wants to preserve a close relation between the notion of normativity and actual practice:

That it is actual human social practices which determine the correctness as a linguistic performance of an utterance on some particular occasion is clear from the fact that the communities in question could just as well use some other noise on the relevant occasions. (1979, 188)

143

Correctness itself bottoms out in community response:

> To specify a social practice is just to specify what counts as the community responding to some candidate act or utterance as a correct performance of that practice. The criteria of identity for social practices appeal to the judgment of the community (where "judgment" here is not to be taken as entailing that the response is an explicit verbal evaluation). What the community says or does, goes, as far as the correctness of performances of their own practices are concerned. (1979, 188)

The issue for Brandom is what "response" amounts to: is it an objective fact, in the sense of "objective apart from community practices," or is it something that is "normative" in a special sense? His answer is this:

> The objective expression of a social practice is then a matter simply of being able to predict when that response will be elicited from the community, a difficult but not mysterious enterprise. But what if the response which for us identifies some social practice is not an objective response, but rather some performance which must be in accord with *another* social practice? (1979, 189)

He notes that if this second practice relies on criteria or justifications, there is "no obstacle to even longer chains, just so they terminate eventually in a practice generated by an objectively characterizable response" (1979, 189). The point of all this is that practices are normatively connected with one another, not causally, so that practices are normative.

What counts as correct is determined by the community, in the form of community response. This sounds like the sociologists' "sanctions" and reactions, and in some sense it is – the "responses" *are* objectively characterizable. The responses, however, do not exhaust the meaning of the practices, which consist in the inferential connections between them, which are not causal, and are therefore, according to the logic of the normativist argument, normative. It would be absurd, Brandom suggests, to try to characterize these facts in terms of predictions, because "the objective description of a social practice for a community for which such chains were the rule rather than the exception (e.g., linguistic practices) would require prediction of everything anyone in the community would ever do" (1979, 189). Does this argument work? The distinction between causal and normative used here is a staple of normativism. In this case there is less to it than meets the eye. Brandom in effect acknowledges that there is a parallel causal process to the things he characterizes in terms of inferential practices. He thinks that knowledge of this domain cannot be understood as causal knowledge because it would require something that is simply unattainable: prediction of everything anyone in the community would ever do. Brandom does not explain why partial predictions of what people would do are ruled out; and he reserves for himself the possibility that individuals operate with partial apprehensions of linguistic practices. But for the learner of the language, matters are different. Predicting people's responses is part of the initial learning process, and must be. Moreover, it is expanded on, and eventually becomes the subject of elaborate folk Good Bad Theories.

The problem with Brandom's version of this account can be seen most directly in the notion of community response. This is the place where Brandom chooses to connect to the actual: community response is the thing that is identical in the normative and the objective, although for him the responses can only be understood properly under their "social" or normative description, which preserves the chain relations of justification and inferential connection underwritten by practices. But what is the "community" here? And what sort of fact is the crucial fact of being "one of *us*" (1979, 193) that it consists in? Are these normative facts? Is there a normative fact of community to which the notion of "us" refers? And what is a community response anyway? Is it normative or causal, or both? We can begin with the last question. In order for people to pass from the prenormative to the normative, to become one of "us," to be initiated into a culture, as John McDowell says, or to go through a process of internalization of norms through correction, they must first deal with responses in a prenormative sense. They cannot do otherwise: they lack anything normative to give them a normative perspective. This also means that the act of responding as experienced by the socialized, initiated, normative person is different from what is experienced by the prenormative person – so that if it is both, it is not both for the prenormative person.

All of this becomes less puzzling when we try to get an understanding of "community" and the sense in which of these are community responses. In the first place, in the experience of the learner, the community does nothing as a community. Responses – sanctions, expressions and acts indicating incomprehension, punishments, and the like – are administered by individuals. Moreover, it is the rough kind of mistake-filled actual experience of the normal social world. It does not come branded or divided into mistakes and correct applications of rules, though of course it includes all the natural indications or concomitants of error: the sanctions, natural signs of incomprehension, and the like. So the sense in which communities respond is already at a remove from the actual. The uninitiated, not-yet-one-of-us, prenormative person learning the ropes has to make something of the mix of events they experience. Of course, these are not empirical claims – all of this simply follows from the way in which the normative-causal distinction works.

Notions like "community" and "us" are not primary facts, at least for the uninitiated. The social science idea of who is and is not a member of the community, or what makes someone a member, depends on what sort of community-like concept, what Good Bad Theory or Theories about who is an "us" are extant in the setting, and on the facts that correspond to these. The sociological study of community in the United States, for example, derived from a fascination with the conflicts between the residents of small towns and the open country that surrounded them, which was a conflict central to the self-conceptions of people who were economically dependent on one another, who shared certain institutions and not others, and who were connected to different individuals. They drew maps that showed such things as the location of the homes of members of churches, subscribers to local newspapers, ownership of power washing machines, and the like to show what kinds of facts the ideological constructions of "town" and "country" were working with. "Community" for them was not some sort of unproblematic natural fact, but a Good Bad Theory about something tangible. The fact that philosophical normativism relies on notions like membership in a community, "*us*," initiation into a culture, and the like is at least odd. These notions are being used as analogies, of course. But they are taken directly from the folk Good Bad Theories, and the analogy is to such rites of passage as baptism, becoming a bar mitzvah (one to whom the commandments apply), or getting a driver's license. Applied to linguistic normativity or rationality they are just fictions, appropriate perhaps to the task of fashioning a normative lens, but at variance with explaining what people actually do.

It should perhaps be added that real and false ideas about groups cannot be disentangled from one another. There is a kind of analogue to the Baldwin effect, in which what is learned eventually becomes instinct, which operates in relation to any collective. On the one hand, it is defined by beliefs that are literally false and often absurd, which its members act on: that the persons in a tribe descended from people who emerged from the earth at some particular hill at some specific moment in history, that they descend from people who had a covenant with God, or that they are bound together by legal facts,

146

such as the signing of sports contracts, which themselves depend on all manner of fictions. On the other hand, there can be something like a group sense, an identity that affects how people behave, who is selected for the group, who is excluded. This sense can drive people's ideas about how their group memberships affect how they behave and relate to others whether or not any of these ideas are true. And the empirical facts of who they encounter, who they empathize with, and who they have a mirroring relation with, among many other things, are affected by these beliefs. So by noting that the appeal to group sense and community reactions is a false abstraction of a complex of real social facts of interaction I do not mean to imply that these ideas, as they are held by the agents whose actions are being explained, are without effect. But I do mean to say that by using them as a naturalistic regress stopper in a normativist argument the normativist appeals to something that is not real in the sense it needs to be for the normativist argument to work – namely, as a hard fact outside the circle of normative reasoning.

What is the underlying factual material that is being constructed through the analogy with initiations into a community with membership boundaries, rituals of taking into the community, commitment, and so forth? Begin with the key issue of error, or the misuse of what Brandom thinks of as an inferential practice, which Brandom thinks cannot be accounted for causally. Even the person wedded to these analogies must admit that practices are learned, and that learning has to be, by the normative hypothesis itself, done on the basis of the "objective" data of community response. Brandom himself acknowledges the reality and irreducibly nonnormative character of facts of reaction. The responses and reactions are in the normal world of explanation, and even for Brandom they are definitive of the facts about error. The idea of "community" is an idealization. Learning is a causal process – even for the learning of false beliefs. Normative inferential relations, as they are actually operative in the social world, are redescriptions of, or idealizations of, causal processes. At no point is a special new "normative" fact inserted into the relevant processes. The same facts are redescribed in normative terms. These terms have no special privilege. They do not correspond to an essence. There is a nonnormativist alternative description at every step.

The history of the social sciences is a history of emancipation from the intellectual propensity to intentionalize social phenomenon – this was very much part of the process that Weber called the disenchantment of the world. If we wish to understand prices in a market economy, for example, we look for a visible hand, and finding none, imagine an invisible hand which we can then explain in terms of the individual decisions of buyers and sellers – which produce the result that an invisible hand would have produced without anyone – collective or not – having had an intention to produce those prices. But speaking this way is ironic. There is no invisible hand. One of the great tropes of nineteenth-century statistics was the image of a powerful ruler who mandated the exact number of suicides every year, as though by law. But here the point, of course, was that there could have been no such ruler – but the result, namely a predictable number of suicides, nevertheless occurred as a result of individual decisions, with no collective agency and no command. From the point of view of this massive body of intellectual development, the idea of collective agency is an archaism and reversion.

The idea of separating the normative element from the natural facts of social life has been an important motive in ethics at least since Rawls. It was prefigured in Kelsen's idea of a pure theory of the law, and it continues in such projects as Gilbert's. This project, however, makes sense only from the side of the normative. The normative-natural distinction used in this way is a normative distinction, depending on the definition of norms, or the normative theory, that supplies the normative elements that are supposed to be separated out and used to reconstruct the phenomenon free from naturalistic or causal considerations. It is not an explanatory distinction found in nature or social reality. It is visible only to those constructing a normative lens.

Notes

1. This is a stark, but nevertheless problematic, formulation, for reasons that will be explored briefly in the next chapter. It should perhaps be noted here that Kripke's own formulation of the problem allows for the group to be challenged in this way only when the relevant language game permits it, and it is not clear that customary law is such a language game. Constitutional interpretation, however, might be understood to permit the opinion of the overwhelming majority about such things as the meaning of a constitutional provision.
2. A simple, standard statement of the problem is found in Velleman 1997, 29–30.
3. One may quibble with many of the examples here: part of an individual's "playing beautifully" *is* playing nondiscordantly, and that is a causal rather than a grammatical fact. So the meaning of this result is not clear, a point to which I will return below in connection with the problem of collective states and collective goods. But it is clear that having the orchestra itself reach the

state of nondiscordant playing is not the appropriate direct object of a single individual intention, at least in the same sense that the bassoon player's own playing is the appropriate object of her intentions.

4   The copy of this volume in Sellars's papers contains extensive underlining and markings. ("The Evolution of Values." Wilfrid S. Sellars Papers, 1899–1990, asp199101, book #779 in the list of annotated books, Archives for Scientific Philosophy, University of Pittsburgh.)

5.   A discussion of Durkheim's model of mind can be found in my *The Search for a Methodology of Social Science*, 1986.

6.   The contrast between the social and the collective approaches is deeply rooted in the history of the relevant disciplines. The first uses of the term "social psychology" are by Durkheim's rival and enemy Gabriel Tarde (Kalampalikis et al 2006, 28) and Charles Ellwood, a student of Dewey and Mead who received a degree in sociology. Ellwood's dissertation on social psychology was published as soon as it was written as a series of three articles in Albion Small's *American Journal of Sociology* in 1899. The dissertation contrasted "mental phenomena dependent on a community of individuals" to "action and reaction of individuals in a group on one another" (1899a, 656), and argued that the latter was fundamental. The text contains the first use by Ellwood of an "inter" term, in this case, "interindividual" (1899a, 256). He was shortly to use "interaction of individual minds" (1899c, 100n1) and "inter-cerebral" in a paper on Tarde (1901, 741). This phrasing marked what was the crucial distinction between interactionism and Durkheimian collective psychology, though Durkheim is not mentioned. The dissertation was reviewed in the *Anneé Sociologique* (Nandan 1980, 65–66), where it was dismissed for using the term "social psychology" rather than "collective psychology."

7.   Metaphors abound in this area. Raimo Tuomela treats this individual aspect of the collective intention as a "slice" of a collective intention (Tuomela 2005). Gilbert speaks of the individual intention as part of a pool of wills dedicated, as one, to a goal (Gilbert 1990, 7). What the metaphors underline is the thought that the collective intention is a fact on its own, which the individual intention partakes of, rather than an agglomeration in which the individual intention retains its identity.

8.   The argument from ubiquity of course cuts both ways. The fact that discussions of the relation I have called S requires elaborate metaphors about the pooling of wills and slicing of intentions indicates that these are not ubiquitous. So the contrast between the collective intentionality analysis and this one is not between one resting on ubiquitous usages and another resting on metaphors, but between one resting on unusual metaphors expressing epistemically dubious facts and one involving ubiquitous metaphors rooted in a commonplace cognitive situation.

9.   But see Fingarette for the interesting argument that intention is absent from Confucian Chinese (1972, 37–56). Fingarette also gives a depiction of Confucian morality that is consistent with the comments made here about morality, where he characterizes the Confucian view of community as a holy rite (1972, 1).

RATIONALITY OR INTELLIGIBILITY

The last three chapters have led to similar results. Normativist arguments either end up becoming circular, typically because they involve
preferred descriptions of facts that can only be accounted for by odd
theoretical devices which we "have to live with," or end up in a regress
that stops in a fiction, such as the fictional notion of community and
membership found in Sellars and Kripke, a fiction that can only be
sustained by immunizing it from rival naturalistic explanations. It is
often argued that these circles are not vicious, but merely innocuous
and inevitable, because they come to the correct result: there is no
way out of the circle only because reason sustains reason, as it should.
But the fact that there are multiple competing circular arguments in
almost every domain in which normativist claims are made belies this
absolution. But this is not the last word. The normativist has a vigor-
ous, and superficially convincing, response to these considerations. It
would go something like this:

*All of the business about the fictional character of initiation, commu-
nity, and the like can be conceded. The important points nevertheless
remain. Throughout this treatment of normativism, the discussion of
the "social science" approach has violated the basic rules of the game
of argument. The use of notions like "belief" is a signal and example
of this violation. The term cannot be used meaningfully apart from the
terms that connect to it (and connect in a normative, justificatory, way).
With such terms, along with intention, meaning, concept, and so forth,
one is in for a penny, in for a pound. There is no taking this and that –
helping oneself – from the package of related concepts. The main thing
that the concept of belief requires is the most transparently normative
philosophical concept of all: rationality. One cannot attribute beliefs
on the basis of utterances, or even treat the utterances as meaningful,*

without assuming rationality on the part of the speaker. And this means assuming intentionality, concept-possession, "concepts" in the normative sense, and all the rest of it.

The discussion of the social science approach, in any event, cheats. It is not really a discussion of social science as a purely causal scientific discipline, which would supply a real alternative. It relies freely on notions like understanding, on getting into the soul of a judge, and so forth. Understanding is a normative concept. The concept of belief is normative. Bracketing these concepts and treating them as Good Bad Theories (as a way of accounting for the human and cultural variation in the language used to express these ideas) is misleading. The core phenomenon of comprehension and understanding cannot be eliminated, so there is no point in bracketing or ironizing the usages in question. The metaphorical language of "community," "us," "initiation," can be ridiculed, but the thing the metaphors are used to explicate, the fact of mutual comprehension and understanding, is real, and it is normative. If the social science approach faced up to this dilemma it would become clear that a regularities approach to rules is required by a metaphysics that admits causes and excludes genuine normativity, and that this approach produces descriptions of human conduct, linguistic action, and thought that are radically at variance with the things we want explained. If the social science approach accepted that understanding, comprehension, rationality, and the like were necessary parts of social science knowledge, it would be accepting that it is a normative enterprise, as Winch argued a half-century ago.

Because of this dependence on understanding, the social science alternative is not genuinely independent of normativism, and thus not really an alternative at all. It is completely parasitic on the very normative language it pretends to replace. True, it is possible to disenchant this or that odd belief – the divinity of the Emperor or the Grundnorm conception of legality – and it is possible to show that notions like "community" are idealizations of empirical facts. But wholesale disenchantment is not possible. There is always something, such as the normative logical relations of modal logic, that is indispensable even for the most resolute disenchanter. And even such things as causal relations, the supposed alternatives to normative relations, cannot be understood without reference to the indispensable normative, conceptual element in causal reasoning, as the failure of disenchanters over the centuries (such as Hume, Comte, Pearson, and Russell) have shown.

The example of logic shows the bankruptcy of the social science approach in the face of these issues. The social science approach depends on redescribing the facts in a nonnormative way. The normativist assumes that if a normative description is possible, it is necessary to accept it, and that failing to accept it means failing to account for some surplus value. The social science approach insists that the surplus

151

is explanatorily superfluous. But the normativist assumption is correct. In the case of logic, no external, causal reinterpretation can possibly capture the relations in question. The only description that can capture the relations is the normative one, and this applies to rational considerations generally. Nor can logic be understood as a matter of belief in a fiction or as a false folk doctrine. The buck stops here, with the only possible correct descriptions of these facts, and the only possible correct descriptions of the facts of logic are normative. The project as a whole, in any case, cannot succeed, for reasons that have been familiar since Aristotle pointed out that to refute logic one needed logic. Rationality is a normative concept. To rationally persuade anyone of anything requires an acceptance of the normative demands of rationality and of the normativity of rationality.

Error accounts, such as those that the social science approach purports to supply, cannot work in the way that would allow them to supply a genuine alternative account. There are many reasons for this, from the obvious that "false" is itself a normative concept, to some more subtle but powerful considerations established by Donald Davidson. Davidson showed that massive error is unintelligible. What this means when we are discussing such interconnected "in for a penny, in for a pound" ways of talking as the intentional action framework for talking about human conduct, is that they cannot be "false." There may be odd accretions to this set of concepts, such as the religious idea that angels and devils prompt our behavior in secret ways, but the big connected notions of intention, action, belief, and desire could not be replaced. At most they could be slightly revised. Consequently they cannot be treated as Good Bad Theories. The fact that odd primitive groups appear to have variant concepts or lack some of these concepts is of no significance – they have to have something like the functional equivalents of these concepts or they would be unintelligible to us. The "in for a penny, in for a pound" character of these concepts also takes the teeth from the charge of circularity. There is no place outside the circle of these closely linked concepts to go to find an explication, so some circularity, or at least the appearance of circularity, is inevitable. What is important is recognizing the inescapability of these concepts, and accepting it. Once this is understood, we can also see that the alternative error explanations the social science approach supplies are not really scientific, but are just an application of the prejudices of materialist metaphysics. As to transcendental arguments, the mere fact that there are many attempted philosophical analyses, and that they conflict, means nothing: if the core things are right, and they are enthymematic, that is to say that there are suppressed premises needed to complete the inferences they depend on, there has to be something that is right that fills in the enthymematic gaps. This is what the normativist account seeks to supply, and to supply in a way that avoids falling into the trap

*of claiming massive error, which any alternative account of our ordi-
nary reasoning would have to do. "Fundamentalism" is just a product
of the recognition that there is no alternative to the acceptance of most
of our beliefs as true.*

This, I take it, is the response that needs to be countered by a defense
of the social science critique of, and alternative to, normativism. The
key issues involve the related ideas of rationality and understanding,
the senses in which they can be said to be normative, and the senses
in which the social science account can be said to rely on normativity.
In this final chapter, I will discuss the question of whether understanding is normative, and the sense of rationality that is relevant to
the problem of understanding, which I will call the "intelligibility"
notion of rationality, as distinct from the more straightforwardly
normative problem of judging reasons as good or bad, which involves
making distinctions among intelligible claims, theories, and doctrines.
This difference is central to the Kantian conception of reason, and to
what I have called "fundamentalism."

The distinction is the analogue to the double sense of normativity we have encountered repeatedly in this book: for example, the
distinction between the sociological sense of legal validity and the
genuinely normative one. The normativist who appeals to the indispensability of normative rationality as the last word and strongest
defense of normativism argues that the buck stops with descriptions
of rational action that involve the genuinely normative, judgment-
supporting sense of rationality. To put it more plainly, the normativist denies that there is a distinction between "sociological" rationality
and rationality *sans phrase*. If there were, the same kinds of problems
would arise as arise in the case of law: one would be the explanatory
sense, and the other would be an account of rationality, potentially
one account among others, outside the stream of explanation and
with a questionable connection to the world it explains. It is to this
distinction that I now turn.

What is Davidson's argument about: Intelligibility or rationality?

Much of the reasoning I have outlined here as the normativist's
response, and especially the crucial closing part relating to what is
intelligible, depends on a particular reading of, and endorsement
of, certain key texts of Davidson's. These texts, as it turns out,

153

are closely related to the core issues discussed in Chapter 4. "The Very Idea of a Conceptual Scheme" ([1973–74] 1984) introduced his attack on the scheme-content distinction. Its treatment of error pointed directly toward Davidson's most controversial claims, in "A Nice Derangement of Epitaphs" (1986), about the nonexistence of "language" as the term is usually understood. Davidson himself thought the implications of his argument were radical, and specifically thought that the argument showed that it was also unintelligible to say "that all mankind – all speakers of language at least – share a common scheme and ontology" ([1973–74] 1984, 198).

The thesis Davidson rejects sounds exactly like the thesis I have put into the mouth of the normativist above. And this is an oddity that is worth exploring. How did this paper become assimilated to the conventional wisdom to which it was opposed? One can reconstruct this process as involving two main steps. The first was to read Davidson as showing that translatability was transitive. If the relation of translatability were not transitive, it would imply the possibility of incommensurable schemes, and if it were transitive, it would imply that our standards are the only standards,[1] which in turn implied that there was after all a universal scheme. Full transitivity requires that a translation from Language L to Language P would include the translations that can be made into L from Language N. If it could not, this would amount to admitting that incommensurable schemes are in fact possible. This interpretation was based on a particular limited understanding of Davidson's objections to the scheme–content distinction, which was interpreted in relation to independence. Davidson had shown only that there could be no understanding of schemes and content independent of one another. Accordingly, one interpretation was that he was proposing a novel "interdependence" model of the relation between the two, rather than getting rid of the distinction entirely (Hurley 1992, 99–101). Another interpretation de-radicalized it in a different direction, by suggesting that his disagreement was with "the metaphors that sustain the picture of an independent scheme and worldly content" (Thorton 2004, 58) rather than the distinction itself.

This reinterpretation was followed by a second step, of interpreting Davidson's explicit denial that there was "a neutral ground, or a common coordinate system" between schemes (Davidson [1973–74] 1984, 198; cf. Hacking 1982, 61) to mean something like the opposite of what it seems to say. Rather than taking it literally as a denial of a common *scheme*, it was taken to rule out an independent realm of *content*. It was then interpreted in terms of the Kantian idea that,

154

as John McDowell put it, the world "cannot be constituted independently of the space of concepts, the space in which subjectivity has its being" (McDowell 1998, 309). This interpretation, though clearly contrary to the main claim of the text (that there could be neither a single scheme nor incommensurable ones), was made plausible through the (interpreted) claim that massive error about widely held beliefs is impossible. If skepticism about significant ordinary beliefs is necessarily incoherent, this fact can in turn be taken to imply that various commonplace metaphysical views about ordinary beliefs are warranted.

The possible intransitivity of translation would be a refutation of the idea that there were no such things as incommensurable conceptual schemes, and an affirmation of the necessity for one common scheme, because the transitivity of explanation would require that we had, so to speak, all the resources for translating all languages in advance. Only this "condition for the possibility of translation" would exclude a case of a Language A such that the speakers of B could translate from A into B, but could not translate A into C. The exclusion of this possibility would mean that in some sense whatever resources are needed to translate A into C have to already be there in C. In the usual forms of this argument, this amounts to saying that "we" must have whatever resources are necessary to translate out of any conceptual scheme.

Error reconsidered

Davidson has a different and much more limited argument: if the speakers of C happen upon speakers of B translating A, if they could indeed translate B, they would, *ex hypothesis*, be able to translate these translations of A as well – the translations from A to B are after all in B. Why is this different? It has to do with error. For Davidson, a translation is not merely the application of a translation manual consisting of sentence correspondences. It is instead a combination of correspondences and explanations of the failures that occur when something is accounted true in one language and false in another. Davidson's central example is a paradigmatic error explanation:

If you see a ketch sailing by and your companion says "Look at that handsome yawl," you may be faced with a problem of interpretation. One natural possibility is that your friend has mistaken a ketch for a yawl, and has formed a false belief. But if his vision is good and his line of sight favourable it is even more plausible that he does not use the word yawl quite as you do, and has made no mistake about the position of the jigger on the passing yacht. ([1973–74] 1984, 196)

The hypothesis that he uses the word differently, in this particular behavioral context, requires us to attribute a whole set of correct beliefs (and norms of correspondence, as Davidson puts it) to our companion: that he or she sees that the smaller mast is far to the stern, that he or she is talking about the same boat, that he or she is not kidding, or testing our knowledge of nautical nomenclature, and so forth. I will have something more to say about these supposedly enthymematic elements later.

The example clarifies why the possibility of "massive error" is excluded. The reason is simple, and has to do with the way error explanations, such as this one, are themselves constructed. They depend on attributing *correct* beliefs that lead the person in error to the specific error that they make when they make an intelligible but false utterance. The number of correct beliefs we must attribute when we attribute error to the false ones is high. And the more extensive the error, the larger the number of beliefs in the web of belief we must rely on to explain the error. Massive error is unintelligible: making massive error intelligible would require an even more massive pool of correct beliefs to draw on to explain the error. But pretty soon one runs out of correct beliefs to provide the background that would allow the attribution of the error.

Translations are thus like theories. They already involve truth claims about the world; they depend on the correctness of explanations and of the theories backing explanations of error, and they are in this respect heir to all of the problems of theoretical explanation not only in the sciences, but in psychology and for that matter the social sciences, where they play a role in backing the explanations of error that translations inevitably involve. The project of translation is bound up with the rest of understanding, which includes making sense of erroneous beliefs, mis-speakings in which what is intended is not what is said, and the other intelligible errors that make up the content of actual speech and action. This dependence on error explanations and on the understanding of the intentions of speakers mean that translations, which are the core to claims about meanings, are also characterized by the usual infirmities of theories: that they are underdetermined by the facts, so that alternative theories may be consistent with the facts, that new data – for example, new behavioral evidence – may require changes in the theories.

Davidson is explicit about this. The method forced on us by the problem of interpretation is to get a first approximation by attributing to a speaker's sentences the "conditions of truth that actually obtain (in our opinion)" and allowing for meaningful disagreement. And the disagreements can wind up in a variety of ways: if we are in the position of the companion, we might find ourselves learning a lesson about the differences between ketches and yawls, and thus we would resolve the disagreement in favor of the hearer. But we might discover that we have a disagreement that present data cannot resolve. If we cut this reasoning down to the basics, we get something like this: interpretive charity is required by the economy of error explanations. The term "charity" means that we need to attribute rationality – in a sense yet to be defined – to the people we interpret, but we also need to attribute a minimum of error because doing so requires attributing lots of correct beliefs, or beliefs we also accept, as well. Among the things we need to attribute are the enthymematic elements mentioned above, and indeed it is these elements that make up the bulk of the beliefs that are needed to account for error and which cannot intelligibly be denied on a massive scale without depriving error explanations of the material they need for their construction.

The upshot of this for everyday metaphysics can be illustrated by a simple example. Consider the Hindu belief that the world is an illusion. We have no trouble translating the relevant sentences, for the simple reason that the translation manages to preserve all our ordinary beliefs. Everything in an illusion appears just as the real thing would – otherwise it would not be an illusion. My belief that the coffee shop down the street serves espresso survives whether or not the espresso, the street, the shop and the rest of it are illusions, because there is no difference between real and illusory espresso other than whether it is real. If we translate the terms, they refer to the same thing, with the exception that we need to add an illusion operator to each sentence in the translation of the target language. But the addition does nothing beyond connecting the sentences to the belief that the world is an illusion. And what goes for illusion goes for the rest of metaphysics – the noumenal world, empirical reality, the phenomenal world, and the rest of it. There are no interesting implications of the problem of massive error for metaphysics, since in these cases there is no massive error. There is only a very economical kind of error, or, alternatively, a kind of underdetermination, about metaphysical facts. There is a question of whether this holds for the "fact" of normativity itself, and here there is an ambiguity. Taken by itself, it seems that the pattern with normativity mimics the pattern for "the world is an illusion." Nothing much changes whether we say that normativity is a fiction or a false belief along the lines of *hau* or fetishes, or whether we say that it is real. But if normativity in the requisite sense is part of the machinery that allows us to speak in this way in the first place, namely, as a condition of interpretation, matters would be different – it would be indispensable.

It might seem that we ought to get more metaphysical bang out of transitivity, especially from the apparent requirement that we somehow have the resources for all possible translation in advance, in some sense. But this is not the requirement it appears to be. Focusing merely on the problem of constructing a truth theory for a language, and ignoring the role of error, obscures important features of translation, and also obscures the reasons translation does not require us to have all the resources for all possible translations – the resources that would define the conditions for the possibility of translating all languages, in advance. Just as theories in science grow, our theories of error and our powers of translation grow in the course of translating from one language to another. This bears on the problem of transitivity. Davidson need only argue that the augmented power of translation we possess when we adequately translate B from A enables us to translate C from B, not that we can translate C with the resources of A. What his explicit argument excludes is the following case: the speakers of C claiming that they can understand B perfectly, but not A as translated into B. This would mean that they couldn't understand the correspondences and the explanations of error. Davidson's point is that this would be grounds for saying that they did not understand B. But without the learning and error theorizing we did when we translated, translators starting with A might indeed be unable to understand C.

This suggests that truncating the discussion of rationality and translation into a discussion of the fixed (and pre-fixed) "conditions for the possibility" of translation is beside the point. The conditions of translation are of a piece with and depend on our ever-changing knowledge of the world. But saying this raises questions about the nature of rationality for Davidson himself, and about the larger problem of normativity that the normative concept of rationality points to. For Davidson, "the concepts we use to explain and describe thought, speech, and action, are irreducibly normative" (Davidson 1999, 460). What does this mean? Even if we de-Kantianize the problem of conditions for the possibility of translation, it seems, we are forced back into another form of the scheme-content distinction by the assumption of rationality and by the normativity of word-world relations. Or is there another, better, interpretation of these two things?

158

Davidson's actual comments are tantalizing. He does say that interpretive charity is non-optional and also sufficient for translation, and he does refer to norms of correspondence, meaning by this something analogous to the correspondence rules of the layer-cake model of scientific theories. He could have said, but did not, that interpretation requires an assumption of rationality and an assumption of certain common human norms of correspondence (1985, 92), and that these are both non-optional and universal. Instead he says the following:

> The ineluctable normative element in interpretation has, then, two forms. First, there are the norms of pattern: the norms of deduction, induction, reasoning about how to act, and even about how to feel given other attitudes and beliefs. These are the norms of consistency and coherence. Second, there are the norms of correspondence, which are concerned with the truth or correctness of particular beliefs and values. This second kind of norm counsels the interpreter to interpret agents he would understand as having, in important respects, beliefs that are mostly true and needs and values the interpreter shares or can imagine himself sharing if he had the history of the agent and were in comparable circumstances. (1985, 92)

The norms of correspondence are norms of interpretation, but not norms in the sense of rules that help decide between interpretations: they are instead a condition of making intelligible interpretations in the first place, which needs to be applied to make any sense out of the task of interpretation. Davidson characterizes these norms as providing "counsel" to the interpreter: the counsel of interpretive charity. The norms of pattern correspond to the notion of rationality. But they are not quite the same as the notion of rationality. There is a telling phrase: "needs and values that the interpreter shares or could imagine himself sharing if he had the history of the agent and were in comparable circumstances."

What, we might ask, is *imagination* doing here? And there is more of the same kind of thing, as when he observes that translation requires a command of the "multitude of finely discriminated intentions and beliefs" required to interpret speech as a form of human conduct ([1973–74] 1984, 186). This is a startling claim: compare it with the idea that what is required to interpret human speech is access (for example by a translation manual) to the normative rule book governing the scoring system underlying linguistic practice. Davidson is saying something different, and decidedly nonbehaviorist, about the kind of knowledge of other people that is required by translation. What is required, in short, is empathy, empathy employing what we know about beliefs, intentions, and values, what we can

159

imagine about them, and what we could imagine about responding to a history we do not have.

The problem of what sort of rationality (and therefore what kinds of normative resources) is required to interpret others needs to be separated from this question. The problem of rationality has the same double structure we have seen repeated in one context after another in earlier chapters. There is an ideal normative form of rationality, and there is the actual way in which people reason. The ideal forms – logic or decision theory, for example – are part of the body of intelligible reasoning, but they are not the whole of it. Certain patterns of inference that are treated as biases in the psychological literature on decision-making are not only understandable to us: we can follow thoughts of that kind, even if we believe them to be wrong or the pattern of inference to be defective. Aquinas, faced with the objection that certain forms of sin seemed to be ubiquitous, and also therefore to be natural, was forced to appeal to the notion of the "fomes" of sin. Natural rationality is full of fomes. But to understand and explain human action one needs to understand the fomes as well as the ideal forms. It is true, as Davidson notes, that the only access we have to the biases of actual decision-making is through correct decision theory: our experiments start with the normative model and identify deviations. But this is an innocuous use of these models, a use that depends on the intelligibility of the model as an ideal-typification of decision-making, not on its normativity in the strong sense.

Intelligible error

Error is not a behaviorist notion. It is normative, perhaps the root normative notion. So to say that considerations of error are inseparable from translation is to accept the role of the normative. And of course there is more normativity to be found in the conditions for translation or interpretation. Rationality is one of the conditions, and it is a normative notion. So to say that assumptions of rationality are necessary for interpretation seems not only to concede that some scheme-like element is necessary, but to refute Quine's "Two Dogmas" (1951) and concede the Kantian point by resuscitating synthetic *a priori* truth. Or does it? One way of putting this issue is to separate two distinct aspects of normativity: one, the sense of the normative as binding, as external and constraining – the Durkheimian–Sellarsian sense – contrasts to a different sense, which can be labeled "intelligibility." We can call this second kind Weberian–Davidsonian.[2]

Durkheim was concerned with the binding character of obligation as it was experienced differently in different societies. Weber was concerned with subjectively meaningful behavior, and with the problem of making the behavior of other people intelligible, something he, like Davidson, thought necessarily meant "intelligible to us in our own terms." There is a normative issue here – intelligibility is also a normative notion. But it is a different kind of normative notion than correctness or rationality in the binding sense. Understanding a subjectively intended meaning, to use the standard translation of Weber's phrase, is, at least on the surface, a normative matter as distinct from a causal one.

Davidson's problem, like Weber's, involves the problem of intelligibility, not the problem of supposed binding norms. The kind of error that concerns Davidson is not deviation from rules, and there is no constraint here, no disciplining by group reactions, as in Brandom. But there is the following: the problem of making oneself understood to other individuals and of understanding other individuals. There are limits, but they are the limits of intelligibility. To go beyond those limits, to speak unintelligibly, is to fail to be understood, to fail to achieve one's purpose in speaking. The errors at issue occur when the speaker has some sort of aim, but fails to speak in a way that is intelligible. Explicable error is intelligible error – the kind of error that we routinely repair in the course of interpretation, by recognizing what the person was aiming for. Translation incorporating a hypothesis that accounts for the error and makes it intelligible extends the limits of intelligibility – extends them as far as they go. Davidson's impossibility argument is about the limits of intelligibility: there is no language recognizable as such beyond the intelligible. But we do not reach the limits of the intelligible without charitably extending the readily intelligible to incorporate the less readily intelligible: namely, that which is not intelligible without a hypothesis about error. And these hypotheses about error necessarily rely on having already made other parts of the web of belief intelligible. As we have seen, this is the basis for the claim that massive error is not intelligible: it is not intelligible because the hypothesis of massive error amounts to denying to the constructor of explicable error accounts the material needed to construct these accounts. To explain the error of a sailor's failed attempt to keep the main from backing, we need to assume that he knows what the main is, has correctly perceived the wind, knows what the sheets and the tiller are supposed to do, and so on. These involve what Davidson calls norms of correspondence. If we deny these "assumptions" (which are of course not experienced as

161

formal Euclidean acts of assuming definitions and axioms, but are, as a matter of psychology, part of our empathic response to the situation of watching the sailor act), we open up the explanation of his actions to such non-empathic, mind-blind hypotheses as these: he is communicating with Martians; he doesn't experience the wind and sea as we do but in some unknown way. And these begin to hit against the limits of the intelligible, because they are explanations of error that are themselves barely intelligible, or unintelligible to us, at least currently.

The concepts-as-possessions picture is different from this picture. Error, in this picture, is not an intelligible mistake, a reparable failure to use words as the hearer expected them to be used, but a violation of rules that are inherent in some sort of external structure – a failure to accept a constraint. But this is an oddly truncated picture of error, because it leaves out the problem of intention – of the aim of the act or the act of speaking. It assumes that the external constraints are owned in some way by the person committing the error – that they apply to the person speaking or acting. This is the point of Brandom speaking about commitments. Without some such background, without the speaker accepting the rules, the "error" is merely error from the point of view of an observer. Is "$2+2=5$" an error? Not if it is intended as a typing exercise, and the object was to correctly copy the expression. Davidson's approach builds this problem of intention into the problem of interpretation itself. For Davidson, interpretation is a hypothesis-testing epistemic process, in which we employ what we know about ourselves and our beliefs to construct accounts of others' beliefs that make sense of their behavior. Behavioral evidence is all we have, and all we want to explain, though we may employ nonbehavioral terms, such as "belief" itself, in order to do the explaining. Error is intrinsic to the process of hypothesis testing, in the sense that we can get the attribution of belief wrong, in which case we can't predict what others will do or say in a way that accords with the attribution of belief we hypothesize. But there is more to it than just predicting. We also want to make sense of the beliefs as beliefs – to make them intelligible. To put the point in a way that will help later, we want to be able to follow others, to follow their reasoning. But this is inseparable from attributing beliefs in the first place, so it is normally not an issue.

Where do the grasp or possession model of concepts and the problem of rules fit in with this account of error?[3] In terms of interpreting other cultures, these things cannot come first. We cannot first grasp others' concepts and then come to understand their utterances.

Yet the possession model has a strong bias toward this kind of formulation: if we are using a concept, it is because we have grasped the rule behind it. Our grasp is presupposed, and it is a necessary condition for "really" using the concept. This is the point of the celebrated arguments about the regress problem made in the first chapter of Brandom's *Making It Explicit* (1994). Really using language, for Brandom, amounts to being able to give justificatory reasons about its use. The chain of justifications has to end somewhere. Because justification is normative, it has to end in something normative. For Brandom it ends in the normativity of language, which is in turn made normative by our commitments to the score-keeping system that allows for the social regulation of error.

Davidson has none of this machinery. Why? The answer is closely related to the reason he also lacks the Brandom–McDowell imagery of constraint. For Davidson, not only does the problem of intelligibility come first and get solved by the process of translation (which resembles hypothesis testing), it ends there. The claim that the rule-following, concept-possessing model deals with something more fundamental, which is common to many of these interpretations and dismissals of Davidson, depends on showing that they are necessary in the first place. They are not, for Davidson. To deal with the behavioral evidence is not only enough, it is all there is. The whole machinery of the concepts-as-possessions model is not so much beside the point in relation to this evidence (it is after all an attempt to account for it) as it is unnecessary for accounting for it. The accounting is done once the beliefs have been identified. There is no higher form of knowledge about these beliefs that results from "grasping" the concepts or having a normative commitment to them, and the like. The only knowledge we have is this hypothesis testing – like knowledge.

For alien cultures, the normativist is inclined to say, this makes sense. We cannot penetrate their inner life, their normative commitments, their space of reasons. We can only make up hypotheses, provide error accounts, and the like. But for our own culture, we are in a different situation. Our statements about other cultures may be behavioral and explanatory. For ourselves, as Joseph Rouse argues, they are "expressivist" (2002, 194). The reasons are our reasons; the normative commitments are ours; we have privileged access to them. Davidson is having none of this, either. One of the most visible consequences of the argument of "The Very Idea" is that the supposed distinction between cultures – between our concepts, our rationality, and theirs – is eliminated. The difference is language, which is treated in a demystified way rather than as a mysterious order of shared presuppositions. But any other explanation of "their" beliefs is in terms – those of error – that equally apply to the people in our own culture using our own language. So there is no "ours" to go with the "theirs." There is no collective fact of shared concept possession behind their beliefs because there is no fact of concept possession in the Kantian sense in Davidson.

The full implications of this reasoning are drawn out in "A Nice Derangement," which extends the use of the notion of error to ordinary linguistic interaction (Davidson 1986). When we deal with other people, we are constantly doing precisely what the anthropologist is doing: we are interpreting their behavior, revising our interpretations in light of our attempts to make sense of it, and attributing beliefs to them. These attributions often include error hypotheses. We could not function as language users or human beings without doing this. Making intelligible is a continuous process. Making inferences about what someone intends to mean, whether they are sincere, ironic, speaking metaphorically, or erroneously, is ubiquitous, and a part of every human interaction. Moreover, this process is logically fundamental and perhaps ontogenetically fundamental: logically, because for the grasp model to make sense there is a two-stage process in which the language learner first needs to identify something – speech as intentional and about something – that is later fully grasped.

Learning, including language learning, is an embarrassment to the possession model. For Brandom, embracing the interdependence of inferences about rationality, together with the idea of meanings as rooted in normative practices of justification underwritten by "commitment," forces him into the odd position of arguing that the prelinguistic individual does not have genuine intentions, which in turn raises the question of how they could have genuine commitments. Davidson avoids this problem by avoiding the collective possessions model. Does he fall into it in another form?

Doing without collective possessions: Is it possible?

Consider the demands and complexity of Brandom's account in *Making It Explicit*. Meanings are not something in the interactional flux, but are rooted in a complex and massive tacit system of normative score-keeping practices which we have access to in filling in the enthymemes of ordinary speech, especially in the context of justification. We and our peers in our linguistic community are committed to this system personally and in the collective voice, as with Sellars's notion of collective intentionality. This commitment, necessarily, is a kind of blank check written by our prelinguistic and thus pre intentional selves. We commit to a system in which individuals participate in a way similar to participation in Platonic forms, which is to say partially, since none of us has within ourselves all the meanings or inferences that constitute the concepts making up the system. The point of Brandom's famous regression argument is to establish this: justification has to end some place, but the place it ends has to be normative, and thus behind each rule is a normative end point which is a commitment to a system of this sort.

For Davidson, this whole machinery of a fixed set of normative practices revealed in the enthymemes of ordinary justificatory usage is simply unnecessary. We have no privileged access to meanings that we can then expressivistically articulate, because there is nothing like this – no massive structure of normative practices – to access. Instead we try to follow our fellow beings and their reasoning and acting, including their speaking: we make them intelligible. And we have a tool other than the normal machinery of predictive science that makes this possible: our own rationality. Rationality is normative, but not in McDowell's sense. It is not the rationality of constraint. Our only constraint is the limit of our capacity to make intelligible. There is no gap between what we can recognize as intentional and meaningful and what we can make intelligible – that is to say, what we can follow, which includes intelligible error. Justification has no special status of the kind accorded it by Brandom. It is just another piece of behavior: the child learns that saying "Why, mommy, why?" gets a reaction. Eventually children come to follow the answers, to make them intelligible to themselves, and to provide them when elicited, but nothing about this activity of giving answers and asking questions gets beyond the behavioral facts, except for the matter of following or making intelligible.

For the normativist, this reply makes a fatal error: it falls back into a variant of the position they themselves hold: that normative rationality is "necessary." The fact that Davidson locates the relevant kind of normativity elsewhere – in the interpreting agent – is to fall back into accepting the synthetic *a priori*, which has to be the source of these normative constraints. But it is worse than their own accounts, because it is mysterious, groundless, and arbitrary. Moreover, they would say, Davidson leaves us with no account of the normativity of that which is generally recognized as normative: rule-following, $2+2=4$, and so forth.

What does Davidson say about this mare's nest of issues? He says something about rationality and its normative character, but not what the normativist wants to hear. For the normativist, rationality is itself a possession, an acquisition like a concept but more fundamental, more universal. Intelligibility depends on something else: the abilities we have to follow the thinking of others. The child's game of "step on a crack, break your mother's back" is intelligible – intelligible error about the causal structure of the world, perhaps – but thinking that one can break a back by stepping on an interdicted crack also represents a form of reasoning that we share with primitive people and indeed all peoples. And it would be hard to construct a "theory" of this kind of inference that would make it rational.

But it is also hard to construct empirical theories of human reasoning: what "empirical" rationality indeed is: how we *actually* infer, rather than how we reason normatively. Worse, there is an odd dependence of empirical theorizing on normative theories of rationality, normative theories that are false as empirical theories. This was among the lessons Davidson learned in the 1950s doing experimental studies of decision-making. Decision theory, which is usually called a normative theory in this literature, is false as an empirical theory of rationality.[4] People do not make decisions in the way that normative decision theory defines as rational. But, as noted, "normative" decision theory is indispensable in at least this sense: to study actual decision-making it is needed as a starting point. Biases and errors are biases and errors *in comparison to it*. And there seems to be no option here. Without notions like bias we don't have a language for describing actual decision-making. There is no "empirical theory" of decision-making that is an alternative to the normative account; there is only one that depends on the normative theory in this odd way.

The normativist would argue that this is a case of *a priori* truth. Normativists read *indispensable* as *necessary*, and necessary in the manner of synthetic *a priori* truth. But this case doesn't fit the pattern. Empirically, it is not truth at all. But it seems to fit with other cases in which the theory is so deeply ingrained in our construction of empirical accounts that we can neither find an alternative to it nor dispense with it. Davidson suggests measurement theory as an example of this: it, too, is a case of empirical theory as classically understood, but as an empirical theory it is also literally false. The oddity has been remarked on in the literature on testing the theory of relativity: measurements were made in accordance with the theory that relativity was to displace, rather than in relativistic terms (Layman 1988). What confirmed the theory were the errors that appeared using the

166

old measurement theory. But this did not displace the old measurement theory, which was as Newtonian as ever.

In the case of rationality, there is an analogous problem. The fact that the theories we have of rationality are false as empirical theories of human decision-making gives us no reason to discard them as normative theory, or to stop treating them as indispensable for our various theoretical and even practical purposes. They are, after all, also part of the universe of the intelligible. But this indispensability does not confer on them any sort of metaphysical status, much less warrant any sort of claim about the metaphysical necessity of the normative as some sort of special ideal realm equivalent and coexistent with the empirically real. Indeed, rationality has properties in relation to the task of making intelligible that point in a different direction entirely.

The different direction is to acknowledge the actual diversity of the relevant kind of rationality. The rationality needed is "rudimentary" (Davidson 1985) and the notion of reasonable belief is "flexible" (Davidson [1994] 2005, 121) – very flexible.[5] Davidson indicates how flexible in the following:

> The issue is not whether we all agree on exactly what the norms of rationality are; the point is rather that we all have such norms and we cannot recognize as thought phenomena that are too far out of line. Better say: what is too far out of line is not thought. It is only when we can see a creature (or "object") as largely rational by our own lights that we can intelligibly ascribe thoughts to it at all, or explain its behavior by reference to its ends and convictions. (2004, 97–98)

The contraposition of this shows how flexible the notion of rationality is for Davidson. If we can recognize something as thought, it is "rational" in the relevant sense. Recognizing something as rational is a matter of being able to follow someone's thought – to simulate his or her thinking well enough that this individual's differences can be allowed for as normal or explained, and thus made intelligible as error. The normative element is not rigidly fixed, unarguable, or even free from conflict between the kinds of inference that we can follow but which also lead to conflicts. This is not the kind of rationality that provides the kind of constraint and ultimate justificatory ground that is the concern of Brandom or McDowell. The only constraints are interpersonal: we are constrained in our understanding by the limits of what we can follow and we are constrained in communicating by the limits of what others can follow, and constrained in what counts as thought by the requirement that for something to be recognized as thought, it must be the kind of thing the recognizer can follow.

What I am calling "following" is what Davidson treats as an act of imagination (1985, 92). This is something different from "possession of a concept." The substance of following is frankly psychological, rather than normative in the sense of Brandom, McDowell, or the rule-following literature. It is perhaps best understood in terms of the idea of simulation in cognitive science. And it is this idea that suffices to account for our capacity to make sense of others, to account for intelligibility as distinct from beliefs about rightness. This is what the rule-following literature stumbles on: it cannot distinguish *possession* of a rule shared with others from *following* another's thinking. Partly this is a matter of the diet of examples: following the idea "addition of two" and possession of the tacit rule governing it if there is such a thing, are the same; translating and possessing, however, are different. Davidson could simply make the point that following is basic to, and sufficient, for both. Our capacity for learning the rule of adding two is our capacity for following the teacher, and there is no additional mystery. We do not need an additional concept of possession of tacit objects to account for the behavioral facts. Nor do we need some notion of the intrinsic normativity of a rule, a notion of commitment, or any reference to community. The concept is "social," but only in the interactional sense of social, rather than the collective idea, the idea of shared frameworks. We are, as individuals, following someone else, and getting feedback from our interactions that reassures us that we are following them sufficiently to say we understand them, but the web of belief that we are constantly adjusting and readjusting in the course of interaction is ours, not a collective fact that is external and constraining. Simulation is also not a causal idea – it is "normative" in a specific sense unlike the Brandom or McDowell sense, not something external and constraining, but linked to the agent's own capacities.

These capacities are naturalizable, not in the sense of the reduction of intelligibility to cause or regularities, or the elimination of intelligibility, but in the sense of "disenchanted." The ability to follow is a capacity of beings with brains with particular kinds of neurons, perhaps, in this case, mirror neurons or the mirroring system, rather than souls participating in the forms, or slates being inscribed on. Part of "following" is following the thoughts and utterances of others about things in the world; so the world is already present in following. "Representing" and similar philosophically mysterious acts are transformed when it is recognized that representing is an interactional act, something done by someone for someone else, within the limits of what the second person can follow, rather than some sort of abstract contact between the mind and reality. And it is these limits, and only these limits, that are the limits of reason itself.

Evidenz and enthymemes

Davidson, as I have quoted him, does not suggest that possession of "rationality" is sufficient for interpretation and understanding. But he dispenses with the machinery of a common coordinating system by virtue of which we understand one another. For the normativist, this produces a major problem. Unless there is a universal coordinating system, what does the coordinating? What does the work of assuring that when we see or hear something, others also see or hear the same thing? That when I speak meaningfully using some language, others retrieve the same meaning from my speech? We can put this objection in the form of a screed.

The strategy of this approach to prize intelligibility apart from ration-ality and from the universal and local coordinating systems doesn't change anything – there is nothing to intelligibility that is not given by rationality. That is the whole lesson of Kant! Intelligibility means jus-tification, justification requires rationality, and rationality requires one common normative coordinating system at a time. Of course the notion of justification leads to a problem about regresses, and we can quibble about the end point of regresses and what regresses matter. But the end point has to be justificatory, and therefore normative, and not causal. Notions like "following the thought of another" and "empathy" are not going to help. They depend on the notion of intention, and intention depends on rationality, the rationality of the relation between inten-tion and action, and is thus inescapably normative. To forget that is to fall into psychologism, and psychological facts can't justify. Of course people will fail to live up to the constraints of rationality, have weak-ness of will, and so forth. There is no understanding outside of inten-tion: intention is inescapable. It is not a Good Bad Theory, but part of the concept of understanding itself. And it is normative. Even "socio-logical" substitutes for intention, such as Weber's notion of subjective meaning, require the notion of meaning, which is not only normative but implies the existence of a normative system that makes things meaningful. Acknowledging these things is the only path to objectivity and truth, both of which are normative notions, and both of which the supposedly "alternative" account relies on – and it is seeking objectivity and truth, if it is really science. The need to end regresses means that the regresses have to end some place, and for the results of any claim to be objective, they must end in some common structure or coordinating system which is normative, and has to be normative to justify anything, to validate even an empirical claim.

Is there a meaningful response to this?

There is an answer, which can be given in terms of two philosophical concepts, both of which, as it happens, figure in the social science tradition in a prominent place: the methodological introduction to Weber's *Economy and Society* ([1968] 1978). The concepts are empathy and *Evidenz*. *Evidenz*, for most (but as we will see, not all) of our purposes may be translated as obviousness. Both terms have had a bad press. Empathy is usually understood as a weak epistemic reed, which fails to warrant truth claims about what is in another person's mind. It is dismissed as an internal feeling rather than a proper experience of actual facts about other people. And it is a poor guide to causal relations, just as introspection is. At the same time it is unnecessary and irrelevant to anything normative or rational, which must be understood as removed from the realm of the subjective. Yet empathy in some sense, namely the sense associated with following, is hard to get rid of: in order to understand or learn from someone, in the sense of following someone's reasoning, it seems that some kind of empathy, some sense of having the same thoughts and recognizing the other's thoughts as thoughts like ours, is indispensable.

Evidenz, as a philosophical concept, derives from the Cartesian notion of self-evidence. The relevant feature of evident concepts is that they are elements of inferences, but they are not inferred from anything themselves. Usually, and problematically in Descartes' case, self-evidence is evidence to me, as an individual. Franz Brentano, the source of the modern form of the idea, formulated it differently, and the difference is significant in relation to empathy. The two elements of his idea of *Evidenz* are (1) that which is evident must also be evident to others, and (2) to be evident is also to be something which cannot be further analyzed – it is the obvious, that which follows naturally. *Evidenz* is philosophically problematic because of this feature of unanalyzability: that which is evident can never be further established. It can't be derived from anything else, but neither can it be gotten rid of and replaced. But the same feature assures its ineliminability. The denial that there is such a thing as *Evidenz* gets caught in a vicious circle – is the denial evident? If so, it refutes the denial. If not, we face a regress, and we must ask at each point whether the grounds for the denial are evident. To prove that there must be such a thing as *Evidenz* or to argue against it presupposes that something *is* evident, either the claims on which the denial is grounded or the

170

validity of the logical connections between the claims in the argument being made against it.[6]

The bad press for *Evidenz* in twentieth-century philosophy was a result of Frege's and Husserl's critiques of psychologism and their insistence on the possibility of some stronger kind of grounding – in Husserl's case, Kant's apodictic certainty, with "consciousness of their necessity" ([1786] 2004, 4:468). Frege's argument was that there is a difference between truth, such as mathematical and logical truth, and taking to be true – which is precisely what *Evidenz* is concerned with. This difference, for him, is related to the difference between what people do and what they ought to do – to normativity. Arithmetic, for him, is a normative science. What people believe about natural numbers has nothing to do with the truths about them. Even a community of arithmetic users could be wrong about doing sums, or could do them incorrectly: nothing depends on what is in their heads or what they do. *Evidenz* is straightforwardly a fact of psychology, a fact about people and their "takings to be." These facts fit into Brentano's category of descriptive psychology, which is phenomenology without the transcendental arguments that there is a structure of fixed and discoverable presuppositions of the experiences that descriptive psychology describes.

Frege treated this approach as an error, the error of psychologism. Psychologism is a shadowy and confused notion, a name for an error it is far from clear anyone has made, but the core of the critique of psychologism is the idea that psychological facts, such as facts about what is taken to be true, are not evidence of truth, and that, more generally, psychological facts are irrelevant to justification. The conventional philosophical view is that there are two distinct kinds of facts here: normative facts about logic and reason, which do justify, and psychological, causal facts that fail to justify or warrant anything. Justifying and warranting are normative rather than causal relations. Facts of psychology are causal facts involving causal relations. The error of psychologism is of confusing the "true" with the psychological fact of "taken to be true." But being true is independent of being taken to be true. Thus, as Frege puts it,

> If being true is thus independent of being acknowledged by somebody or other, then the laws of truth are not psychological laws: they are boundary stones set in an eternal foundation, which our thought can overflow but never displace. ([1893] 1964, 13, sec. xvi)

Frege himself has no solution to the regress problem. As he concedes, the basic laws of logic cannot be justified. Logical justification comes to an end when we reach these laws. To argue that our nature or constitution forces us to abide by the laws of logic is no longer a logical justification, but a change in subject from logical to psychological or biological considerations. (Kusch 2007; Frege [1893] 1964, sec. xvi-xvii; cf. Kusch 1995, 30–41). So in a sense, Brentano's point stands – there is no getting rid of *Evidenz* or something like it, because even on Frege's account we must take these laws to be evident.

Worse, even Frege must resort to psychological language in his discussion of concepts ([1893] 1967). People must somehow relate to these concepts in order to understand and use them. So he uses a term that appears repeatedly in the analytic tradition, "grasping." This term is a surrogate for psychological terminology, but it is loaded: it makes sense only if there is something to be grasped. But it is difficult to see what grasping consists in other than the achievement of *Evidenz* described by Weber and Brentano. If the only difference is that grasping implies that there is something being grasped, the usage is misleading: it pre-decides the issue of the nature of concepts and conceptual experience in favor of the idea that concepts are external and objectlike. If we return to the point where this particular intellectual shortcut has not gained currency, it becomes apparent that grasping and *Evidenz* are closely related ideas – perhaps indistinguishable in practice (though as we will see with different implications in relation to truth). And this apparent indistinguishability points to a set of possibilities. Brentano's solution to the regress problem is to end it with something that is not hidden but evident: a set of premises for arithmetic, for example, that are not part of ordinary practiced arithmetic.[7]

If we understand evidence as "evident to me," the objection that *taking to be true* and *being true* are different makes sense – something can be evident to me but still be wrong. "Wrong" would mean that someone could be right. But Brentano excludes this possibility. He points out that

> One usually says "This is evident" and not "This is evident to me." Probably because of the faith that what is evident to one is evident to all. ([1930] 1966, 126)

He also says,

> Truth pertains to the judgment of the person who judges correctly – to the judgment of the person who judges about a thing in the way in which anyone whose judgments were evident would judge about the same thing; hence it pertains to the judgment of one who asserts what the person who judges with evidence would also assert. ([1930] 1966, 122)

172

Evidenz is thus a judgment about what "anyone whose judgments were evident would judge." In short, it is a claim about what others *would* think – an empathic claim. If it is correct, it would exclude the possibility traded on by Frege's critique – as well as the raft of similar arguments associated with Kripke's cryptic comment about rules that everyone in the community could be applying incorrectly – that there could be something normative about which everyone could be wrong. If no one would think otherwise, no such possibility could materialize.

Empathy as part of social science, and as a subject of science: From behavioral data to empathic fact

"*Evidenz*" and "empathy" appear together in a key passage in the first pages of Max Weber's classic *Economy and Society* ([1968] 1978), where Weber discusses his requirements for the explanation of social action, which he has already stipulated is by definition "meaningful."[8]

All interpretation of meaning, like all scientific observations, strives for clarity and verifiable accuracy of insight and comprehension (*Evidenz*). The basis for certainty in understanding can be either rational, which can be further subdivided into logical and mathematical, or it can be of an emotionally empathic or artistically appreciative quality. Action is rationally evident chiefly when we attain a completely clear intellectual grasp of the action-elements in their intended context of meaning. Empathic or appreciative accuracy is attained when, through sympathetic participation, we can adequately grasp the emotional context in which the action took place. The highest degree of rational understanding is attained in cases involving the meanings of logically or mathematically related propositions; their meaning may be immediately and unambiguously intelligible. We have a perfectly clear understanding of what it means when somebody employs the proposition 2 X 2 = 4 or the Pythagorean Theorem in reasoning or argument, or when someone correctly carries out a logical train of reasoning according to our accepted modes of thinking. In the same way we also understand what a person is doing when he tries to achieve certain ends by choosing appropriate means on the basis of the facts of the situation, as experience has accustomed us to interpret them. The interpretation of such rationally purposeful action possesses, for the understanding of the choice of means, the highest degree of verifiable certainty. With a lower degree of certainty, which is, however, adequate for most purposes of explanation, we are able to understand errors, including confusion of problems

173

of the sort that we ourselves are liable to, or the origin of which we can detect by sympathetic self-analysis. ([1968] 1978, 5)

This is not quite the same as Brentano, who does not treat *Evidenz* as a matter of degree. But it is the classic articulation of the sociological use of the notion of *Verstehen*. Note that it accounts for "error" in empathic terms – this is intelligible error, made intelligible empathically, that is to say, an error that we can in some sense follow as an error.

The obvious objection to appeals to empathy of any kind is this:

> *Empathy is not a reliable guide to anything. Indeed, it is not a fact about the world, or about others, at all. It is merely a fact about one's own mental life or responses. Our empathic attributions often go wrong. Empathy produces results with* Evidenz *only in simple cases, such as Weber's example of a man chopping wood. And even these empathic imputations are fallible. So the assumption underlying empathic universalization, on which this whole account is based – that empathy is an autonomous source of knowledge – is simply false.*

In what I have said here I have tried to separate empathy and empathic universalization from truth and objectivity by arguing that while empathic universalization leading to intersubjective agreement is enough for truth and objectivity, empathic universalization is a broader phenomenon; it applies to anything that another person can follow. This formulation inverts the relationship between *Evidenz* and truth that informed the earlier discussion: the evident is not a problematic subtype of truth, as it is in the earlier picture. It is a feature of mutual reasoning, which may or may not lead to truth. We may understand the caste system in terms of its notions of uncleanliness and contagion, for example, without believing in it. Such beliefs are always, in any case, more complex than their elements, such as the intelligible notion of contagion, and it is these beliefs, such as the concept of ritual cleanliness, that we can reject as an intelligible error. So empathic universalization fits better with intelligibility than it does with truth, reason, rationality, and the like. The true, the normatively rational, and Right Reason are subcategories of the intelligible, and the intelligible is that which can be empathically understood. This leads to a different picture of empathic universalization – not as a criterion for the acceptability of "certain" or evident statements, but as a commonplace and essential part of ordinary human interaction.

If empathy is error prone, how could it have any sort of meaningful role in establishing fundamental facts? This was the kind of objection that would have occurred to Frege and Husserl. Here the critics of empathy are half right: empathy is not a mechanical means of producing truths. But it is also more than a "method." Weber, again, makes the crucial point:

> Understanding may be of two kinds: the first is the direct observational understanding of the subjective meaning of a given act as such, including verbal utterances. We thus understand by direct observation, in this case, the meaning of the proposition 2 x 2 = 4 when we hear or read it. This is a case of the direct rational understanding of ideas. We also understand an outbreak of anger as manifested by facial expression, exclamations or irrational movements. This is direct observational understanding of irrational emotional reactions. We can understand in a similar observational way the action of a woodcutter or of somebody who reaches for the knob to shut a door or who aims a gun at an animal. This is a rational observational understanding of actions. ([1968] 1978, 8)

Direct understanding is non-inferential and ungroundable. It is a matter of *Evidenz*. But something interesting happens in direct understanding: the data are behavioral – the woodcutter is observed cutting wood, but the "intentions" of the woodcutter are not "observed." Nevertheless we understand this act as having a meaning, and attribute this meaning to the woodcutter. One might employ the language of intention here, but appealing to this Good Bad Theory of mind is not necessary at this point. One is understanding the behavioral facts *as* meaningful action. Behaviorism disallows this as a matter of smuggling in theoretical content – a theory of mind that needs to be independently established. So the behaviorist would deny that this kind of direct understanding is possible. The critic of empathy would cite the error-prone character of such understandings. This problematic kind of understanding is necessary to provide the elements for inferential understandings, which Weber calls explanatory understanding. This would include cases in which we infer from directly observed actions an understandable connection between the actions, such as the case of choosing a means or making an error.

Empathic universalization: Justifying Brentano's faith

Brentano spoke of the assumption that others will take as evident what we take as evident as a matter of faith. But something very significant has happened in the intervening years that has altered dramatically the status of empathy: the discovery of mirror neurons in monkeys and the subsequent development of inquiries into empathy and the mirroring systems of human beings. Mirror neurons activate both in the performance of actions and in the perception of actions. They enable the brain to operate on a dual-use basis, so that the neurons used for acting are also used for what Weber would call the direct observational experience of a meaningful action such as chopping wood. We may be born with some capacities of this sort, which would be what enables very young infants to do such things as respond to smiles with smiles, and to distinguish between human intentional touching and robot arm touching, as in the experiments discussed in Chapter 2, and more generally to recognize intentional behavior. The dual-use character of this system suggests that "we recognize someone else's action because we manage to activate our own inner action representations using mirror neurons" (Keysers et al. 2003, 634). But we don't manage anything – the brain does. But it does so on the basis of our own abilities to perform similar actions, and especially "from the massive experience we have accumulated over the years in planning and executing self-produced activities" (Blake and Shiffar 2007, 56). Dancers can see things about dance moves that other people can't see (Cross et al 2006), male and female ballet performers see the typical gender-specific dance moves of their own gender better (Calvo-Merino et al 2006, 1907). There is also research on the visual cues that allow motions and emotions to be identified. What this research suggests is that the cues needed by the system are very modest, and that the preconscious work of perceiving is done largely by the perceiver constructing perceptions of whole actions on the basis of very limited inputs. Even a very small set of visual cues, for example, allows someone to identify motions and emotions of certain kinds (Tomasello and Carpentier, 2005, 141; Loula et al., 2005; Blake and Shiffrar, 2007).[9]

The brain, in short, performs the trick Weber attributes to direct observational understanding – of transforming behavioral cues into action-identifications, which is to say into meaningful actions. And having a location in the brain changes the status of empathy – it ceases to be an intellectual process bound up with the error-prone folk language of intentionality, and becomes a fact of science with a discoverable set of features located in specific neuronal processes. Moreover, it is these processes that deal with *subjective meaning*, in an recognizable sense of that term. Error-prone or not, these processes fall squarely into the realm of fact, and nonnormative fact at that. Our action capacities form a *natural* basis for interpretation which functions as a default mode, subject to correction or revision, similar to the way that the assumption of rationality and the same norms of correspondence and the default mode of interpretive charity functions for Davidson.

The use of norms and the normative in these contexts by Davidson is, as we have seen, somewhat peculiar. He does not use these terms to refer, as other normativists do, to the presence of some sort of fixed, autonomous, normative structure that binds individuals and to which they submit. But the cognitive mechanisms involved in mirroring are not normative at all, and do the same work at a pre-intentional, prelinguistic level. And the way they work sheds a good deal of light on the issue of meaning. Empathic universalization, the projection that we make when we respond to the man chopping wood as a man chopping wood rather than as a set of behavioral data points about which we must construct a theory and derive intention as a theoretical term in the theory, is not a faulty meta-physical assumption, but a default response that improves through feedback, the kind of feedback we receive in social interaction and in interaction with the world itself, as in the case of the infants with their sticky mittens. We "know" or "assume" the man is chopping wood because we can rely, to some extent, on the default setting of empathic projection. "Know" and "assume" are misleading terms here – we are not yet in the context of justification. But saying that the man is chopping wood is verbalizing or stating something that is rooted in this interactive process, and thus statements of this kind more or less closely correspond to something that is part of a very basic pattern of human interaction that appears at the earliest stages of human development.

The fact that these processes are so basic tells us something about the standard hot-button issues of normativism. Begin with Brentano's own famous argument that the mark of the mental or thought is that it is *about* something, the thing that distinguishes our understanding of people from our understanding of things. If we accept this, we can also say that our empathy with respect to aboutness is also the minimum that is needed to begin to apply mentalistic terms. And it is also sufficient to apply these terms – we know what it is about because we can successfully project this aboutness empathically. Aboutness is the key to Searle's argument for normativity and collective intentionality with respect to meaning, and it is one of the places in which Davidson uses normative language – his reference to norms of correspondence. And this poses a question about whether any reference to norms is needed here. Recognizing that a gesture is about something is an empathic projection. The "norms" that govern meaning, the meanings of terms applied to the world, may be readily understood in nonnormative terms: as empathic projections that are confirmed, sustained, corrected, and improved through interaction with others.

This same kind of well-understood process of social interaction, understood in terms of empathic projection, allows us to make sense of the authority of the speaker to articulate the meanings of terms that expressivism trades on – the muddled business about "rights" to speak for a group that we found mentioned in Kripke and central to Sellars's account of "ought." For the expressivist, the speaker explaining a meaning is articulating something hidden: the system of meanings, rules, scoring systems, collective intentions, and whatnot that the normativist takes to be hiding behind meaningful speech and making it possible by coordinating meanings and determining what expression is correct. The empathist can say something parallel to this, but better: that the authority one has in saying what one means is a product of the confirmation of one's empathic projections through interaction – a process full of potential correction, redundancy, and so forth, governed by the constraint of making oneself understood.

Much of the time our empathic errors are corrected by feedback: if we think we understand the arithmetic teacher, but do not, we are liable to be unable to account for what needs to be accounted for. The question is whether empathy plus feedback – including the social feedback that Haugeland has in mind when he mentions conformity – is enough, or to put it differently, whether there is anything more to be had. In the case of "+2" it is doubtful that anything more is needed. To the extent that there are actual deviants who are unable to match their use of "+2" to that of their teachers and fellow students, it is likely that there is a more serious and pervasive problem of understanding other people or performing mathematical tasks. And Kripke and Frege also appeal to this kind of deviance. Intersubjectivity of the sort produced by mutual comprehension based on empathy plus feedback produces as much "objectivity" in this case as there is to be had. And universal intersubjective agreement – literal rather than analogical agreement behind the surface agreement – is as much as there is to objectivity. But more than one intelligible inference may fit the facts, and the facts may underdetermine our judgments, and allow for more than one intelligible alternative in a given situation.

But limiting empathic universalization to these philosophically central cases is misleading. Empathic universalization is *not* restricted to the evident, the obvious, or the truths of logic, and the implications of the notion go beyond these issues. Empathy may, in fact, account for a great deal of actual conduct and social interaction. This was a point made by Weber and later by Alfred Schutz ([1932] 1967). The sociologist Charles Horton Cooley a century ago wrote of the looking-glass self, the idea that we are constituted as selves by the way we are reflected back to ourselves by others (1902). The same can be said for things like meanings: we live in a looking-glass world, and what we mean is something confirmed for us by the looking-glass interactions that make up our social and linguistic lives. These interactions provide a highly redundant means of correcting for empathic errors about such things as meanings.

As with *Evidenz*, empathy is impossible to eliminate as a part of social interaction and the explanation of social interaction. This becomes clear when we consider failures of empathy, cases where our capacity to understand is challenged, or in which we cannot initially understand, empathically or rationally, what the behavior in question means. If we are to explain a Hindu ritual of purity, such as the treatment of untouchables, which initially seems strange, even unintelligible to us, we attempt to give an account of it which in some sense normalizes it, and normalizing it amounts to making it intelligible. But making it intelligible in this context amounts to bringing to bear facts that enable us to describe it in a way that allows us to empathize. The idea of defilement by touch is already intelligible to us as a part of our own thinking. We already know, and find intelligible, the kind of thinking that goes into the notion of contagion by touch – from such diverse sources as the laying on of hands of the apostolic succession to the child's game of tag. So our problem of making the Hindu practice intelligible in the end relies on us filling in the rest of the context in such a way that we can match it up with something intelligible to us.

Intelligibility here bottoms out not in a theory of rationality, but in an actual point of empathic contact. Contagion thinking seems to be universal, and thus universally intelligible. But contagion inferences are not "necessary": we can follow them without accepting them. They are ungroundable, final. Perhaps they are rooted in the primal mirrorable experience of the nonmechanical effects of touch, which provides a template for the notion that touching produces nonmechanical transformation. But there is no reason for us to think that this kind of inference will always be correct. As with Weber's discussion of indirect understanding of action, based on inferences, we need to confirm contagion inferences if they are inferences about actual causal relations: if they concern disease, for instance. But whether they predict or not is a separate question from the question of whether we can follow the thinking. Following is empathic, final in the sense that there is no further explanation of it. One might say

179

that contagion reasoning itself is a matter of *Evidenz*, in the sense that there is no additional justification of it to be had. But of course it is not evident in the sense that it is necessary or necessarily "true." We can understand with complete clarity reasoning we reject.

The last word?

The problem of explaining the normative brings us to a stark choice: between normativism, in its endless varieties, with its reliance on a vast array of problematic arguments as well as *faux* facts, such as presuppositions that arise instantly, preintentional commitments, community memberships, *Grundnormen*, and so forth, on the one hand; and a "naturalistic" account that relies on or at least can point to genuine cognitive mechanisms that account for the facts nonnormatively, on the other. The burdens of the normativist's arguments are immense. There is the problem of queerness: that is, admitting the existence of an unusual class of facts, one that harks back to the undisenchanted world before science, involving entities with a spooky relationship to the actual causal world and the world of ordinary experience. There is the problem of description: the need to insist on the unique validity of particular descriptions of events that require explanation in terms of these unusual facts. There is the number of unusual devices necessary to sustain this argument: the problem of the construction of the facts themselves, which were made by analogies – rules which are not ordinary explicit rules, but tacit; spaces, for example, of reason, which were not spatial; presuppositions that are not, as in Euclid, actually presupposed, but were rather conditions for the possibility of the normative fact that are retrospectively constructed for the purpose of explaining them; commitments, for example to scoring systems, which are undertaken by people, such as infants, who are, according to the particular normative theory in question, prelinguistic and consequently preintentional – the list could go on indefinitely. There is the constant reliance on notions that, on examination, turn out to be circular, such as appeals to communities, for example the community of rational beings, which were not communities in any sense other than that they are composed of people who adhered to the rules that the fact of community is supposed to explain. There is the reliance on transcendental arguments to make what amounted to causal claims – claims about why we distinguish correct and incorrect, for example. There is the problem of separating the "normative" from the pragmatically successful, for

180

example in the task of speaking meaningfully, and the insistence that this has to involve odd normative entities, such as meanings which were infinite commitments into the future, rather than the ordinary facts of human interaction and feedback, which seem to explain actual linguistic behavior just as well. There is the problem of the empirical inaccessibility of the normative facts that were provided as explanations, which seems to immunize the normativists' claims from any competition with alternative explanations. And there are burdens of explanation: the problem produced by dismissing the diversity of morals and of the normative as irrelevant to the truth of the particular normative claims favored by the normativist; and the consequent problem of explaining why it doesn't matter that one can't explain how it could be that most of the people in history and in the present were and are living in normative error.

The case for normativism is that the things normativism accounted for, such as legal validity understood as fact or rationality, could not be given up, or given up for any supposed alternative, such as legitimacy or rationality understood as a natural fact. There is, normativism insists, no alternative description of these facts that captured their significance, and therefore no alternative to accepting the normative presuppositions that these things required to in order to be intelligible. These arguments necessarily come as a package. Normativism cannot claim to be just another theory. It must insist that there is no alternative to normativism. The project depends on transcendental arguments – arguments that certain presuppositions are required for the thing in question. To say that there is an alternative explanation is to say that they are not required. This is why insisting on the privileged character of descriptions that require these presuppositions is critical to the argument. Alternative descriptions are always available that do not require the presuppositions. And it is thus especially useful for the normativist to claim that the supposed alternative "helps itself" to the facts as described by the normativist, and cannot avoid doing so.

Normativism was a reaction – to the disenchantment of the world in general, and to the specific disenchanting produced by psychology and sociology. Frege and Husserl rejected "psychologism." What they were rejecting in fact were the innocuous claims of Brentano, whose arguments about *Evidenz*, its character, and its indispensability did not provide the kind of additional justificatory force, necessity, they craved. Kelsen rejected Weber's sociology of law out of the same kinds of motives: he wanted an account of the validity of law that rested on more than mere human belief. Fundamentalists recoiled at the acknowledgment of diversity as anything other than error,

181

and insisted that actual diversity implied nothing about the truth of the alternatives. They also could not accept the actual diversity of morals as a case of the underdetermination of theory by data, perhaps because they regarded such an acknowledgment as uncontainable, and as a long step toward relativism. But their biggest problem was the application of the arguments of social science to their own views.

The traditional issue with social science accounts of this sort was the concern that the application of these arguments to the normativist's own views was that the normativist's claims to universality would be undermined by relativizing them to specific circumstances, cultural backgrounds, and historical periods. The normativist could reply that the origins of an idea have nothing to do with its validity or its universal rationality. Inductively, however, the picture is different: every form of philosophical reflection on the normative in the past has turned out to "validate" or articulate parochial (and often very peculiar) moral ideologies, such as the morality of a small coterie in Edwardian Bloomsbury in the case of G. E. Moore, or the Victorian morality of such intuitionists as W. E. H. Lecky, who affirmed the universal validity of the intuition that chastity was a basic good, or the political ideology common to the precincts of 1970s Harvard in the case of John Rawls. Such reflections on the normative have also been, as MacIntyre argued, attempts to resolve, through philosophical abstraction, the concrete moral dilemmas of people living through periods of social change in which acting in accordance with the received morality no longer produced the same results.[10] But the problems run deeper than this. The devices that the normativist uses to explain normativism – the odd constructions that are ubiquitous in normativism – are difficult to distinguish from the fictions that figure in "native" accounts – *hau*, fetishes, and the like. They have the same properties of queerness, spookiness, empirical inaccessibility, and the rest.

The alternative picture we get from the empathist is this: ordinary language about the mental and concepts has no special validity – it is highly diverse and only vaguely connected to the realities of the brain. Regresses are everywhere, and they end. But they do not end in analogical facts, such as agreements or assumptions. Nothing is hidden. They end at the point that people find that they can follow each other, and that the step in their reasoning is evident. *Evidenz* – that is, ending a regress at a point that the parties each can find their way to – is indispensable. Seeming to be evident and being evident are, in this setting, the same thing. Being evident means being evident to everyone – subject to the usual limitations of "everyone" being sane, similarly situated, and so forth. But being evident is not necessarily permanent and thus is not a guarantee of truth. What seems evident can cease to be evident, as Euclidean space ceased to be evident. And "similarly situated" is not the same as "sharing a framework." It is merely being able to empathize over these same things. The only evidence we have of successful empathy is indirect – through the success of our interactions. But it is not reducible to these interactions, or to any evidence. But experience does modify our capacities to empathize. As Weber says, we "understand what a person is doing . . . on the basis of the facts of the situation, as experience has accustomed us to interpret them" ([1968] 1978, 5). Our experiences, and thus our capacity to empathize, vary individually. And what and how we experience is itself partly the product of this variable capacity to interpret. The fact that we can empathize is not derived from anything like a premise and needs no justification.[11] It is a natural fact, which the mirroring system causes and physically realizes. To deny it is to deny one of the causal conditions of learning such things as language, communicating, and much more.

MacIntyre joked that "the temptation to tell anthropologists that taboo is the name of a non-natural quality would be very strong for any Polynesian who had read G. E. Moore" (1970, 68). MacIntyre's point was that this is a problem for Moore, not for the Polynesian: it immunizes claims about the good from refutation, but at the same time removes any ground for Moore to reject *tabu*. So it produces a kind of relativistic Babel, because their nonnatural quality is not his. If we regard *tabu* as a Good Bad Theory we are in a better position. We can reject it for being false and therefore bad, but grant that it serves some good, such as the purpose of co-ordination. The normativist could perform a parallel analysis. The theory of *tabu* could easily be converted into the kind of theory the normativist would respect: *tabu* is a paradigm example of the kind of normativity that is everywhere. The normativist defender of *tabu* could alter the theory of tabu by adding philosophical devices that further immunize it by making it less empirically accessible and less open to intelligible and empirically correctable revision. But immunizing a Good Bad Theory does not transform it into a good theory. The normativity of *tabu* is sustained by belief. The belief is intelligible. But it is false, like normativism itself, and for many of the same reasons: it only appears to explain.

This sketched picture is obviously not the only possible approach to this material, nor is it meant to be anything more than evidence that an empirically oriented alternative to normativism can be constructed, and constructed for the subject matter of "reason itself," without falling into contradiction. But as we have seen, normativism must deny the existence of an intelligible alternative. The argument for normativism is a transcendental one. To the extent that we are compelled to accept it, we must accept it because there is no intelligible alternative. For the normativist to admit that there is an intelligible alternative is to admit defeat. To be sure, the normativist appeals to something attractive: the idea that one could somehow extract, through transcendental arguments, true legality out of the actual facts of ordinary legitimate legal orders; that one could find, through some special method of analysis, some foundation of thought more compelling and necessary than that which is evident to all; or that a single standard of normative rationality could be extracted from mere intelligibility and used as a standard of judgment. These projects derive from the understandable desire to have, as Nagel puts it, the last word. But the record on these projects is one of failure, failure to square with the world followed by a turn to reliance on usages outside the stream of ordinary explanation and devices that make the projects immune to criticism and evidence. This is not a result we need to learn to live with.

Notes

1. Susan L. Hurley (1992); Thomas Nagel (1986); Mark Johnston noted in Susan L. Hurley (1992, 108n23).
2. The similarities between Davidson and Weber are far more extensive than anything I have indicated here. I have discussed them in "Weber on Action" (1984) and "The Continued Relevance of Max Weber's Philosophy of Science" (2007c). On Weber's philosophical views generally, see Bruun (2007).
3. A much more nuanced account of the problems of talking about mistakes is given by Paul Roth (2003).
4. Kahneman and Tversky (1974, 1981).
5. I have provided a more extensive discussion of Davidson's complex development in relation to these topics elsewhere (Turner forthcoming).
6. A useful discussion is found at http://de.wikipedia.org/wiki/Evidenz
7. Brentano gives a variety of examples of the regression problem (Brentano [1930]1966, 123).

> Consider . . . the *regressus ad infinitum* which would be involved if a man wished to know, or to judge with evidence, that "*A* is." He could not affirm or acknowledge *A* with evidence unless he could also affirm or acknowledge the "being" of *A* with evidence. (Brentano [1930] 1966, 85–86)

This is the first step of a potential regress produced by talking about "the being of the being of A," the being of the being of the being of A, and so forth. Brentano's solution is that one accepts, "with evidence", that acknowledging the being of A is a justification for "A is," and that "A is" amounts to acknowledging the being of A ([1930] 1966, 86).

8. "Meaningful," as Weber uses it, is close to, if not identical to, Brentano's notion of intentionality (cf. Brentano [1874] 1973, 88). Weber did not speak of meanings as a kind of autonomous realm of fact, but of meaningfulness, as Brentano did not speak of intentions, but of such things as intentional relations. Brentano later altered his usage to avoid some implications of the Scholastic use of the term (cf. Speigelberg 1971, 40).

9. There is a large and growing literature on these issues, in the philosophy of cognitive science (e.g., Hurley and Chater 2005), social theory (Lizardo 2007; Turner 2007b) as well as across many other disciplines (Lanzoni and Brain, forthcoming). The last of these includes an expanded discussion of some of the issues in this chapter (Turner, 2008).

10. See MacIntyre, *A Short History of Ethics* (1966). One "methodological" reason for this is that deliberation or reflection has to operate on some set of materials – moral intuitions, for example – that are present in the historical situation in question. The range of intuitions that are relevant at any given moment in history is characteristically small, and ethics is concerned with the questions thrown up by the moral problems of the time. The philosophy of science operates on the science and the issues thrown up by the science of its own time and in the history of science. Ethics is no different. So the practitioner of deliberation has everything to fear from a social science or historical account that identifies the omissions, prejudices, cultural assumptions, exclusions, and the like that limit the content of the material which is reflected on. Indeed, given the historical record of parochialism in ethics, it is a kind of historical vanity – and a groundless one – to proclaim that one has liberated oneself from these limitations and can address these questions from the resources of reason alone.

11. The literature in this area is deeply influenced by the kinds of considerations that Brentano was attempting to bypass with his notion of descriptive psychology, especially the idea that there is some more fundamental set of facts from which psychological facts of the sort available through empathy can be "derived." This term recurs repeatedly in the literature. In a critique of Alvin Goldman, for example, it is asked "how a conception derived from introspection could possibly give us a concept of experience that we can intelligibly apply to other people" (Child 2002, 27). Brentano's point would be that "derivation" is irrelevant here, for there is nothing to derive from that does not depend on the thing itself.

Epilogue

THE ARGUMENT IN HISTORICAL PERSPECTIVE

Normativism begins with a big idea: that there are mundane and undeniable things, like the meaning of what we say or the logical relations between the things we say, that cannot be explained by science. Often this claim is treated as obviously true and in no need of justification. All that is needed to support this claim is to recognize other obvious facts: that we distinguish between promises and expectations, acting in accordance with routines and following the law; that we use normative language and take claims about normative topics to be true; that there are correct and incorrect ways to use terms, and so forth. Claims about promises, the law, and correct usage are justified. But science is not the place to find such justifications.

There is a familiar rejoinder to this. There may be a distinction between expectations and promises, routines and law, and so forth. But we can explain what people are doing when they are promising, following the law, speaking correctly, and so forth without deciding whether a promise is valid, a law is genuinely a law, or whether the use of the term is genuinely correct. To explain what people actually do we need only appeal to the beliefs that people have about what is correct, genuine, and the like. Judging is unnecessary for the explanation-giver. The factual content of promising, laws, and accepted usage – what people actually do – is entirely explainable without resort to considerations about genuine validity or correctness. There is nothing that is within the realm of fact that is beyond ordinary explanation.

The issue between these two accounts comes down to this: is there a special domain of fact that cannot be explained as part of the ordinary stream of explanation, but can only be understood, and accessed, in a special way? "Normativism" is a portmanteau term for the doctrine

186

that there is such a special class of facts. (Little hinges on the term "facts," though it is widely used in this literature.) Different forms of normativism claim that there are different things beyond science or explanation. In the case of the distinction between routines and laws, for example, the claim is that there is such a thing as legal validity that attaches to genuine laws only. Nothing about people's beliefs about laws makes laws valid. Validity is a fact of its own special kind.

One way of handling claims about validity would be to treat them as questions that have nothing to do with explanation. Judging the validity of a law, for example, can be treated purely as a normative problem, to be answered solely by reference to normative considerations. Whether we can get agreement on these considerations, or even whether they make sense, has nothing to do with the problem of explaining what people actually do. The problem of explanation and the problem of evaluation proceed, so to speak, in different containers of thought. Explanation never needs to take anything from the container marked "validity, correctness, etc.," except when we evaluate explanations themselves – but explanation is something distinct from the evaluation of explanation.

The normativist rejects this solution. For the legal normativist, for example, one cannot explain the law apart from the normative properties of the law. To ignore these is to change the subject into something other than "the law." Explanations need to be about adequately described things. To adequately describe the law one cannot omit its central feature – its validity. Explaining some substitute set of facts – legal behavior – for example, is an evasion. The facts that need to be explained are intrinsically normative. This becomes even more obvious when the issue is something like "rationality." There is no notion of rationality that is not normative. In any case, normativity is built into to usages like "belief," "intention," and so forth, so any explanation that appeals to these terms is already normative.

How does one settle this dispute?

Normativists have a standard set of arguments about how this dispute is to be settled. The antinormativist always cheats, and loses when he is caught cheating. Cheating, in this context, is using normative language while pretending to avoid it; changing the subject; and failing to acknowledge the normative nature of all reasoning. The antinormativist thinks the normativist cheats too. The way the normativist cheats is to reason in circles; to pretend not to understand the difference between normative and nonnormative senses of terms; and, most important, to appeal to something bogus – the supposed facts of normativity and the supposed facts associated with it, such as collective intentions or commitments. These explain nothing: they are fictions that have no place in the world other than to justify normative usages that are themselves either bogus or make sense only as opinions rather than fact. Sometimes even the normativist admits that normativism requires one to live with some strange ideas. But the normativist says "Get over it," and the antinormativist refuses to get over it. For the antinormativist, the lesson is that normativism and its predecessors have constructed the facts in question in a way that produces the problem artificially, and, by appealing to explanations involving normativity, given an artificial solution to an artificial problem.

This makes more sense if it is put into some historical perspective and translated into different vocabularies. In the earlier part of the twentieth century, Ernst Cassirer, who was steeped in the conventional neo-Kantian tradition, formulated this generic argument in terms of representation and meaning: "it is the symbolic functions of representation and meaning which first give access to that objective reality in which we are justified in speaking of substantial relations and causal relations" (1957, 101). In short, the normative always comes first, as a matter of logic. Cause presupposes the category of causation. A psychology based on causal regularity would be a contradictory project, for it presupposes, in the use of the concept of causality itself, a different and conflicting psychology, a psychology revealed by and accessible only through transcendental philosophical reasoning. In this alternative psychic world, the objects of thought and perception are constituted by presuppositions such as the constituting idea of causality itself.

The causal world, or at least the world of non-psychic stuff, nevertheless is still there, even for the normativist, and has a peculiar relation to the world revealed by transcendental reasoning. Could it be that the things that need to be accounted for *can* be accounted for as part of the normal stream of explanation, without appealing to a realm of the normative? Normativism says "no." The causal world is insufficient to explain the world revealed by transcendental reasoning – the psychic world and order of symbolic relations, in Cassirer. The neo-Kantians themselves saw that there was a problem with this claim. Nikolai Hartmann, speaking for the Kantianism of his time, puzzled over the fact that there were physical facts that paralleled the events in the realm of the spirit. Hartmann could only treat this as a mystery. He said that there was a *hiatus irrationalis* between the physical and the psychical. This gap, he argued, could only be overcome by seeking a common source. But since the source could not be found in the realm of experience, by science, since science presupposes the psychical, it must be, as Cassirer explains, "sought in the transcendental realm – and this implies that it can be no longer *known* in the strict sense but must be surmised or at best posited as a hypothesis" (1957, 97).

This is a more detached view of what transcendental arguments can produce than one finds in Kant or in present day Kantians and Sellarsians. It reflected the experience of neo-Kantianism: that transcendental philosophy did not lead to the univocal results that were implied by the term "necessary," but only to the claim that something had to be there in the transcendental realm to do the necessary work of validating and grounding. Later normativists forgot this experience, and convinced themselves that they were capable of identifying the genuine transcendental conditions of this or that. In short order they reproduced the Babel of late neo-Kantianism, what Gadamer called "the dissolution of neo-Kantianism," which led to Heidegger and Carnap.

Hartmann reproduces the core reasoning of normativism: that science can't explain some range of facts, and that the only account of these facts, and of the logical, psychic, rational, or normative conditions of a large body of undeniable fact, including the phenomenon of science itself, must be sought in the transcendental realm. Cassirer was more modest about what one can get through transcendental reasoning. But the basic reasoning is the same. Normativism still trades on the claim of explanatory failure. There is a realm of special facts (though nothing much hinges on the use or avoidance of the term "fact"), which cannot be accounted for by science, but which nevertheless is there, presupposed by all our thinking, and by science itself. As the Heideggerian slogan has it, this presupposed stuff is "always already there," ineliminable and indispensable. The term "normative" is a way of marking this distinction that encompasses rationality, the language of intention, belief, and so on, as well as the language of correctness and appraisal and the notion of logical necessity, all of which are held to be irreducible to science, and inexplicable by science.

Variants of these arguments can be found throughout the current normativity literature. The basic structures reproduce themselves. For Brandom, the relation between normative facts and other kinds of facts is this: "the realm of the normative includes the factual, since facts are intelligible only as claimable contents" (1997, 197). This presupposes the claim that I placed as an epigraph to Chapter 1: "Normative facts (e.g. about who is committed to what) are just one kind of fact among others. Normative facts are facts statable only using normative vocabulary (compare: physical facts)" (Brandom 1997, 197n6). For Heideggerians, the constitutive is always already there. The reasoning is simple: there is normative language, therefore there are normative facts. If there is a language of legal validity, or meaning, or ought, there must be something that corresponds to this language and makes it true or meaningful.

The Heideggerian form of this argument is frankly hostile to scientific explanation as a false attempt to usurp the right to truth about Being. Being is something to be sought *through*, not in opposition to, the "always already there." In contrast, the versions of normativism influential in Anglo-American philosophy typically attempt to accommodate science and avoid claims about the special Being of the spiritual world, but also without accepting any sort of "reduction" of the normative to the nonnormative. The shorthand, polemical form of the argument is contained in the claim that the facts (or claims) in question, facts (or claims) about our understanding of one another or about inferential relations, cannot be reduced to facts about causal regularities. The solution to the problem of accounting for these things is to posit a realm of the normative – a space of reasons – which science and thought in general depend on.

But what do these arguments really establish? Are there facts here? Is there a fact that there are meanings and oughts? Or is there merely a fact that people understand one another and that they have beliefs about obligations, or that (given that obligation is a local notion of our culture and time) we can interpret as being about obligations? The normativist treats these questions as a kind of skepticism, and treats skepticism itself as a kind of self-undermining claim. If we mean things, make inferences that we expect to be binding on others, and so on, we are, the normativist thinks, always already acknowledging the normative. To turn around and question any of this can only be a kind of self-refutation.

The step of erasing or ignoring the distinction between "people understand one another" and "people understand one another through shared meanings" is a familiar one, so familiar that we are inclined not to recognize the transition from meaning something to there being such a thing as a "meaning," or from saying someone ought to do something to saying that there are "oughts." This transition may not be seen as a step at all. But it is, and there is a philosophical tradition, through Quine, that questions precisely this step.

In a sense, taking this step is conservative – a cheap solution to the problem of explaining such things as the fact that we understand one another, however imperfectly. It saves the phenomenon of meaning something or feeling an obligation in a way that allows us to keep everything as it is – to treat our ordinary usages as being *about* something, the something being a realm of things that hide just behind our ordinary usages and more or less correspond to them.

There is even an important bonus to this solution. The idea that there are real meanings helps explain some very pervasive usages – those involving correctness, for example, the correct use of a term, or what counts as fulfilling an obligation. Correctness, real correctness, is to be found in the ideal realm, to which actual behavior, with its mistakes and failures of comprehension, can be compared and judged. But this solution works on one side of the reasoning described above: the presuppositions side. The explanatory side is still shrouded in mystery.

The troubles with this solution become clear when we ask what oughts and meanings are. Whatever they are, they are not medium-sized dry goods, the sorts of things we usually take to be the paradigm of things. Calling what we know about them "facts" is trouble too: they aren't the kinds of things there are ordinary facts about. Nor are they part of the world known to science. They exist, if they exist, in a special nether world. And if there is a special nether world, we have all of a sudden found ourselves with an exotic ontology that we need to make sense of. But making sense of it gets us into deeper trouble.

We know that the history of philosophy is littered with attempts to comprehend this world – from Platonism and the theory of forms on to Hegelian world spirits, Frege's concepts, and C. I. Lewis–Sellars–Brandom inferentialism. The idea that there is a coherent realm or space here is challenged by the very fact of the extraordinary diversity of attempts to comprehend it. Nevertheless, all of these attempts to construct this alternative, ideal world have something more or less in common. They involve regress arguments that begin with some fact, or rather with some description, and identify, through a series of steps of justification, an ultimate justifier.

So where do these regress arguments take us? To a variety of places, depending on who is doing the regressing: to Reason with a capital R, to the basic laws of logic that only a person with a hitherto unknown form of insanity would deny, to the place where Wittgenstein said "my spade is turned," to phenomenological certainties, to the concepts that are constitutive of the reasoning in question, to *Grundnormen*, to practices ordered in relation with one another into

191

a large hidden structure underpinned by commitments and a scoring system. The sheer diversity of the answers creates its own problems. Each account has a strong tropism: to the idea that there is a hidden ordering structure behind our thinking that authorizes or justifies it. But the huge variety of justificatory end points, and the difficulty of deciding between them or deriving one from another, suggests not so much hidden order as chaos.

If we decide that the end points are merely a matter of our various and diverse hidden commitments, we seem to be giving up on the idea of justification we started out with: it seems uninformative in the extreme to be told that the ultimate justification of some inference we are making is that we are tacitly committed to it. This is why a hidden *structure* is so important to this kind of analysis. There needs to be some sort of intermediary between us as the source of the justification and the justificatory work itself, or it is not justification at all. But to arrive at a large array of hidden structures – to the point of having a hidden structure behind every inference or term – defeats the idea of structure itself. The neo-Kantians discovered this on their own, which led to the idea that the structures were deeper than mere presupposed constitutive categories, and this idea led to Husserl and Heidegger, as well as to Frege, and of course to such present normativists as Brandom and McDowell. But unless there is one deep structure to be found, the strategy reaches multiple dead ends, as neo-Kantianism itself did.

Real explanation

There is another problem. At some point there needs to be some sort of transformative process by which what is not a justification becomes a justification. The paradigm for this is the transformation of the will of individuals to the will of the collective, which somehow then simultaneously becomes binding on the individuals who are part of the collective. One can translate this into the language of commitment and say that there is no mystery because commitment is already normative, or one can perform any one of a variety of other tricks with this material, as we have seen. But the basic problem remains: something normative has to come out of something nonnormative. Hiding this problem within the problem of collective structures seems like a good solution, because one can make a plausible case for the explanatory necessity of the collective structure in question. But at some point this problem needs to be faced.

All of these answers to the puzzle of normativity evade this crucial question. What is taken for granted and serves as a condition for thought, the *a priori*, had to get there somehow. But more important, the taken-for-granted has a history, it gets into the individual, who thinks, from an environment, which does not think, and does so through such explainable mechanisms as learning. The process of the production of the taken-for-granted can be studied and theorized about, though not necessarily in terms of "regularities." The reason this kind of social theoretical or sociological account is of no interest in this context is that these accounts don't authorize or justify anything.

But is there a realm of spirit, or a space of reasons? Is it really true that psychology and other relevant sciences cannot explain these things? This turns out to be a less straightforward question than it seems. In their polemical mode, normativists like to draw a sharp distinction between causal regularities and normative facts, and simply dismiss scientific explanation of normative facts as impossible in principle. But much scientific explanation comes in forms other than appeals to causal regularities. At other times, in a quest to avoid appearing to be irrationalist deniers of science, normativists make some important concessions. One concession is to acknowledge, however grudgingly, that the "always already there" is not always already there. McDowell, as we have seen, concedes that our rational capacities have to be the product of evolution. But this is true more generally about the conditions of thought. The already there is there as a result of a specific history which is part of its explanation.

The normative, understood in this "spiritual" way, clashes with something we also hold dear: science, or at least the scientific image of the world. Much of post-Kantian philosophy has been concerned with this conflict. Its roots, which are still evident in neo-Kantianism and the neo-Kantian construction of the problem, are in the conflict between spiritualism and materialism that animated the immediate post-Kantians, the German Idealists. But under the neo-Kantians the problem evolved into something different: a struggle with the emerging sciences of the mind and society over what could and could not be explained scientifically. Yet the conflict between transcendental philosophy and psychology, as well as that between logic and psychology, remained abstract. The "psychologism" that Frege and Husserl had in mind was Brentano's, not the actual discipline of psychology.

The claims that psychology could not explain an important set of facts, that causal explanation itself presupposed a category or concept of causality, are a template for the core issues about normativity. The general claim is this: there are things or facts that cannot be explained by normal explanations. These presuppositions were among these things or facts that fell into this important set of facts. These presuppositions had to be accounted for. But they had to be accounted for in a special way outside the limits of normal explanation. This is what Boghossian is saying when he describes "meaning properties" that "appear to be neither eliminable nor reducible," and then suggests that "perhaps it is time we learned to live with that fact" (1989, 548). Normativism is defined by this thought: that we must accept an anomaly, something beyond normal explanation, that corresponds to normative language – to "correctness" in the case of semantic normativity, which is Boghossian's concern in this passage.

Is there a way out of this reasoning that is consistent with the use of normative language, and that allows for the possibility of philosophy as a discipline concerned with the normative? Can one have normative talk without normativity? One way out is suggested by Michael Friedman in his discussion of the causal explanations of scientific belief offered by the sociology of science: that philosophical claims about good science or the nature of scientific truth need not conflict with causal explanations of science, if we consider the task of philosophy of science to be the fashioning of a normative lens with which to view an activity that is indubitably in the normal world and subject to normal explanation. Understood in this way, the normative beliefs of scientists would be taken as part of the same stream of explanation as other beliefs of scientists – both explainers and things to be explained. They would have no special, anomalous, status.

The normativist would of course object to this solution by claiming that this kind of explanation is impossible, because normal explanation presupposes something normative – the category of causality itself, and the standards of explanation that explanatory claims appeal to. So we are back, it seems, to the same problem. But this time there seems to be an answer to the normativist: that the presupposed standards are themselves subject to normal explanation, and are not anomalous. All the normal explanation of science claims for itself is that it makes scientific belief part of the normal stream of explanation. The standards of good explanation are themselves part of this stream. The normal explanation of these standards is reflexively consistent. The question of whether the normal standards are the correct standards is a normative matter, to be sure. But one reply would be that it is a question that belongs to the people who are in the business of fashioning normative lenses, philosophers of science, not to the problem of explanation itself.

194

The idea that beliefs and presuppositions were open to normal explanation was not contemplated by the early post-Kantians. By Hartmann's time there was a threat, but one that could be turned away. The "science" he was concerned with was psychophysics. It was evident enough that *Geist* was not going to be accounted for by the Weber-Fechner law. But with the advent of the social sciences, the *Geisteswissenschaften*, things changed, and social science and history became a meaningful alternative with the development of the intrusive sociological approaches of Weber and his successors, such as Mannheim, and with the Durkehimians, who sociologized moral doctrines by explaining the origin of morality in terms of religion and primitive religion as a kind of erroneous belief in which God was substituted for Society – the transcendent entity that primitive people were in fact dependent on.

This is a different kind of rivalry, in one key respect. It is not about the reality of some realm of spirit or about the abstract problem of whether causal regularities can ever, in principle, account for some phenomenon such as necessity or consciousness. It is about the nuances of description. The normativist must claim, and routinely does claim, that the descriptions the social scientific explainer employs are defective. But the issue of description is a strange one. The defect is not that there is some failure to include some of the things being described, that there are things missing in a sense that scientific objectivity would recognize, or that there is a failure to include something that the user of the norms learns in the process of learning and mastering the norms. It is a failure to include the specifically normative component of the norm – the thing that makes it binding and therefore a genuine norm.

With Kelsen we see the issue for the first time in this form. He is perfectly aware that the explanation of law and the history of law can be done without reference to the normative claim that the law is actually binding, and that indeed, as Weber pointed out, the bases of legitimacy and accommodation to the legal order were a variety of beliefs, habits, interests, and preconscious choices to do what is convenient, as well as the credible threat of sanctions, rather than any sort of collective force compelling people by its demands to obey. But the real world of legal power, he thought, did not account for the specifically legal: genuine legality itself, which was normative.

The idea that these constituting ideas or presuppositions were normative was then read back into these earlier conflicts. The different source involved the problem of what I have been calling local

195

normativity. The laws of logic and the structures of consciousness of interest to phenomenology were taken to be universal. But there are other laws that are also said to be binding, which define obligations, and which indeed are the paradigm for such concepts as "rule": the laws that are in statute books and enforced by courts. These laws are diverse – different countries or legal systems have different laws, different cultures have different obligations and practices, different languages different meanings. Local bindingness places normativism into a direct rivalry with anthropological and sociological accounts of law, religious belief, and norms, and also culture and meaning.

For local normativity, Hartmann's idea that the common source of the psychic and the spiritual needed to be sought through transcendental arguments was ironically prophetic. Both a dominant strand in social science and the direct ancestors of present normativism in philosophy drew from the same sources: the idea of a collective psychic structure. The many variations on this idea – from the notion of shared *Weltanschauungen*, *Denkgemeinschaften*, *Consciences Collectif*, central value systems, all the way to paradigm – served as a more or less common resource. The difference between social science and present-day normativism rooted in Sellars is in the different aims of the two. Social science did not concern itself with the genuinely normative; normativism was eager to avoid the metaphysical implications of the idea of collective minds.

The two could not be kept entirely separate. There had to be some factual substance to the idea of collective structures – even for normativism. Without this connection normativism would collapse into the Friedman solution: that the normative appeared only when the normative lens rather than the explanatory lens was used. For Sellars this took the form of the idea of collective intentionality. For Winch it was society as constituted by the joint "possession" of concepts understood in terms of (tacit) rules. For Brandom it was collective reactions. These accounts linked the normative to the actual social world, however abstractly. But they also amounted to an alternative substantive social theory.

Circularity and the added fact explained by normativism

With Hartmann, the issue looked simple: could a science with the limited capacities of psychophysics explain *Geist*? The answer was clearly no, and the solution was to accept *Geist* as an irreducible mystery that only transcendental philosophy could approach, and, because psychophysics was never going to be able to explain both *Geist* and the Weber-Fechner law, transcendental philosophy was going to have to take on the task of explaining both – or at least of providing a common source for both the world of spirit and the physical and psychophysical world. With Kelsen and Weber, however, the issue is reversed. The only fact about the law that can't be accounted for by sociology or the historical sciences is the "fact" of legal validity. But by Kelsen's time this "fact" was already under criticism as a piece of magical thinking by Axel Hägerström, the founder of Scandinavian legal realism, who was on his own journey of emancipation from neo-Kantianism (Hägerström ([1929] 1964). So the thing left over when the social science explanation was done was not something undeniable and unproblematic, but something that seemed to have no role in explanation, that depended on a preferred description of the law as valid, and that merely recapitulated the dogmatic presuppositions of legal science. The defenders of normativity were defenders of what had come to be regarded as a piece of legal mythology.

Description thus became all-important for the normativist, and the argument for normativism narrowed, at least in this central context, to a claim about the essential character of the legal as captured in descriptions that included the notion of genuine legal validity as distinct from "believed in" legal validity, and the claim that law described in this correct or fully adequate way can't be explained as part of the normal stream of explanation but requires transcendental reasoning, a regress, leading to a normative grounding fact that is itself outside the normal stream of explanation.

This kind of argument is a standard template for normativism: the preferred description warrants the preferred explanation, which in turn validates the preferred description as capturing the real thing. And with this we reach an impasse. The normativist can dismiss the rival description provided by the social sciences as "changing the subject," and therefore not really a rival at all. Doing this is essential to making a transcendental argument stick. If there are alternative possible non-transcendental explanations, no transcendental explanation is a necessary and therefore genuine condition for the possibility of the thing being accounted for. So securing the preferred description is the key to any normativist argument. The fact that this exercise results in a circular argument can be dismissed – circularity can even be embraced as a necessary feature of these arguments, even celebrated, under such names as reflexive equilibrium.

Relativism and rationality

The problem with such arguments, as social scientists and the public at large knew, was that there is a spectacular variety of human practices, beliefs, usages, moral standards, definitions of the moral, ideas of what is right, and so forth. Reflexive self-affirmation and self-dogmatization was open to all of the different world views. The Columbian Exposition of 1892–93 held a world Parliament of Religions which illustrated the point perfectly. Such speakers as Swami Vivekananda, who made Hinduism seem less a miserable superstition and more a meaningful alternative with something to teach the West, were tremendously successful. He said that "Sectarianism, bigotry, and its horrible descendant, fanaticism, have long possessed this beautiful Earth. They have filled the earth with violence, drenched it often with human blood, destroyed civilization, and sent whole nations to despair. Had it not been for these horrible demons, human society would be far more advanced than it is now" (1893). The Christian representatives responded to these successes by opining that it was all well and good that there were other religions, but Christianity was still the best because only Christianity provided salvation through Jesus Christ.

The lesson was obvious enough. Each tradition had the resources to provide explanations of why their view was right and everyone else was wrong, subhuman, in error, and so forth. And the existence of these different cultures, different religions, and different moral standards challenged our own certainties. If we believed that a certain kind of sexual compact or family was "normal," for example, we would soon discover that there were many alternatives, each of which had advantages of one kind or another. The existence of alternatives that are not obviously wrong poses a problem for transcendental justifications – they cannot claim to be the necessary preconditions of something that is itself necessary, because the arrangements being justified are not themselves necessary. They were reduced to such circularities as the Christian response to the Parliament of Religions: that only their views justified their views.

What the good Swami established was that Hinduism was an intelligible alternative. One might differ with the beliefs, and thus with the conclusions, take different books to be Holy Books, and so forth, but these were differences that could be discussed in a more or less normal way as differences of belief in a highly underdetermined context in which differences in belief were themselves intelligible. What the Christians did in response was simply to invoke their own religious

198

theory as a justification for its superiority: an empty self-compliment. But others who were more rational could see that there might indeed be advantages to the alternative, and problems with their own views that the contrast with the alternative could illuminate. The Christian theologians succumbed to the temptation to assert the global superiority of their own views. One can easily see, in this context, why this is circular and derationalizing – and one can see how little help "reflection" provided. Why is the analogous temptation, to think that one can appeal to the dictates of reason, also provided by self-reflection, to validate one's own ethical, scientific, and philosophical views in the face of intelligible alternatives which also fit the relevant data, not also clearly absurd?

One reason is this: the distinction I have been making between intelligibility and rationality is routinely erased by treating any intelligible but wrong doctrine as irrational rather than simply in error. Bernard Williams's treatment of Nazism and egalitarianism is a simple example of this. For Williams, the Nazis were guilty of a contradiction: they said they were against equality, but their arguments showed that they acknowledged equality as a moral principle but rejected its application to those they oppressed. Thus the principle is universally rational, and the Nazis weren't rational. They failed to accord with the dictates of reason, which dictate this doctrine. But this results in the conclusion that the Nazis were, mysteriously, irrational, and that their doctrines are unintelligible. But the doctrines of the Nazis, however false and repugnant, are intelligible. To make them intelligible we identify the errors of their racial theories which justify the exceptions they make to the principles they acknowledge. There is nothing contradictory about their views in this respect. The dictates of reason are of no help here. To condemn the Nazis as irrational one must smuggle in the claim that their substantive beliefs about the inferiority of those they oppressed were also irrational. This may be true, but it is a case that would need to be made by showing the errors in the way they arrived at these false theories.

The normativist wants to use this kind of conclusion to say "there is that word error again – a normative term." And to conclude that "in the end, it comes down to universal principles of rationality." After all, judging the inferences on which the beliefs were constructed is a judgment about rationality. But what do we get to in the end? What if we get to different inferences, each of which is intelligible, and each of which leads to different substantive beliefs? This is the situation of the Christians responding to the good Swami. For them, the promises of the Bible were a sufficient inferential ground. And this is intelligible. We can give plenty of good reasons for rejecting reliance on the Bible as a general way of reasoning. But these are grounds in the normal world of belief and inference – places in which there are intelligible disagreements, and which might, in many cases, be settled by new facts, by the demonstration of the superior results of thinking and inferring in a certain way, and so forth. The Swami, indeed, made a few recruits himself. Natural science managed to overcome reliance on the Bible in the West, but it did not do so through a general face-off over who was more rational.

What makes the "dictates of reason" model tempting is the fact that there are places that we seemingly don't have alternatives that are intelligible. This seems to imply that there are at least some universal principles of rationality. If these can be used to judge, we can then hope to validate our own views in general – about ethics, science, politics, and so forth – as the views that uniquely conform to these universal principles. What Davidson showed was that every idea we can say is false, indeed every idea we can understand, is always already rational. This means that to "judge" some doctrine to be irrational is also to show it to be unintelligible, and thus to judge it to be not a doctrine, or sentence, at all. The strategy described above simply collapses in the face of this: there is no situation in which we can say "the following views are intelligible, but when hauled before the tribunal of reason, they must be judged irrational." To get to the tribunal in the first place they must be intelligible, and thus rational.

Endpoints

Nevertheless, there does seem to be something right about the idea that there is an endpoint to justification, and that this has something to do with rationality, correctness, or understanding. And here the idea that the endpoint is a hidden structure by virtue of which such things as understanding, mathematical correctness, and rationality become possible gains its plausibility. What is not plausible are the ways in which these hidden structures are conceived.

The problem can be restated in this way. There is something to these things that needs explaining that cannot be easily or obviously explained using the simplest kinds of explainers, such as causal inputs or learning through feedback. This is the problem familiar from Kant's response to Hume. The radical (Kantian) solution to the problem is to release the explainer from the ordinary constraints of explanation, to free the explainer from the obligation to make sense of the thing

200

that needs explaining within the ordinary stream of explanation. The basic solution is to say that there is some sort of *a priori* element that allows us to account for the things we wish to account for, either directly or in conjunction with things that are part of the ordinary stream of explanation, such as habits acquired through feedback. But this release from the limits of ordinary explanation turns into a festival of circular argumentation and requires the invention of a host of theoretical entities whose role is to account for the missing, unexplained, element: the "normative," a term whose meaning is vague and largely negative. The category includes Hartmann's *Geist*, but it could be taken far more narrowly: limited, say, to "conceptual content" narrowly construed in terms of its linguistic function. It is more or less identified with the parts of human interaction that are supposed to be left over, unexplained.

The description of the normative things to be explained becomes all-important in this body of thought, because it provides the only real constraint on explanation: transcendental "solutions" to the problem can be generated, and are generated, free of any connection to anything that is part of the ordinary stream of explanation. The solutions range from claims about the dictates of reason, fixed and immutable, to David Lewis's idea that presuppositions spring up whenever they are needed. These are unconstrained by anything "natural," such as the psychological mechanics of learning, though in moments of intellectual conscience it might be conceded, as it is by McDowell, that there ought to be an evolutionary explanation that would place it partially back in the ordinary stream of explanation, but acknowledging the special, novel, and normative character of the thing to be explained. These pangs of intellectual conscience reflect the truth recognized by Hartmann: that there are ordinary processes that accompany everything that is in the category we are now calling normative. So the problem of explanatory sufficiency never goes away. There are rival explanations, and the question of whether they are in fact insufficient recurs. The defense against these rivals is to reassert the novel and special character of the normative by insisting on descriptions of the normative that preclude normal explanation.

Normativists concede that there is something mysterious about the normative understood in this way. They can say that we must simply learn to live with these mysteries. Another is to find ways to preserve the distinctly normative while at the same time demystifying it. These attempts tend to produce new mysteries, for example by appealing to such things as collective intentions, which are theoretical objects outside the ordinary stream of explanation which nevertheless mimic features of ordinary explanation. The appeal to "practices" as a normative grounding can be understood as another attempt to preserve the normative by demystifying it. Jürgen Habermas paraphrases Brandom by endorsing the idea that the normative is "implicit in . . . practices" and adds the thought that "Ideas enter into social reality via the idealizing presuppositions innate in everyday practices and inconspicuously acquire the quality of stubborn social facts" (2006, 413). This makes for what he calls "detranscendentalized reason, the normative content of which is incorporated into social practices" (2006, 423). The dual structure is retained in such formulations: there is what people do, and there is the hidden normative structure, in this case implicit in another structure, that of practices. Practices are themselves objects of social theory, and more or less natural. But every step in the direction of detranscendentalization brings the theory closer to ordinary explanation.

From the point of view of explanation, there is a standard response to these dual structures. Weber formulated it in connection with the idea of the *Weltanschauung* of the Middle Ages. This was an idealization that only erroneously was taken to be real or to add anything explanatory. The explanation was to be found in the diverse and heterogeneous facts of what and how people in the Middle Ages actually thought and believed. The idea of a medieval world view was an idealization of these facts – a fiction useful for historical purposes, which became a problem when people forgot that it was an idealization. Davidson made the analogous point about language when he denied that there was such a thing as a language as usually conceived. There is what people say and understand – which we idealize into a "language." This is a useful fiction, but a fiction nevertheless.[1] The normativist would respond to this by saying that without appealing to the hidden structure there would be things that could not be explained.

But what is left unexplained? And are there means available to account for the leftover, unexplained things, at least what is there at the level of what actually happens, including what people actually believe, say, and do about such things as correctness, without appealing to a hidden structure? We are back to the undeniable facts: are they undeniable, or are they facts described in a tendentiously "normative" way that adds nothing in the way of empirical completeness or specificity, but merely inserts properties that then appear to be irreducible and ineliminable? With respect to such things as legal validity, the answer is clear: "genuine" validity is not intrinsic to the law, and everything that needs to be explained about the beliefs, behavior, even the meaning of legal acts can be accounted for by the participants' beliefs about these things, and the actually operative notions of correctness and legal validity can be abstracted from the mass of actual decisions and actions performed in terms of beliefs about validity and correctness. This was Weber's point about the legal historian's task in assessing past legal decision-making: the sociological understanding and the assertion of normative theories about validity that could be imposed on the past or constructed out of past legal materials were two different enterprises. There are no "undeniable facts" about genuine legal validity, however much it appeared that there were to Kelsen at the beginning of his career. The idea that there is such a thing at all is a (questionable) normative theory, of a kind that might also be held by the participants in legal actions, but of no greater or different standing than the theological theories held by churchgoers. In these cases we can suspend our endorsement of these theories and still understand what is going on – though in the theological case, as with the legal one, there will be those who insist that full understanding is given only to the true believer.

What appears to be different about rationality, inferences, meanings, and the like is that this option, for understanding without endorsement, is not open to us. To understand basic arithmetic is also to see that it is true, or correct. Similarly for meaning. To understand what a word or sentence means is to subscribe, as Oakeshott put it. And this might seem to require the kind of hidden normative structures that the normativist appeals to. For the normativist, there is no option like the one given by Humpty Dumpty in Alice's Adventures in Wonderland.

> "When I use a word," Humpty Dumpty said in rather a scornful tone,
> "it means just what I choose it to mean – neither more nor less."
> "The question is," said Alice, "whether you can make words mean so
> many different things."
> "The question is," said Humpty Dumpty, "which is to be master –
> that's all." (L. Carroll, 1872, 72)

I can make words mean what I want them to mean. But to do the work of communicating or persuading requires more. It requires that the words be understood by others. And this goes for inferences, reasons, and the like. But to understand what I mean is to understand what I am trying to say. Does this require going back to a hidden structure of meanings to which we both assent? No. If you understand what I am trying to say you understand what I mean. And this kind of understanding can be accounted for more directly and simply

203

by means that do not refer to hidden normative structures, norms concealed in practices, and so forth.

Empathy, in the sense of following the thought of another, explains what is necessary to explain. Empathy is important as an addition to this discussion because it goes beyond the traditional Humean inputs and means of learning. To the extent that we have, and actually employ in ordinary interaction, a primitive capacity for following the thought of another – "primitive" meaning that we can do this "following" the thought of another without constructing a theory or invoking presuppositions – we have a surrogate for the kinds of *a priori* content that Kant thought Hume was lacking, a surrogate without the mysteries of transcendental philosophy. How much of a surrogate? The content of the thing that needs to be explained is not well-specified, in spite of the reliance of these arguments on claims about irreducibility and ineliminability. What is irreducible and ineliminable are facts that are described in questionable ways and can be redescribed without loss of empirical content. The explanatory relevance of empathy and empathy-like capacities is vast: the child understanding what the teacher wants when basic arithmetic is taught, as well as the attribution of sense to the talk and acts of others that Lewis seems to have in mind when he discusses presuppositions that spring up whenever they are needed, are both cases that make psychological sense in terms of these capacities.

Mathematical reasoning, as we have seen, has a different property: understanding *is* subscribing. Is there a way of accounting for this? To answer this we need to go back to the moment when the evident became a subject of dispute. Regresses have to end somewhere. Justification requires that the end-point of justification is something that the justifier and the recipient of the justification accept. Justifications end with what is taken to be evident. There is no getting rid of the evident – which is to say the case where understanding is subscribing. What came under dispute in the late nineteenth century was the *nature* of the evident. The traditional doctrine, ascribed to Descartes, was that self-evidence was wholly individual, and that it made sense to doubt, as not self-evident, such things as the existence of the world or of other people, their mindedness, and so forth. But self-evidence was subjective. Brentano's contemporaries opted for theories that eliminated subjectivity by accounting for the evident character of such things as mathematics by reference to something objective that warranted the sense of evidence but was itself objective, a hidden structure of some kind.

Brentano's strategy was to rehabilitate evidence. Brentano's critics, such as Moritz Schlick, dismissed *Evidenz* because it was a "feeling." This is also the literal meaning of *Einfühlung,* the term translated by "empathy" – it is an in-feeling. According to a traditional account, feelings are subjective. Similarly, self-evidence is a subjective fact – the evident is evident *to me.* But by defining *Evidenz* as evidence to everyone, Brentano provided a way of accounting for the case where understanding is subscribing. Understanding is understanding as others do: for meaning facts, and fundamental mathematics or the evident steps in a proof, this is the end. Regresses can go no further. But no explanation of evidence in terms of hidden structures is needed. Empathy does the work of explanation that hidden presuppositions did for Brentano's rivals. The reason empathy works to produce genuine *Evidenz* is that there is a natural process underlying it: both the capacity, actually employed, of emulating or following the thought of another and the feedback generated by actual social interaction. These are facts of social theory (and of neuroscience). This kind of social theory does not involve collective facts, such as practices, collective intentions, or collective responses, as in Brandom and Habermas. But it detranscendentalizes "reason" just as effectively.

Note

1. The same problem of dual structures arises in the naturalistic social theory of practices. It is supposed by the collective versions of this theory that there are practices that are in some sense "out there" which individuals need to master, incorporate, or otherwise download them so that they are reproduced internally in the individual, where they can guide action, belief, feeling, and so on. The implausibility of this account was the concern of other writings of mine, especially *The Social Theory of Practices* (1994) and has been restated in different ways in many other places, including *Brains/Practices/Relativism* (2002), which contains discussions of other aspects of normativism. Relativism is discussed in a chapter in that volume, and in "Practice Relativism" (2007d).

REFERENCES

Anscombe, G. E. M. ([1976] 1981). The question of linguistic idealism. In *Collected Philosophical Papers: From Parmenides to Wittgenstein* (pp. 112–33). Oxford: Blackwell Publishing.

Austin, J. L. (1962). *How to Do Things with Words*. Cambridge, Mass.: Harvard University Press.

Bennett, M. R., and Hacker, P. M. S. (2008). *History of Cognitive Neuroscience*. Malden, Mass.: Wiley-Blackwell.

Bergson, H. (1935). *The Two Sources of Morality and Religion*. (R. Ashley Audra and C. Brereton, trans., with W. H. Carter). New York: H. Holt & Co.

Blake, R., and Shiffrar, M. (2007). Perception of human motion. *Annual Review of Psychology* 58, 47–73.

Bloor, D. ([1976] 1991). *Knowledge and Social Imagery* (2nd edn). Chicago: The University of Chicago Press.

Bloor, D. (1981). The strengths of the strong programme in the sociology of knowledge. *Philosophy of the Social Sciences* 11, 199–213.

Bloor, D. (1996). The question of linguistic idealism revisited. In H. D. Sluga and D. G. Stern (eds.), *The Cambridge Companion to Wittgenstein* (pp. 354–82). Cambridge: Cambridge University Press.

Bobbio, N. (1981). Max Weber e Hans Kelsen. *Sociologia del Diritto* 8 (1), 135–54.

Boghossian, P. A. (1989). The rule-following considerations. *Mind* 98 (392), 507–49.

Bosman, William ([1704] 1967). *A New and Accurate Description of the Coast of Guinea: Divided into the Gold, the Slave, and the Ivory Coasts*. New York: Barnes & Noble.

Bouglé, C. (1926). *The Evolution of Values: Studies in Sociology with Special Applications to Teaching* (H. S. Sellars, trans.). New York: Henry Holt.

Boyd, R., and Richerson, P. J. (1985). *Culture and the Evolutionary Process*. Chicago: The University of Chicago Press.

Brandom, R. (1979). Freedom and constraint by norms. *American Philosophical Quarterly* 16 (3), 187–96.

Brandom, R. (1994). *Making It Explicit: Reasoning, Representing & Discursive Commitment*. Cambridge, Mass.: Harvard University Press.

206

Brandom, R. (1997). Replies. *Philosophy and Phenomenological Research* 57 (1), 189–204.

Brentano, F. ([1930] 1966). *The True and the Evident* (ed. O. Kraus; R. M. Chisholm, I. Politzer, and K. R. Fischer, trans.). London: Routledge & Kegan Paul.

Brown, J. R. (2001). *Who Rules in Science: An Opinionated Guide to the Wars.* Cambridge, Mass.: Harvard University Press.

Bruun, H. H. (2007). *Science, Values and Politics in Max Weber's Methodology.* Ashgate Publishing.

Calvin, J. ([1536] 1960). *Institutes of the Christian Religion* (ed. J. T. McNeill; F. L. Battles, trans.). Philadelphia: Westminster Press.

Calvo-Merino, B., Grèzes, J., Glaser, D. E., Passingham, R. E., and Haggard, P. (2006). Seeing or doing? Influence of visual and motor familiarity in action observation. *Current Biology* 16, 1905–10.

Carrithers, M., Collins, S., and Lukes, S. (1985). *The Category of the Person.* Cambridge: Cambridge University Press.

Cassidy, J. (2008). Economics: which way for Obama? (Review of *Nudge: Improving Decisions About Health, Wealth, and Happiness* by R. H. Thaler and C. R. Sunstein, Yale University Press). *New York Review of Books* 55 (no. 10; June 12), 32.

Cassirer, E. (1970). *The Philosophy of Symbolic Forms.* Volume 3: *The Phenomenology of Knowledge* (R. Manheim, trans.). New Haven, Conn.: Yale University Press.

Cassirer, E. (1996) *The Philosophy of Symbolic Forms.* Volume 4: *The Metaphysics of Symbolic Forms* (ed. J. M. Krois and D. P. Verene; J. M. Krois, trans.). New Haven, Conn.: Yale University Press.

Cassirer, E. (2000). *The Logic of the Cultural Sciences* (S. G. Loftus, trans.). New Haven, Conn.: Yale University Press.

Child, W. (2002). Reply to Alvin I. Goldman. In Dokic, J., and Proust, J. (eds.), *Simulation and Knowledge of Action* (pp. 21–31). Amsterdam: John Benjamins Publishing Company.

Collingwood, R. G. (1939). *An Autobiography.* Oxford: Oxford University Press.

Cooley, C. H. (1902). *Human Nature and the Social Order.* NewYork: Scribner's.

Cross, E. S., Antonia f. de C. H., and Grafton, S. (2006). Building a motor simulation de novo: observation of dance by dancers. *NeuroImage* 31, 1257–67.

Cummins, D. (2005) Dominance, status, and social hierarchies. In Buss, D. M. (ed.) *The Handbook of Evolutionary Psychology* (pp. 676–95). Hoboken, N.J.: John Wiley and Sons.

Davidson, D. ([1970] 1980). Mental events. In *Essays on Actions and Events* (pp. 207–27). Oxford: Clarendon Press.

Davidson, D. ([1972] 2005). The third man. In *Truth, Language, and History* (pp. 159–66). Oxford: Oxford University Press.

Davidson, D. ([1973–74] 1984). On the very idea of a conceptual scheme. In *Inquiries into Truth and Interpretation* (pp. 183–98). Oxford: Clarendon Press.

Davidson, D. ([1976] 1980). Hempel on explaining action. In *Essays on Actions and Events* (pp. 261–76). Oxford: Oxford University Press.

Davidson, D. (1985). A new basis for decision theory. *Theory and Decision* 18, 87–98.

Davidson, D. ([1986] 2005). A nice derangement of epitaphs. In E. LePore (ed.), *Truth and Interpretation: Perspectives on the Philosophy of Donald Davidson* (pp. 89–108). Cambridge: Basil Blackwell.

Davidson, D. ([1994] 2005). The social aspect of language. In *Truth, Language, and History* (pp. 109–26). Oxford: Oxford University Press.

Davidson, D. (1999). Reply to Pascal Engel. In L. Hahn (ed.), *The Philosophy of Donald Davidson* (pp. 460–63). Chicago: Open Court Press, Chicago.

Davidson, D. (2004) Representation and interpretation. In *Problems of Rationality* (pp. 87–100). Oxford: Clarendon Press.

De Vries, W. (2005). *Wilfrid Sellars*. Chesham, Bucks, UK: Acumen Publishing.

Dodds, E. R. (1951). *The Greeks and the Irrational*. Berkeley: University of California Press.

Dumont, L. ([1966] 1970). *Homo Hierarchicus: An Essay on the Caste System* (M. Sainsbury, trans.). Chicago: The University of Chicago Press.

Dumont, L. (1994). *German Ideology: From France to Germany and Back*. Chicago: The University of Chicago Press.

Durkheim, É. ([1893] 1933). *The Division of Labor in Society* (G. Simpson, trans.). NewYork: Free Press.

Durkheim, É. (1920). Introduction à la morale. *Revue philosophique* 89, 79–97

Ellwood, C. (1899a). I. Prologomena to social psychology: The need of the study of social psychology. *American Journal of Sociology* 4 (5), 656–65.

Ellwood, C. (1899b). II. Prologomena to social psychology: The fundamental fact in social psychology. *American Journal of Sociology* 5 (1), 807–22.

Ellwood, C. (1899c). III. Prologomena to social psychology: The nature and task of social psychology. *American Journal of Sociology* 5 (2), 98–109.

Ellwood, C. (1899d). IV. Prologomena to social psychology: The concept of social mind. *American Journal of Sociology* 5 (2), 220–27.

Ellwood, C. A. (1901). The theory of imitation in social psychology. *American Journal of Sociology* 6, 721–41.

Emmet, D. (1986). Foreword. In B. Hallen and S. J. Olubi (eds.), *Knowledge, Belief and Witchcraft: Analytic Experiments in African Philosophy* (pp. 1–4). London: Ethnographica.

Evans-Pritchard, E. P. (1937). *Witchcraft, Oracles and Magic Among the Azande*. Oxford: Oxford University Press.

Fehr, E., and Fischbacher, U. (2004). Social norms and human cooperation. *TRENDS in Cognitive Science* 8 (4), 185–90.

Fingarette, H. (1972). *Confucius: The Secular as Sacred*. New York: Harper & Row.

Finnis, J. (1980). *Natural Law and Natural Rights*. Oxford: Oxford University Press.

Freyer, H. (1998). *Theory of Objective Mind: An Introduction to the Philosophy of Culture* (S. Grosby, trans.). Athens: Ohio University Press.

Friedman, M. (1998). On the sociology of scientific knowledge and its philosophical agenda. *Studies in the History and Philosophy of Science* 29 (2), 239–71.

Friedman, M. (1999). *Reconsidering Logical Positivism*. Cambridge: Cambridge University Press.

Friedman, M. (2000). *A Parting of the Ways: Carnap, Cassirer, and Heidegger*. Chicago: Open Court Publishing Company.

Garfinkel, H. (1991). Respecification: evidence for locally produced, naturally accountable phenomena of order, logic, reason, meaning, method, etc. in and as of the essential haecceity of immortal ordinary society (I) – an announcement of studies. In G. Button (ed.), *Ethnomethodology and the Human Sciences* (pp. 10–20). London: Routledge.

Gawande, A. (2008). The itch: Its mysterious power may be a clue to a new theory about brains and bodies. *The New Yorker*, June 30, 2008. Accessed January 27, 2009. http://www.newyorker.com/reporting/2008/06/30/080630fa_fact_gawande

Gennap, A. van. (1960). *The Rites of Passage*. Chicago: The University of Chicago Press.

Gewirth, A. (1978). *Reason and Morality*. Chicago: The University of Chicago Press.

Gierke, O. von. ([1880] 1939). *The Development of Political Theory* (B. Freyd, trans.). New York: W. W. Norton & Company.

Gilbert, M. (1989). *On Social Facts*. London & New York: Routledge.

Gilbert, M. (1990). Walking together: A paradigmatic social phenomenon. *Midwest Studies in Philosophy* 6, 1–14.

Gilbert, M. (1996). *Living Together: Rationality, Sociality, and Obligation*. Lanham, Mass.: Rowman and Littlefield Publishers.

Gopnik, A. (2008). Babies and the sticky mitten test: How babies of only three months can learn to have a theory of mind. *Times Literary Supplement*, September 3. http://entertainment.timesonline.co.uk/tol/arts_and_entertainment/the_tls/article4666842.ece Accessed January 27, 2009.

Guttman, B. (1926). *Das Recht der Chagga*. Munich: Beck.

Habermas, J. ([1981] 1984–1987). *The Theory of Communicative Action* (T. McCarthy, trans.). Boston: Beacon Press.

Hägerström, A. (1953). *Inquiries into the Nature of Law and Morals*. Uppsala: Almqvist & Wiksells.

Hägerström, A. ([1911] 1971). On the truth of moral ideas (T. Mautner, trans.). Canberra: Department of Philosophy, The Australian National University.

Hägerström, A. ([1929] 1964) A summary of my philosophy. In *Philosophy and Religion* (pp. 33–76; R. T. Sandin, trans.). London: George Allen & Unwin.

Hallen, B., and Olubi, S. J. (eds.) (1986). *Knowledge, Belief and Witchcraft: Analytic Experiments in African Philosophy*. London: Ethnographica.

Hamlin, J. K., Hallinan, E., and Woodward, A. (2008). Do as I do: 7-month-old infants selectively reproduce others' goals. *Developmental Science* 11 (4), 487–94.

Hansen, C. (2007). Philosophy of language in classical China. Chuang Tzu (Zhuangzi). http://www.hku.hk/philodep/ch/lang.htm Accessed January 27, 2009.

Hart, H. L. A. (1961). *The Concept of Law*. Oxford: Clarendon Press.

Haugeland, J. (1998). *Having Thought: Essays in the Metaphysics of Mind*. Cambridge, Mass.: Harvard University Press.

Hempel, C. G. (1961–1962). Rational action. *Proceedings and Addresses of the American Philosophical Association* 35, 5–23.

Hempel, C. G. (1965). *Aspects of Scientific Explanation: And Other Essays in the Philosophy of Science*. New York: The Free Press.

Henderson, D. (2002). Norms, normative principles, and explanation. *Philosophy of the Social Sciences* 32, 329–64.

Holt, M. P. (1995). *The French Wars of Religion, 1562–1629*. Cambridge: Cambridge University Press.

Howard, D. (1990). Einstein and Duhem. *Synthese* 83, 363–84.

Howard, D. (2003). Two left turns make a right: On the curious political career of North American philosophy of science at midcentury. In G. Hardcastle and A. W. Richardson (eds.), *Minnesota Studies in the Philosophy of Science*, vol. 18 (pp. 23–93). Minneapolis: University of Minnesota Press.

Huff, D. and Turner, S. (1981). Rationalizations and the application of causal explanations of human action. *American Philosophical Quarterly* 18, 213–20.

Hunter, I. (2005). Kant's religion and Prussian religious policy. *Modern Intellectual History* 2 (1), 1–27.

Hurley, S. and Chater, N. (eds.). (2005). *Perspectives on Imitation: From Neuroscience to Social Science*. Cambridge, Mass.: MIT Press.

Ihering, R. ([1872] 1915). *The Struggle for Law* (J. J. Lawlor, trans. of the 5th German edn., *Der kampf ums recht*). Chicago: Callaghan.

Ihering, R. ([1877–83] 1924). *Law as Means to an End* (E. Husik, trans. of the 4th German edn., *Der Zweck im Recht)*. New York: Macmillan.

Kalampalikis, N., Delouvée, S., and Pétard, J.-P. (2006). Historical spaces of social psychology. *History of Human Sciences* 19 (2), 23–43.

Kant, I. (1968). *Critique of Judgment* (J. H. Bernard, trans.). NewYork: Hafner Publishing.

Kelly, D., and Stich, S. (2007). Two theories about the cognitive architecture underlying morality. In P. Carruthers, S. Laurence, and S. Stich (eds.), *The Innate Mind* (pp. 348–67). Vol. 3, Foundations and the Future. http://www. rci.rutgers.edu/~stich/Publications/publications2.htm Accessed January 28, 2009.

Kelsen, H. ([1925] 2006). *General Theory of Law and State* (*Allgemeine Staatslehre*) (A. Wedberg, trans.). New Brunswick, N.J.: Transaction Publishers.

Kelsen, H. ([1934] 2002). *Introduction to the Problems of Legal Theory* (*Reine Rechtslehre*, 1st edn.), (B. Paulson and S. Paulson, trans.). Oxford: Clarendon Press.

Kelsen, H. (1946). *Society and Nature: A Sociological Inquiry*. London: K. Paul, Trench, Trubner & Co.

Kelsen, H. ([1960] 1967). *Pure Theory of Law* (*Reine Rechtslehre*, 2nd edn.), (M. Knight, trans.). Berkeley: University of California Press.

Kelsen, H. ([1979] 1991). *General Theory of Norms* (M. Hartney, trans.). Oxford: Clarendon Press.

Keysers, C., Kohler, E., Umiltà, M. A., Nanetti, L., Fogassi, L., and Gallese, V. (2003). Audiovisual motor neurons and action recognition. *Experimental Brain Research* 153, 628–36.

Korsgaard, C. (ed.). (1996). *The Sources of Normativity*. Oxford: Oxford University Press.

Kripke, S. (1982). *Wittgenstein on Rules and Private Language: An Elementary Exposition*. Cambridge, Mass.: Harvard University Press.

Kurzban, R., and Neuberg, S. (2005). Managing ingroup and outgroup relationships. In D. M. Buss (ed.), *The Handbook of Evolutionary Psychology* (pp. 653–69). Hoboken, N.J.: John Wiley and Sons.

Kusch, M. (2006). *A Sceptical Guide to Meaning and Rules: Defending Kripke's Wittgenstein*. Chesham, Bucks, UK: Acumen.

Lacey, N. (2004). *A Life of H. L. A. Hart: The Nightmare and the Noble Dream*. Oxford: Oxford University Press.

Lanzoni, S., and Brain, R. (forthcoming). *Varieties of Empathy in Science, Art, and Culture.*

Lask, E. (1907). *Rechtsphilosophie.* In *Die Philosophie im Beginn des zwanzigsten Jahr hunderts: Festschrift fur Kuno Fischer,* 2nd edn. (pp. 269–320). Heidelberg: C. Winter.

Levy-Bruhl, L. ([1922] 1923). *Primitive Mentality* (L. Clare, trans.). London: George Allen & Unwin.

Lewis, D. (1969). *Convention: A Philosophical Study.* Cambridge, Mass.: Harvard University Press.

Lewis, D. (1979). Scorekeeping in a language game. *Journal of Philosophical Logic* 8, 339–59.

Lillehammer, H. (2008). In hope of an answer (Review of *Oughts and Thoughts: Rule-following and the Normativity of Content* by Anandi Hattiangadi, Clarendon Press, Oxford; and *The Nature of Normativity* by Ralph Wedgewood, Clarendon Press, Oxford). *Times Literary Supplement* 5482 (April 25), 11.

Lizardo, O. (2007). "Mirror neurons," collective objects and the problem of transmission: reconsidering Stephen Turner's critique of practice theory. *Journal for the Theory of Social Behaviour* 37, 319–50.

Loula, F., Prasad, S., Harber, K., and Shiffrar, M. (2005). Recognizing people from their movement. *Journal of Experimental Psychology* 31 (1), 210–20.

Lukes, S. (2000). Different cultures, different rationalities? *History of the Human Sciences* 13 (1), 5–18.

Lukes, S. (2008) *Moral Relativism.* New York: Picador.

Luria, A. ([1974] 1976). *Cognitive Development: Its Cultural and Social Foundations.* Cambridge, Mass.: Harvard University Press.

MacIntyre, A. (1962). A mistake about causality in social science. In P. Laslett and W. G. Runciman (eds.), *Philosophy, Politics, and Society* (pp. 48–70). Oxford: Basil Blackwell.

MacIntyre, A. (1966). *A Short History of Ethics.* New York: Macmillan.

MacIntyre, A. (1970). Is understanding religion compatible with believing? In B. R. Wilson (ed.), *Rationality* (pp. 62–77). New York: Harper & Row.

Mackie, J. L. (1977). *Ethics: Inventing Right and Wrong.* Harmondsworth: Penguin Books.

Mandelbaum, M. (1938). *The Problem of Historical Knowledge: An Answer to Relativism.* New York: Liveright Publishing.

Mauss, M. ([1925] 1967). *The Gift: Forms and Functions of Exchange in Archaic Societies* (I. Cunnison, trans.). New York: W. W. Norton. Originally published in *L'Année Sociologique,* n.s. 1: 30–186.

Mauss, M. ([1938] 1985). A category of the human mind: The notion of person; the notion of self (W. D. Halls, trans.). In M. Carrithers, S. Collins, and S. Lukes (eds.), *The Category of the Person: Anthropology, Philosophy, History* (pp. 1–25). Cambridge: Cambridge University Press.

McDowell, J. ([1984] 2002). Wittgenstein on following a rule. In A. Miller and C. Wright (eds.), *Rule-Following and Meaning* (pp. 45–80). Chesham, Bucks, UK: Acumen Publishing.

McDowell, J. (1996). *Mind and World.* Cambridge, Mass.: Harvard University Press.

Mead, M. (1928). *Coming of Age in Samoa: A Psychological Study of Primitive Youth for Western Civilization.* New York: W. Morrow.

211

Miller, A., and Wright, C. (eds.). (2002). *Rule-Following and Meaning*. Chesham, Bucks, UK: Acumen Publishing.

Mises, L. von (1960). *Epistemological Problems of Economics*. Princeton, N.J.: Van Nostrand.

Mommsen, W. ([1959] 1984). *Max Weber and German Politics 1890–1920* (M. S. Steinberg, trans.). Chicago: The University of Chicago Press.

Nagel, T. (1986). *The View from Nowhere*. New York: Oxford University Press.

Nagel, T. (1991). *Equality and Partiality*. New York: Oxford University Press.

Nagel, T. (1997). *The Last Word*. Oxford: Oxford University Press.

Nandan, Y. (ed.) (1980). *Émile Durkheim: Contributions to* L'Année Sociologique. New York: The Free Press.

Needham, R. (1972). *Belief, Language, and Experience*. Chicago: The University of Chicago Press.

O'Neill, O. (1996). Introduction. In C. Korsgaard (ed.), *The Sources of Normativity* (pp. xi-xv). Oxford: Oxford University Press.

Pareto, V. (1935). *The Mind and Society*. New York: Harcourt Brace.

Parfit, D. (1984). *Reasons and Persons*. Oxford: Clarendon Press.

Patterson, E. W. (1950). Introduction. In *The Legal Philosophies of Lask, Radbruch, and Dabin* (K. Wilk, trans.; pp. xxvii-xxxix). Cambridge, Mass.: Harvard University Press.

Paulson, S. ([1934] 2002). Introduction. In H. Kelsen, *Introduction to the Problems of Legal Theory* (B. Paulson and S. Paulson, trans.; pp. xvii-xlii). Oxford: Clarendon Press.

Paulson, S. (1997). On the Kelsen-Kant problematic. In E. G. Valdés, E. Garzón, W. Krawietz, W. Werner, G. H. von Wright, and R. Zimmerling (eds.), *Normative Systems in Legal and Moral Theory. Festschrift for Carlos E. Alchourrón and Eugenio Bulygin* (pp. 197–213). Berlin: Duncker & Humblot.

Pettit, P. (1990a). Affirming the reality of rule-following. *Mind* 99, 433–39.

Pettit, P. (1990b). The reality of rule-following. In A. Miller and C. Wright (eds.), *Rule-Following and Meaning* (pp. 188–208). Chesham, Bucks, UK: Acumen Press.

Pettit, P. (1996). *The Common Mind: An Essay on Psychology, Society, and Politics*, 2nd edn. Oxford: Oxford University Press.

Pettit, P. (1997). *Republicanism: A Theory of Freedom and Government*. Oxford: Oxford University Press.

Postema, G. J. (1987). The normativity of law. In R. Gavison (ed.), *Issues in Contemporary Legal Philosophy: The Influence of H. L. A. Hart* (pp. 81–104). Oxford: Clarendon Press.

Pound, R. (1911–12). The scope and purpose of sociological jurisprudence. *Harvard Law Review* 24 (June), 591–619; 24 (December), 140–168; 25 (April 1912), 489–516.

Pound, R. ([1958] 2002). Later forms of juristic realism. In *The Ideal Element in Law* (pp. 288–320). Indianapolis: The Liberty Fund.

Pufendorf, S. von. ([1688] 1964). *On the Law of Nature and Nations* (C. H. Oldfather and W. A. Oldfather, trans.). London: Wiley & Sons.

Quine, W. V. O. (1980). Sellars on behaviorism, language and meaning. *Pacific Philosophical Quarterly* 61 (1&2), 26–30.

Railton, P. (2000). Normative force and normative freedom: Hume and Kant. In J. Dancy (ed.), *Normativity*. Oxford: Blackwell Publishers.

212

Raz, J. (1999). Explaining normativity: reason and the will. In *Engaging Reason: On the Theory of Value and Action* (pp. 90–117). Oxford: Oxford University Press.

Raz, J. (2009). Reasons: Explanatory and normative. In C. Sandis (ed.), *New Essays on the Explanation of Action*. New York: Palgrave/McMillan. http://josephnraz.googlepages.com/publicationlist Accessed January 28, 2009.

Rokeach, M. (1964). *The Three Christs of Ypsilanti: A Psychological Study*. New York: Alfred A. Knopf.

Roth, P. A. (2003). Mistakes. *Synthese* 136, 389–408.

Rouse, J. (2002) Two concepts of practices. In T. Schatzki, K. Knorr-Cetina, and J. von Rouse, *How Scientific Practices Matter: Reclaiming Philosophical Naturalism*. Chicago: The University of Chicago Press.

Rouse, J. (2007). Social practices and normativity. *Philosophy of the Social Sciences* 37, 46–56.

Sacks, O. (1995). An anthropologist on Mars. In *An Anthropologist on Mars* (pp. 244–96). New York: Alfred A. Knopf.

Saji, M. (2009). The division between reason and unreason in Kant. *Human Studies* 32, 201–23.

Savigny, E. (ed.). *The Practice Turn in Contemporary Theory*, London: Routledge.

Schmaus, W. (2007). Categories and classification in the social sciences. In S. P. Turner and M. W. Risjord (eds.), *Handbook of the Philosophy of Anthropology and Sociology* (pp. 429–58). Amsterdam: Elsevier.

Schuhmann, K., and Smith, B. (1993). Two idealisms: Lask and Husserl. *Kant-Studien* 82, 448–66.

Schutz, A. ([1932] 1967). *The Phenomenology of the Social World* (G. Walsh and F. Lehnert, trans.). Evanston, Ill.: Northwestern University Press.

Searle, J. (1990). Collective intentionality and action. In P. R. Cohen, J. Morgan, and M. E. Pollack (eds.), *Intentions in Communications* (pp. 401–16). Cambridge, Mass.: MIT Press.

Searle, J. (1995). *The Construction of Social Reality*. New York: The Free Press.

Sellars, W. ([1956] 1963). Imperatives, intentions, and the logic of "ought." In H.-N. Castañeda and G. Nakhnikian (eds.), *Morality and the Language of Conduct* (pp. 159–214). Detroit, Mich.: Wayne State University Press.

Sellars, W. ([1956] 1997). *Empiricism and the Philosophy of Mind* (R. Brandom, ed.). Cambridge, Mass.: Harvard University Press.

Sellars, W. (1967) *Philosophical Perspectives*. Springfield, IL: Charles C. Thomas.

Sellars, W. (1968). *Science and Metaphysics: Variations on Kantian Themes*. London: Routledge & Kegan Paul; New York: Humanities Press.

Sellars, W. (1980). Behaviorism, language and meaning. *Pacific Philosophical Quarterly* 61 (1&2), 3–25.

Seyfarth, R. M., and Cheney, D. L. (1984). Grooming, alliances, and reciprocal altruisms in vervet monkeys. *Nature* 308 (April5), 541–42.

Simmel, G. ([1908] 1964). *The Sociology of Georg Simmel* (K. H. Wolff, trans., ed.). New York: The Free Press.

Sommerville, J., Woodward, A., and Needham, A. (2005). Action experience alters 3-month-old infants' perception of others' actions, *Cognition*, 96, B1-B11.

Spiegelberg, H. (1971) Franz Brentano (1838–1917): Forerunner of the phenomenological movement. In *The Phenomenological Movement: A Historical Introduction*, 2nd edn., vol. 1 (pp. 26–52). The Hague: M. Nijhoff.

Steiner, F. B. ([1954] 1999). Chagga law and Chagga truth. In J. Adler and R. Fardon (eds.) *Taboo, Truth and Religion: Franz Baermann Steiner Selected Writings*, vol. 1 (pp. 235–50). Oxford: Berghahn.

Thomas, W. I. , and Znaneicki, F. ([1918–1920] 1958). *The Polish Peasant in Europe and America: Monograph of an Immigrant Group*, 2nd edn., republ. in 2 volumes. New York: Dover Publications.

Thornton, T. (2004). *John McDowell*. Montreal: McGill-Queen's University Press.

Tilly, C. (2006). *Why?* Princeton, N.J.: Princeton University Press.

Tomasello, M., and Carpenter, M. (2005). Intention reading and imitative learning. In S. Hurley and N. Chater (eds.), *Perspectives on Imitation: From Neuroscience to Social Science*, vol. 1 (pp. 134–48). Cambridge, Mass.: The MIT Press.

Tuomela, R. (2005). We-intentions revisited. *Philosophical Studies* 125, 327–69.

Turner, S. (1979). Translating ritual beliefs. *Philosophy of the Social Sciences* 9, 401–23.

Turner, S. (1980). *Sociological Explanation as Translation*. Rose Monograph Series of the American Sociological Association. New York and Cambridge: Cambridge University Press.

Turner, S. (1981). Interpretive charity, Durkheim, and the "Strong Programme" in the sociology of science. *Philosophy of the Social Sciences* 11, 231–43.

Turner, S. (1989). Depoliticizing power (Review of Joseph Rouse, *Knowledge and Power: Toward a Political Philosophy of Science* and Barry Barnes, *The Nature of Power*), *Social Studies of Science* 19, 533–60.

Turner, S. (1994). *The Social Theory of Practices: Tradition, Tacit Knowledge, and Presuppositions*. Oxford: Polity Press; Chicago: University of Chicago Press.

Turner, S. (2002). *Brains/Practices/Relativism*. Chicago: The University of Chicago Press.

Turner, S. (2003). What do we mean by "we"? *Protosociology: An International Journal of Interdisciplinary Research* 18–19, 139–62. http://www.protosociology.de/Volumes/Volume18.html Accessed January 28, 2009.

Turner, S. (2004). The new collectivism (Review of Keith Graham, *Practical Reasoning in a Social World: How We Act Together*). *History and Theory* 43, 386–99.

Turner, S. (2005a) Normative all the way down. *Studies in History and Philosophy of Science* 36, 419–29.

Turner, S. (2005b) Attitudes. *Dictionnaire de la pensee sociologique* (pp. 40–43). Paris: Presses Universitaire de France.

Turner, S. (2007a). Explaining normativity. *Philosophy of the Social Sciences* 37(1), 57–73.

Turner, S. (2007b). Mirror neurons and practices: a response to Lizardo. *Journal for the Theory of Social Behaviour* 37, 351–71.

Turner, S. (2007c). The continued relevance of Weber's philosophy of science. *Max Weber Studies* 7 (1), 37–62.

Turner, S. (2007d). Practice relativism. *Crítica, Revista Hispanoamericana de Filosofía* 39(115), 3–27.

Turner, S. (forthcoming). Davidson's normativity. In J. Malpas (ed.), *Dialogues with Davidson: On the Contemporary Significance of His Thought*. Cambridge, Mass.: MIT Press.

Turner, S. (2008). Following the thought of another: Normative or naturalizable?

REFERENCES

In S. Lanzoni and R. Brain (eds.), *Varieties of Empathy in Science, Art, and Culture.*

Turner, S., and Factor, R. (1984). *Max Weber and the Dispute Over Reason and Value; A Study in Philosophy, Ethics, and Politics.* London: Routledge & Kegan Paul.

Turner, S., and Factor, R. A. (1994). *Max Weber: The Lawyer as Social Thinker.* London: Routledge.

Turner, V. ([1966] 1977). *The Ritual Process: Structure and Anti-Structure.* Ithaca, N.Y.: Cornell University Press.

Tversky, A., and Kahneman, D. (1974). Judgment under uncertainty: heuristics and biases. *Science* 185 (September 27), 1124–31.

Tversky, A., and Kahneman, D. (1981). The framing of decisions and the psychology of choice. *Science* 211 (January 30), 453–58.

Vaihinger, H. ([1911] 1935). *Philosophy of "As If": A System of the Theoretical, Practical and Religious Fictions of Mankind* (C. K. Ogden, trans.). London: Routledge & Kegan Paul.

Velleman, J. D. (1997). How to share an intention. *Philosophy and Phenomenological Research* 57, 29–50.

Vivekananda, Swami. (1893). Opening Welcome Address at the World Parliament of Religions. Chicago.

Weber, M. ([1904] 1949). Objectivity in social science and social policy. In *Methodology of the Social Sciences* (E. Shils and H. A. Finch, trans., eds.; pp. 49–112). Glencoe, Ill: Free Press.

Weber, M. ([1907] 1977). *Critique of Stammler* (G. Oakes, trans.). New York: The Free Press.

Weber, M. (1949). *The Methodology of the Social Sciences* (E. A. Shils and H. A. Finch, trans, eds.). New York: The Free Press.

Weber, M. ([1968] 1978). *Economy and Society: An Outline of Interpretive Sociology,* 3 vols. (G. Roth and C. Wittich, eds.). Berkeley and Los Angeles: University of California Press.

Weber, M. (2000). On legal theory and sociology. In A. J. Jacobson and B. Schlink (eds.), *Weimar: A Jurisprudence of Crisis* (B. Cooper, trans., pp. 50–65). Berkeley: University of California Press.

Williams, B. (1973). The idea of equality. In *Problems of the Self: Philosophical Papers 1956–1972* (pp. 230–49). Cambridge: Cambridge University Press.

Wimsatt, W. C. (2007). *Re-engineering Philosophy for Limited Beings: Piecewise Approximations to Reality.* Cambridge, Mass.: Harvard University Press.

Winch, P. (1958) *The Idea of a Social Science and Its Relation to Philosophy.* London: Routledge & Kegan Paul.

Winch, P. ([1964] 1974). Understanding a primitive society. In B. R. Wilson (ed.), *Rationality* (pp. 78–111). Oxford: Blackwell.

Wittgenstein, L. ([1953] 1958). *Philosophical Investigations,* 3rd edn., (G. E. M. Anscombe, trans.). Englewood Cliffs, N.J.: Prentice Hall.

Woodward, A. (1998a). Infants' encoding of grasping by humans vs. machines, *Infant Behavior and Child Development* 21 (April), 766.

Woodward, A. (1998b). Infants selectively encode the goal object of an actor's reach. *Cognition* 69, 1–34.

Wright, C. (1986). Does *Philosophical Investigations* I.258–60 suggest a cogent argument against private language? In J. McDowell and J.-P. Petit (eds.), *ubject, Thought, and Context* (pp. 210–66). Oxford: Clarendon Press.

INDEX